NO HANDCUFFS

Eddie Richardson (born 1936) became one of the most feared and respected powers of Britain's gangland, having survived the Blitz and on the turbulent streets of post-wartime South-East London. 'The Richardsons' became infamous in the 1960s and the stuff of screaming headlines. Famously loyal to his trusted family and friends, Eddie Richardson, the tough guys' tough guy, is a much-travelled man who has seen and experienced the best and worst of the world. He did hard time in jail but through his often violent protests won better prison conditions for all. He remained his own man during his long incarceration and by dedication to his talent became a renowned and award-winning artist. Today his paintings are much sought after and he devotes himself to his art and is a popular after-dinner speaker when he recounts, with wit and hard-won wisdom, his life as a legendary gangster. Tread carefully, for even with *No Handcuffs* he still packs an almighty punch.

Douglas Thompson is a biographer, broadcaster and international journalist, and a regular contributor to major newspapers and magazines worldwide. His twenty-eight books, published in a dozen languages, include the TV-based anthology *Hollywood People*, and have been serialised in newspapers and magazines throughout the world. He collaborated with the dancer Michael Flatley on his *Lord of the Dance*, and worked with Christine Keeler on her revealing memoir *The Truth At Last*, an immediate bestseller. Recent successes include *Stephen Ward: Scapegoat*, a study of the rakish charmer at the centre of the Profumo Scandal. He is a director of one of Britain's popular literary festivals, and commutes between Suffolk and Hollywood, where he was based full time as a correspondent and columnist for twenty-two years.

NO HANDCUFFS

THE FINAL WORD
ON MY WAR WITH THE KRAYS

EDDIE RICHARDSON

with Douglas Thompson

with a foreword by Martina Cole

JB

JOHN BLAKE

Published by John Blake Publishing,
The Plaza,
535 Kings Road,
Chelsea Harbour,
London SW10 0SZ

www.johnblakebooks.com

www.facebook.com/johnblakebooks 🖪
twitter.com/jblakebooks 🅴

First published in hardback in 2019

ISBN: 978-1-78606-881-1

British Library Cataloguing-in-Publication Data:

A catalogue record for this book is available from the British Library.

Design by www.envydesign.co.uk

Printed and bound in Great Britain by Clays Ltd, Elcograf S.p.A

1 3 5 7 9 10 8 6 4 2

John Blake Publishing is an imprint of Bonnier Books UK
www.bonnierbooks.co.uk

For my loyal family and friends

Eddie Richardson's membership card for
J. Arthurs, his club in Catford.

CONTENTS

BOOK TWO: CRIME AND PUNISHMENT

FOREWORD BY MARTINA COLE

A few years ago I edited Eddie's first manuscript *The Last Word*. It was a real honour and a great read so I was looking forward to reading the next instalment, *No Handcuffs*.

I wasn't disappointed.

It's another no-holds-barred read that chronicles Eddie's life from his childhood to his eventual stints in prisons.

Over the years I have had many a long lunch or a night out with Eddie and he is a natural raconteur, he can be hilarious, especially when telling a story against himself. He is good company, and as I have remarked on more than one occasion he has a better social life than most people I know. We had a lunch date booked and he rang explaining that he was off to Belfast the next morning to watch a boxing match – he was going with the trainer and the boxer etc.... That really epitomises Eddie: he is always out and about, always looking to the future and always enjoying his life.

NO HANDCUFFS

In many ways he's a force of nature. In *No Handcuffs* he tells stories that give a unique insight into the British penal system and the treatment of offenders, which can only give one cause to think long and hard about what we need to do to try and give young men and women a better chance of rehabilitation.

The book is peppered with reminiscences about his time away and the people he was banged up with, or those whom he met over the years when he was on the outside, a lot of them household names.

I read this manuscript in one sitting and then I immediately read it once more. There's plenty to keep the reader interested, but it also has the ability to make you feel like you are eavesdropping, and that is a big part of this book's charm.

There's an innate fairness in Eddie that I think is a large part of his own charm. Even enemies are given their due although, as always, he doesn't hold back if he feels anyone has taken liberties.

This book is a great read. It's insightful and interesting and most of all it's immensely readable, but the bottom line is the reader is being given the opportunity to experience Eddie's life in the raw as Eddie experienced it.

No Handcuffs is a testament to one man's determination to live his life to the fullest no matter what, and I know for a fact that Eddie has done just that!

Read and enjoy – you won't be disappointed.

Eddie reminds us of an age that is long gone but will never be forgotten; he brings back the Golden Era of the 1950s and 1960s with his usual astute eye for detail.

There are painful reminders of what life was really like for a lot of people, and how the 'you-never-had-it-so-good' generation had to fight tooth and nail to get a stake into a better life for themselves and their families, and that often this came with a very high price tag.

He reminds us of the changes in criminality that the 1980s brought, and how the whole landscape changed with them. His book is a real eye-opener in many ways, and it leaves the reader with a sense of having a better understanding of a world that is still fascinating, if frightening.

Eddie is a good man, fair and kind in equal measure, but after saying that I wouldn't want to be on the receiving end if he felt he was being mugged off. He wasn't and never will be anybody's fool.

No Handcuffs is his story and only his to tell, and he tells it with humour and with honesty.

MARTINA COLE
April 2019

A NOTE FROM EDDIE RICHARDSON

No Handcuffs is something I am truly excited about. Circumstances have allowed me to open up totally about my life, my family and the many infamous and famous and corner-shop scallywags I have encountered and endured in and out of prison for the past seventy years and more. I know that crime fans will be fascinated – and I believe many, many others will be too – for I am able to offer revelations which will surprise and shock them.

With hindsight, and the wisdom of time, I find the ability to be free about what I say brings a new perspective to all of it. I no longer need to protect or cover up for past associates or associations. Time has taken care of those obligations. It is not about settling scores, but putting right the history. It is also as a tribute to my friends for, with friends, you don't weaken. The stories are all mine and are not extravagant. They're a hard lump of truth, the truth and nothing but...

EDDIE RICHARDSON
London, England, 2019

MEET THE GANG

When it's too late to be good, you have to be careful. Eddie Richardson is very careful about cherishing the life he has and, importantly, the lives of others. He has been wicked and vicious and been punished, but in the years since becoming a free man for the second time, he has taken every chance to fulfil his life, to live it. He has, he says, no handcuffs on him any more; and not just the ones he wore when being taken by armed guard from one secure prison unit to another during his many years of incarceration.

His brother Charlie is dead. Also gone are his mother, Eileen, whom he tried to protect in the most lurid of his felonious times; his notorious and sometime partner, 'Mad' Frankie Fraser; and many of the other 'legends' whom he fought with or against during his turbulent years when London was the Wild West and the sheriff was on the outlaw payroll. He is able to abandon much of the artifice of the narrative that has gone before. Eddie Richardson is not only free, but he feels free to speak, to tell his remarkable and disquieting story without looking over his shoulder. Yet, yes, he is careful. It's played a part in his survival.

You can still see the ferocity of the young gangster in the walk and the stance: weight on the back heel, the way he carries himself, careful like a cat, evidence of the dangers of the past, the crimes not atoned for, the faith placed rashly in weak strangers and, chillingly, family, an awareness that even now, around the next corner, might be an enemy with intent.

Being astute got Eddie Richardson to age eighty-three in 2019. Not being so, his restless energy, found him locked up in Britain's most secure prisons, often for long stretches in solitary confinement, in 'chokey', for nearly a quarter of a century. Inside or out, he was dangerous and clever. And, with his brother Charlie, the most feared: public enemies who crashed through an invisible barrier to lifetime notoriety. He grew up in a post-World War Two world when life was so much different from today, no street cameras, no mobile phones; if you wanted to call for help you had to find a telephone box that worked. Everyone had to look after themselves.

'It was,' he says, 'the way it was.'

But decadent dreams were not for everyone. He admits to an incorrigibility, a jack-the-lad boyhood camaraderie with his older brother Charlie, but larks became serious and you had to be tough, ruthless, to survive and to profit.

If you wanted gold or glory you had to fight for it, be brutal, hard and fast, and Eddie and Charlie Richardson emerged as determined conquistadors from an exceptional, if deceptively so, training ground, the terraced back streets of Camberwell, South-East London. By the late 1950s, so very, very quickly, they were a myth, a pair followers believed could work miracles, and, as such, not men others were willing to explain their limitations to. They were easily offended. No one was ever brave enough to tell them what they needed to know. Their fluency with violence led their way. It was a society within society. Eddie Richardson is succinct: 'We couldn't, we wouldn't, let anyone take a fucking liberty. That was never an option at that time.'

That time, as Britain emerged from World War Two and into the 1950s and many of the blitzed streets of London were being demolished for the social misfits of housing, the high-rise estates, was the environment in which Eddie Richardson struggled and fought to cope with and conquer. That Eddie is not a man, he says, he would like to meet today. There was, he admits, a pleasure in the power, an enjoyment in being fearless and willing to take on anyone, any obstacle which could be broken down and crashed through.

It is, the psychologists would tell us, human nature. There is always plenty of that around. When Eddie and Charlie Richardson were establishing their business endeavours, myriad schemes and enterprises where cash trumped legality in any game, the extent and growth of their empire could never have happened without the connivance of the police. Eddie says it wasn't the policemen, the bobbies on the beat or the cops on their 'Z Cars' patrols who profited most: it was the hierarchy, the officer class playing true life snakes and ladders climbing up to commanders; patrolmen were instructed when not to interfere in the Richardsons' business.

Paradoxically, many of these policemen were corrupt out of principle. They didn't want to be thought of as stupid, of being slow on the uptake. It wasn't pure venality. Being bent was traditional.

This melancholy fact meant you didn't drink alone in the pub when Eddie or Charlie sent over a drink, a bottle. You weren't an 'outsider'; you were clever for the profit to be had in looking the other way, a simple act which turned every Friday night into a birthday: there was always a present waiting.

The cash payments were discreet but enabling, and when they had grown strong and confident and into their early thirties the brothers were feted and feared; this feeling of immunity defeated any self-awareness, any thoughts that the scaffolding around the enterprises might be shaky.'

Eddie didn't get away with it. He's spent more time in prison than many people of his parents' generation lived. He's not proud of it but he's pleased with the way he handled the punishment he was given. Yet, some of it, he has always believed, was harsh. So were the crimes and the times.

'It was the Wild West out there for a long time,' says Eddie as he sits in his London club next to the River Thames in 2019, but it was real bullets not the comic book bang-bang-and-get-up-again version. If you got hit, you bled. It was a brutal world we were in and brutal things were done.

'I was there, but I was a different man then. But they were done. 'There is no question of that.'

Eddie found himself throughout his life surrounded by boys, young men, older bruised and battered men, many who were so off their heads, such a mess, that having anything to do with them devastated the mind. Being on the same planet was tough enough, but they were so turned around they were totally unpredictable. That's what brought the headaches – if you were involved in a bit of business, business of an entrepreneurial variety, you wanted people to keep to the script. Not be unpredictable.

Eddie, then as now, liked to know his fellow man and he liked them to be like him, tough and willing to battle for his corner, to take chances to protect his own territory, but be experienced enough to respect pain. He admired and wanted reliability, for, in the world of criminal chance, a player had to stick to his word, be that rare, remarkable oxymoron: an honest crook.

Eddie Richardson has also always carried the awesome weight of his brother Charlie, a man whom Eddie now believes was warped by his early days in reform school. And Charlie was heavy, even as a brother. They are linked by birth, myth and history, but Eddie Richardson learned a Biblical lesson as his brother grew more and more imaginative in his plans.

Eddie and Charlie Richardson were untouchable. Legend said they owned the police. They could buy any witness, no jury could be secured. Charlie believed the publicity. Others sold it. Tabloid history has offered fact and fiction about the Richardsons, making mufti and uniform interchangeable, but Eddie is straight about the intensity of his so often furious fraternal relationship.

When Charlie Richardson died in September 2012, from peritonitis following years of wheezing, suffering with emphysema aggravated by his decades-long passion for tobacco (from aged eight) and cannabis (all his prison life), it gave Eddie the moment to confront his own mortality. He pondered on the crazy days when neither mortality nor any other obstacle was a problem for him, a young man then on the up.

He says he won't pretend, the way he used to, that he will

never die. He's gained an understanding with himself of what is inevitable.

Yet, with men like Eddie Richardson, although intellectual thought tells them that's so, there's a cavalcade of bravado which can never quite believe it, no matter how great the evidence.

Charlie gave him more trouble than his own supposed enemies. This extraordinary fact of his life is what made him, forced him, to be very much his own man: he had to be so to survive.

Eddie Richardson has over many years disguised some of the animosity with his brother, offered a rather oblique view, the Venetian blinds snapped down on the actuality. The torture, the horror, the nastiness were all shaded by suggestions of fake news, of bent coppers being snide, of brothel-creeping-suede-shoe journalists inventing outrage for lurid headlines. Charlie Richardson had proclaimed long and loud that the library of stories about 'torture and the rest' was a nonsense.

In the Wild West London of the Richardsons' prime there were other brothers who could happily be cast in that fiendish frame; even now, with the twenty-first century well out of the starting blocks, there remains for many the wonder, the eternal curiosity, and what was, for some, a fatal fascination for the detritus of the rivalry between the Richardson Brothers and the Kray Twins.

It had its spectacular moments. Ronnie Kray, in his manic agitation, became so determined to wipe out Eddie and Charlie Richardson that, his requested limpet mines and Mills bombs (fragmenting hand grenades) not being available, he armed himself and his brother Reggie with new Browning machine-guns ('a hundred and fifty quid well spent,' said 'Colonel' Ron Kray). Events, as the gangsters' much discussed Prime

Minister Harold Macmillan knew, can upset any plans, and the shoot-out puttered out like a damp squib. Eddie believes any confrontation would have gone his and Charlie's way: 'Put it this way, if the Twins were put in a cell with Charlie and I and told to fight it out I know Charlie and I would have walked out the next day. No question.'

DOUGLAS THOMPSON
London and Suffolk, England

GRAVE MISTAKES

With the twenty-first century arriving, several good friends and family have had the solemn words spoken over or about them. Most took secrets with them, but my friend Danny Pembroke left us with one of the biggest, a story I couldn't reveal until he'd gone.

I'd known Danny most of my life; we grew up round the corner from each other, he was in Crown Street just off from Wyndham Road in Camberwell, South London, where I was brought up. He was in the Army, did his National Service in Malaysia. He was a very sound man was our Danny; I called him 'DP'. He was steady and careful – which is why he got away with his role and his money from the Great Train Robbery.

They still rabbit on about Ronnie Biggs and all his nonsense, but Danny was on the train, an active member of the team, and escaped with a fortune. It was tens of thousands of pounds in 1963 and that's millions today. With all the bullion robberies and high-tech cyber crimes and this 'genius' and that 'mastermind', the train job still had an impact that's never been forgotten. They stole banknotes, £2.6 million in cash [the gang held up a Glasgow to Euston mail train at Sears Crossing, near Cheddington, Buckinghamshire on 8 August 1963], which is £40 to 50 million, depending on who's counting, half a century or more later. Bruce Reynolds, who led the job, 'Napoleon' we called him, gathered a strong team around him. It should never have gone wrong.

I shared a few prisons with the Train Robbers over the years. Some who served their time and got out of prison did OK but it went bad for others: 'Buster' Edwards ended up hanging himself [1994], Charlie Wilson got knocked by a hitman in Spain [1990].

Danny Pembroke waltzed through it all and stayed a free man. He was pulled in, but they had nothing on him. [Pembroke's home was searched on 6 September 1963, by Flying Squad officers, including the then Detective Sergeant Jack Slipper, 'Slipper of the Yard'.] Danny had worn gloves for every moment that mattered during and after the robbery that the papers called the Crime of the Century, and the job itself probably was – give or take the ones that no one ever heard of.

The rest of the boys were nicked and convicted through fingerprints and forensic evidence linking them to their hideout, Leatherslade Farm, near Aylesbury, Buckinghamshire. They'd taken a hundred and twenty sacks of notes – used fivers and one-pound notes – and planned to sit it out for a few weeks at the farm. They had food and drinks and played Monopoly with real cash – they had plenty of it. Paranoia got them; they were spooked. RAF planes that had nothing to do with the hunt for them flew low over the farm. It happened a few times, they were training flights, and the boys panicked, split the money – Danny got £140,000 plus – and fled. The plan had been to torch the farm but we know that never happened. When the police got to the farm they found all the debris, the Post Office sacks, the remains of food, and lots and lots of fingerprints.

The police took Danny's prints and even checked samples of his pubic hair from the sleeping bags they found at the farm. There wasn't a match. He was free to go and look after his money.

All the others got time, not money. People like Biggs were an afterthought for the robbery but Danny was wanted on the train job, a good man. He went in with the South London lads, Bobby Welch, Tommy Wisbey and 'Big Jim' Hussey. The South-West Gang had a huge reputation and had done business on the London to Brighton trains and this was a big job, lots of people involved, so an experienced man like Danny was a bonus. He was like so many of us around our way, eager to get on, to make a living, and after he left the Army he drifted into doing a bit of work here and there. The train robbery was a big opportunity. He got away with it but he spent his life afterwards working hard to make a living for his family and doing all hours as a London cabbie. So, where did all the bank notes go? Well, that's more twisted than a Roald Dahl story.

After the train job, Danny lived in Chislehurst, Kent, working his cab to bring up his five children. He had a whole load of grandchildren and one great grandson by the time he died, aged seventy-nine, on 28 February 2015. He had a heart attack in his sleep, so there was not a lot of suffering. A week or so later I was with his family and friends for his funeral at Kemnal Park Cemetery near where Danny lived. We all got together after the ceremonies at The Manor at Bickley in Bromley, Kent. I was talking to Danny's son Danny – DP Junior – and he was concerned that people would think that his father had done something wrong, that he'd grassed to the police to stop being arrested for the train robbery. There was a story about fifty grand being left in a phone box that was a pay-off for the Flying Squad.

I assured DP Junior that his father was a straight man. He had nothing to do with pay-offs or doing deals with the police. He'd just been careful, and it was not nuclear physics to think to keep his gloves on at Leatherslade Farm where the foolishness happened. Later, there was no way he could give himself away by making a mistake and spending too much.

Not, as it turned out, that he had cash to splash out.

After the train robbery Danny took care of his money and also the shares of Bobby Welch and poor Tommy Wisbey, another of the trainmen who's gone [Wisbey died in December 2016]. He had cash from a couple of the others too. He was trusted. Danny went down to Devon, to a village called Beaford near Great Torrington. They hid their money there. It was a fortune.

And right at that time Charlie was on his quest to turn himself into South London's version of De Beers and become a diamond and mining zillionaire in South Africa. Charlie was into 50-guinea suits then, tycoon togs and a puffed-out chest.

But quick as he got money, and he had tens and tens of thousands invested, he needed more. Bruce Reynolds had a favourite saying: 'A friend in need is a friend you don't need.'

Danny and his South London lads, with 'hot' money they wanted laundered, were open season for Charlie. He was a good salesman, don't worry about that. He was also desperate for cash to chase a fortune.

'It's a doddle, I'll double it. No, I'll treble it. And, I'll see there's even a little bonus on top of that.'

Danny and the others got the cash out of safekeeping in Devon. Charlie was going to make them the richest men in the world, partners in the biggest mining business ever. It was, as his sales patter went, the greatest opportunity in the history of opportunities. Danny personally invested a lump of the Great Train Robbery take, £25,000, and no one ever saw the money again.

They got nothing back, not a penny of their 'investment', not even retribution.

For the celebration of Danny's life at The Manor at Bickley a photograph of our onetime football team, Soho Rangers FC, was blown up and given pride of place on the wall. It was quite a team.

The names, as they run across the photograph include me, our managers, Stanley Baker, and Albert Dimes, Billy Rawlins, Reggie Saunders, George Wisbey [Tommy's brother], goalie Danny Pembroke, Bill Staynton, Tommy McCarthy, Frankie Fraser, Bert McCarthy, Peter Warner, Ronnie Jeffrey and Ronnie Oliver.

My brother Charlie isn't in the picture.

He wasn't much of a team player.

BOOK ONE
FAMILY MATTERS

CHAPTER ONE

LAST ORDERS?

It had all started as a laugh-a-minute night, a few drinks and jokes in the pub after a long day and no worries other than where to have one more drink. My mate Dickie Martin, who worked on a demolition team and did business at our scrapyard, suggested we go to a club in Peckham. Now, to run a club in Peckham in the late 1950s and 1960s needed more than charm and a backdoor licence for after-time drinks. You needed to be tough, to be able to look after yourself. That was Bill Slack.

I'd never met the man when I went to his club for a drink with Dickie Martin. I was twenty-three years old and very happy-go-lucky, but I wasn't happy moments after we knocked on the door of Slack's club. It wasn't much of a place, a lick of paint was overdue, but you could get a drink. It was around midnight, not too late for a place like that. We knocked again when there was no answer. I might have knocked again but the doors swung open and about fifteen of them came steaming out. I'd no idea what it was all about. They were screaming and cursing, we were 'fucking arseholes' and we were going to get done over. One of them had a shovel and he belted Dickie Martin with it. I banged one and he shoved off but in that time Dickie got a terrible beating and ended up with thirty stitches in his face. They had left Dickie alone now and were after me. I lumped another one and got around the corner of the place where a big bastard was standing, but I dodged around him. The odds were not on – I went back home and Charlie was still up. He was livid, as angry as me when I told him the story. We got some tools, jemmies and coshes, and we raced back to the club but Slack had closed and locked up. But that wasn't the end of it for me.

I don't think he knew who I was when he came at us. He did a little later. We jemmied open the locked doors and we were in the place. We smashed it to pieces, anything that could be broken we broke. We smashed bottles, drinking glasses and the mirrors and windows. We kicked in cupboards. We took all our anger out on the property because we couldn't do it to that bunch of bastards who attacked Dickie and me. It was a pleasure taking the place apart. I wanted to do the same to Bill Slack.

I was determined to find and beat the shit out of him. I was ready for a tear-up. For you who don't know, a tear-up is a good going fight where iron bars or the like are the weapon of choice. I wanted to find Slackie – and I wanted a big blunt instrument to hammer him with.

And Slack knew I was coming. All of Peckham did.

It became a vendetta for me and Charlie and my dad, who was a tough man especially with his temper up. He had a way with him, especially with women, he'd twinkle-eye them into his arms, but if things got rough he could match it. He'd been a prizefighter in the war, in the Norfolk Regiment with the Army in India, the Merchant Navy, and now he was at Bill Slack's front door.

We tracked Slack down, found his house. My dad, Charlie Senior, was a big man, not burly but tall, around six foot. Slack was if anything an inch or so taller and vicious but he didn't trouble me. I was going to have him. It was a matter of honour; I was going to sort out Slack. People couldn't take liberties. I had a really short fuse.

Charlie and I had synchronised our watches with our dad: he'd knock on Slackie's front door, Charlie and I would nip over the back fence and into the house. Which was much how it went. Except Slackie was expecting us. We were all but silent, but his nerve ends were up and he heard us. In turn, I heard a nervous cough, quiet, like a deep breath, and there he was in front of me. His eyes were so bloodshot I couldn't tell what colour they were but the gun held tight in his fist was clear enough. It was pointed at my head. He stared at me, his eyes beaded like a stuffed toy. The gun in his hand magnified him, he seemed to have got taller, his shoulders wider.

His only way out was to put bullets in Charlie and me. And that didn't bother him one bit. His problem was it didn't bother me either. He was warning us to back up, steadying himself to fire. The gun he held was well used and I could smell the gun oil; it was cleaned, loaded and ready for action. Slackie himself wasn't so well prepared. He glanced away and I lashed out with the bottom end of a pneumatic drill and the gun flew out of his hand and thumped across the brittle linoleum. I belted all kinds of hell out of Slackie and the bloodied bar slipped out of my hand. Charlie had kept an eye out and we left Slackie moaning on the floor.

As I said, Dickie Martin got a terrible beating and needed thirty stitches in his face and never went to the police. Bill Slack got a terrible beating, and he never called the police. People didn't do that in them days. It was different culture entirely; you had to look after yourself. We never heard of or about Bill Slack again. But everybody heard about us. *The Richardsons* were a family business, the old man, Charlie and I. None of us knew what an extraordinary story it would be. I should have guessed, given my childhood, but I am not inviting sympathy. I never have. The deal always was that if you handed it out, you took it in the same way; no complaining. We were just getting started and it was all going our way. There wasn't much to complain about.

———

The only time I ever felt hard done by, sorry for myself, was when Hitler was making a bloody nuisance of himself. I was a toddler when his Luftwaffe started dropping bombs on London. I didn't mind the bombs, they made life exciting and I had a collection of bits of shrapnel. It was being evacuated that upset me. It's when I learned, a long, long time ago, to be careful about who I trusted.

Of course, we're all born trusting: I was [on 29 January 1936], and into a world of women who could cope with anything, who grafted and loved their families. Around our way you stopped unconditional trusting the moment you got out of the pram.

My mother Eileen never complained and she had Charlie my dad to put up with. Dad was a charmer and my mother fell for him. She was born in Camberwell and her mother Lizzie was a tough one too. She'd come over from Ireland as a baby and never went back until she was eighty years old. In between she married Bill Allen who was a printer and she ran the newsagents' shop on Wyndham Road, Camberwell. My mum was the first of their three daughters. When she married my dad they lived in a little flat, it was just a room, in Twickenham over a shop in Hamptons Road. Charlie was born there [18 January 1934] and then they moved back to Camberwell and got a place on Wren Road near the police station. I came along and then, with years in between, we'd moved to Victoria Mansions on Wyndham Road and my brother Alan [1943] and our sister Elaine [1951] arrived.

There was a toilet and washstand but no bath; God forbid a shower, at Victoria Mansions. I had to line up with everyone else for a proper clean-up at Manor Place Baths every Saturday. You took a number and called out if you wanted hot water. My mum helped out at the newsagents' shop and worked at a Lyons café near the flat: she was a 'nippy', a waitress who moved quickly, nipped about serving the tea and cakes. Dad was from a huge brood – thirteen kids, seven from his mum and dad, and half a dozen others after his dad died and his mum married again. The Richardsons and the Hummerstons. They were mostly tough nuts.

They say the boy is the father of the man and that's what I grew up around. Tough, hard men. My father was a boxer – he did it for cash, fighting as Charlie Binks. He knocked out my Uncle Wally with one punch at a family wedding. Wally was pissed, but then, so was my dad. Dad's criminal trouble began when he knocked out a sergeant in the Army and had to desert from India; a clever bastard, he signed on with the Merchant Navy and cruised away from trouble.

I don't recall much of it, but he was jailed for robbery, got a couple of years inside. Charlie remembered being taken by Mum to see him. I used to trail along after Charlie when we were little boys. There's a picture of the two of us at the seaside with a stuffed Donald Duck and we looked a lot more innocent than the daffy duck. Charlie was five when he started at infants' school at Comber Grove. I'd walk after him to school. I was only three years old and I wanted to go in with Charlie. He took me into his class and the teachers just accepted it. When I think back... here was little Charlie watching over all the little kids. Every afternoon there was a half-hour nap and all the kids had to lie down and sleep. Charlie claimed he went around every one of them, me included, and tucked us in our blankets.

Amazing, for he spent the rest of his life tucking people up.

But he was the oldest, man of the house if you like, for our dad was not about that much; when he was it was great fun for a time because he'd come back from sea with exotic bits, stuff you couldn't get a look at at home.

But most of the time it was Mum and mostly our grandparents who watched us and we got away with more mischief than other kids. My best mate, Whippet Tear, he was one of thirteen kids, got backhanders from his folks for being a rogue, but not us. The grown-ups were too busy worrying about surviving from moment to moment than what we were up to.

When the Germans started dropping bombs on us every night we moved into our grandparents' flat above their shop. We'd huddle up, crushed in beneath the kitchen table to sleep. I wasn't aware of the dangers – it was different, so it was fun. My mother got more and more concerned about the bombing – half the road had vanished, flattened by the bombs. She started telling Charlie and me stories about the countryside, the cows and the sheep and how nice it was. It was as big a fairy story as Hans Christian Andersen.

We got shifted off to a farm in Dorset and it wasn't Old MacDonald's. There was a load of us and we all met at Camberwell Town Hall and then got on buses. I was lucky in that Charlie and I were kept together; some of the kids were split up from their brothers and sisters, which was cruel. It was bad enough having to leave London and your family and here was authority getting it wrong and creating problems that never needed to be there. Charlie thought it was a great adventure and cheered me up on the way – little did we know. We were boarded in a big farmhouse; it seemed to have room after room and after room but we got stuck in a dormitory with a gang of other boys. There were about twenty boys, six or so to a room, and they told us what bastards our 'guardians' were. They were three ugly-sister types who were being paid to have us. I was no Cinderella and neither was Charlie, but the sisters' animals got a better deal than we had. Charlie made friends with another boy and I kept up with them, so we had our team, but the rules were strict: all day at the village school, a flint and brick building, a nasty mess for tea and then bed. I was only a toddler but I learned you had to push hard to get anything. They were fucking horrible lessons to be given so early. My mother was fretting about us all the time and sent down food parcels but we never got a sniff of any of that. We were stuck in the long village of Piddletrenthide – yes, Piddletrenthide – in Dorset and Mum was four hours, if things went well, away from us by train in London.

It was hellish. The food was awful, we got skinny and we got scabies. Finally, we got out. First, Charlie did what he spent the rest of his life at – running away, trying to escape from the consequences. This first time he took me with him and another kid came along. We must have gone for a mile or so, it seemed like a marathon, but we – three scruffy little kids –were picked up by the local policeman and taken to the local nick. From there we were taken back to the farm where it was cold baths, six of the best with a cane on the bare backside, and a week without tea after school.

When our mother came on a visit we poured how badly we were being treated and fed and she twigged that we weren't getting the food parcels she'd worked so hard to be able to send. She could see how rough we looked but there wasn't much she could do. However, on her next visit both Charlie and I had scabies, our skin was covered in infected scabs. She took me away immediately but the nurses insisted Charlie was too ill to leave hospital. He was in a right state, a real mess with the sores, in agony with them. It took a lot to keep him down but the scabies did that. Reluctantly, Mum left Charlie and took me back to Camberwell. It was a tearful journey on the train. When Dad found out that Charlie was still stuck down there he went off like a rocket. And took off down to Dorset by train. By all account he marched into the hospital like the 8th Army, chucked Charlie over his shoulder like a sack of spuds, and marched him out of there at a quick one two. Dad's morality might have been as light as a pound note but he had his moments of being a hands-on dad. But only moments. His money from the shipping line would come into Mum every week, so there was that security; there weren't cascades of cash but we didn't go short. There was no childhood trauma which led us to a life of crime.

If anything, it was Dad's tales of adventures, which he'd bring back along with our presents when he came home on leave, which put us boys on the lookout for excitement. We knew they had to be great adventures for when he was home Dad spent most of his time sleeping them off. Mum was busier, promoted to manageress at the Lyons teashop at Camberwell Green, and we were wilder. Charlie would be up to stuff and I would get dragged along. Bombed-out South London was like a playground, a devastated area like one of those end-of-the-world black-and-white movies.

Much of it was gangs of us kids 'playing' at war, beating all kinds of hell out of each other. We had the location: for me, messing about in the wartime debris of buildings was fun. We weren't stuck in front of a television, there wasn't one, we were out on our own adventures. There always had to be an adventure. The school of hard knocks was established for me, I learned the lessons by heart. I was able to give out a kicking but I've always been able to take it, too. Charlie and I used to gather other kids around us and Charlie led the way but Charlie didn't half push his luck.

Everything was a commodity, sweets, fizzy drinks it was like living with Steptoe and Son, they were on every corner the horse and cart merchants, everything for sale at the right price, the post-war version of Ebay. Whatever you had someone somewhere would want it. When the bombs stopped the shortages didn't. Clothes were scarce, there were no frills on ladies' knickers, no turn-ups on men's trousers, and second-hand suits, and coats and all else were valuable. A pair of boots would get you up the West End for days. Wool had added value – everything has more value when you don't have it. I grew up watching all this, the harsh mechanics of day-to-day life of those who didn't have much of a life. Those who prospered were tough, singled-minded, hagglers, scam artists, the chisellers [con artists] who cheated by sneaking a toe on the scales when rags or scrap metal were being weighed; even an ounce meant extra currency.

It was another world and it was my world and it was a world of looking out for yourself and your family. We were kids but we were also junior businessmen and we had a lively number in lovely bunches of coconuts. Being little, we could get our way into the Bermondsey Docks on Jamaica Road and get off with coconut shells under our jumpers. We sold the bits – the white 'meat' was a treat – in the school playground. We'd nick canned food off the docks and knock the tins about a bit, as if it was 'damaged stock' it could be sold outside the rationing laws. We were up to all the tricks; Camberwell in the post-war years was a huge classroom for me. We figured out how to get traffic lights to change by jumping up and down, putting weight on the pressure pads in the street, and when lorries stopped at a red light we'd be onto them. Our road, Wyndham Road, was one of the popular ones for lorries taking fruit and veg through Camberwell to Vauxhall and into Covent Garden. It was well planned out: a points lad would signal that a likely lorry was coming our way, we'd jump about on the traffic pads like kids playing, red light, the lorry braked and stopped, we nipped on the back, grabbed everything we could carry and we were off at the next stop light. It was usually food but whatever was on board was for the taking.

Charlie got nicked for stealing books of a lorry and ended up in juvenile court. They read out his school reports, which were rotten; he was playing truant all the time. He got a couple of years' probation and from that he learned: he would be as nice as pie to people, perfect manners, polite and subservient but at the same time regarding these same people as wankers. Charlie could always talk the talk, find an excuse, an alibi, a reason why the fucking tragedy he'd caused had nothing whatsoever to do with him. Our mum – I always tried to protect her from our antics – didn't really have much chance with us, although our grandmother would keep an eye on us. We'd try not to get them upset but we weren't worried about anyone else.

By the time I got to The Avenue Secondary Modern School just off the Walworth Road, Charlie had graduated from there to approved school for stealing a load of lead. He'd been grassed up by another lad who confessed all to the police in return for a better deal in court. It was yet another lesson about choosing the friends you work with.

School wasn't for me: I was born with a bad ear, a hearing problem which makes it hard for me to catch what's being said; I can lose the sense of what people are saying and that's a huge handicap in the classroom. The teachers didn't have the time or the patience to repeat for one lad in the class. I'm also dyslexic, which slows up my reading. I get there fine in the end but in schooldays it was no fun. But I didn't mind school. Charlie hated it. When they raised the school leaving age from fourteen to fifteen years old he was furious, effing this and that. I don't know why, he never went anyway. He spent more time in and out of juvenile court than at school. His first proper conviction was in May1948 – I was twelve – for stealing lead, valued at one-pound sterling. When he went to approved school he was 'away', just like Dad, was 'away' at sea, and it just seemed part of my life, part of growing up.

It still makes me smile when I think of the time Charlie aged fourteen escaped from Ardale approved school at Upminster and Dad went to pick him up. Charlie got out by knotting bed sheets together and shinning down a wall where his accomplice, Dad, was waiting with a change of clothes. Here was Charlie, absconded, on the run, and on a bus with Dad. Charlie was trying to vanish into his seat and not be noticed. Nobody cared about him, but as far as he was concerned the whole of British law enforcement was on his tail. He tried to be a shadow of himself. Dad was sitting there and bored. He turned around and decided some bloke was staring at him. Charlie loved telling the story of how Dad had stood up in the middle of the bus. It was Dad's particular pantomime.

'Am I on fire?

'Am I on fucking fire? What are you looking at?'

He pretended he was in flames. He had the whole bus looking at him. He started waving his arms around and flapping at himself to put out this fantasy fire.

'Am I on fucking fire?

'Oh, yes I am.

'Oh, no, I'm not.'

As kids we used it as a catch phrase when we got funny looks. But, really, we weren't kids any more.

Charlie's return home was, of course, just a little break and he soon went back at Ardale. Yes, we still had the two-year age gap, but we were more equal. He'd changed then, become brasher and more confident: the system that was supposedly rehabilitating him from his criminal tendencies was just pumping them into his blood: everyone he met at approved school or lining up to meet a probation officer was another influence and not for the better.

Everybody he met and I met through him were lads on the make, tough nuts who were happy to do anything required to get what they wanted. And it worked. I soon found out the system was shite. I loved motors, and me and a couple of friends were out collecting conkers near Dulwich Hamlet's football ground. As we wandered along there were cars parked up and down Red Post Hill and we were looking in the windows of them. One car was unlocked and there was a torch on the passenger seat. I picked it up and stuck it in my bag of conkers. Somebody must have seen me for by the time we got to the end of the street there was a police van parked up. Me and the kids I was with – John Daly who made it big producing movies, and Jimmy Hutton – gave the coppers some cheek, some verbal. One copper found the torch and asked which car I'd taken it from. I hadn't a clue ('just one of 'em) and this big fat copper started slapping me about the face. He really belted me, gave me a smacking, and he enjoyed it. They took us all to Camberwell nick and John and I said we'd taken the torch. The sergeant at the police station was OK. Then Dad, who was home on leave, pitched up. He went mental, truly mental. He shouted and wanted to 'bash up that bastard cop who'd hit his son'. The police sergeant eventually calmed him down but only a bit; this older cop knew that his policeman had been out of order with me. Dad never got to have a proper go at him but we never saw that particular cop again.

I encountered plenty of other cops. It wasn't a Professor Moriarty job, that much of a crime, but it taught me that there was no such thing as 'a fair cop' and that no one in authority was going to cut me any slack. I was lucky, I could look after myself and the bullies got it or they kept away. Nobody bothered much if we missed school. This brave new world they were pushing at the time gave us free time in school hours – time to contemplate our navels – but we'd take off because no one was watching us, keeping us where we should have been.

We always seemed to be on to something, up to some devilment or other. All the kids were. Getting lead off a roof was easier than algebra and a lot more profitable even when I had to use an older bloke, a middle man even then, to do a deal with the scrapyards as they wouldn't entertain us for being so young. That's where I saw the business potential in scrap. Everybody seemed to leave the yards with something, usually a bundle of pound notes. Supply and demand, you've got it, they want it, what's the price? It was simple, easy to understand: my formal education might not have been up to much but I was smart. I was angry and frustrated too because it was difficult to settle down to simply learn. It had been a haphazard upbringing – lively is the word. Lively, loving home life.

It was even harder for me not being able to hear the teacher clearly. The teachers use to shout at me and ask if I was listening. I was bloody listening but I couldn't hear what they were saying and I got upset at them because it was so infuriating. I took off class as much as possible.

What I learned most at school was that I was not afraid of

confrontation, of a bare-knuckle fight. Having a punch-up or a tear-up and coming out on top meant you got respect. In turn, I learned early, in having that respect you could make people do what you wanted. There were teachers at school who liked to cane kids just for their perverted pleasure. They got no respect. Those who did were the ones who played it fair and resorted to physical punishment when you'd pushed them too far and you knew it. I liked to fight to make my ground, every reason was an excuse to go at it. It was quick and fair and got the job done.

For me, having no fear was not a handicap; not in life and not playing football – I'm a lifetime Millwall fan – for I went into everything willing to hand it out but take it if the other bloke was strong enough to hand it out. Physically, I was well co-ordinated, an all-rounder at cricket and I played it quite seriously, but like all post-war kids we imitated those around us and smoked. I'd buy 'a single', one cigarette, because that's all I had; any kid with a packet of five Woodbines had got lucky somewhere. Dad always had a Capstan Full Strength on the go. I wanted to be like Dad. *Men* smoked. That was the life and the way to get on.

I don't know exactly when it happened but in our teenaged years we stopped just being known as local kids: we became *the Richardsons*.

Metamorphis? That's what they call it. Two tough little kids from the wrong end of nowhere were suddenly the boys to follow, to look up to, the men to fear. I loved it. But it wasn't any sort of preparation for a nine to five 'normal' life in 'Fifties' Britain; the Richardsons were perky pegs in a square world looked at through net curtains with lots of snide gossip. Girls who wore a sleeveless cardigan were tarts and housewives who didn't scrub their front step on a Friday were not much better. Everyone was constantly judged by other people's perceptions. With all the ducking and diving I did there was never much chance of being granted a halo. London had plenty of dark corners and we found them all. The society columns were still big in the newspapers, with double-barrelled names spilling out of them; even early on we were more likely to be looking down double-barrelled shotguns. It was a tough time and crazy with it, the bad guys would cut, shoot and kill – often each other – for power and profit. Each territory had its own rules and risks. And bosses. There was certainly a sense of anything goes, an overspill of the Blitz mentality, of the blackout; for the wide boys, the chancers at every level, there were many opportunities. Around every corner.

Food rationing did not end until midnight on 4 July 1954 and trains still ran on steam. We were running on adrenalin with extra shots of gall, a wicked chutzpah. There wasn't much money or anything else about, but the proper villains were rolling in cash. And we spotted that, witnessed it first-hand. Money was about if you knew how to go about getting it. I was willing to work for it but not to be taken advantage of. I've always looked for and been open to an opportunity. You have to be enthusiastic to get on. At school, I was enthusiastic to leave. The only classes that grabbed my interest were woodwork and technical drawing and so that's what I was really good at: the skills that took me as a fifteen-year-old boy to a company called Durrants in Great Dover Street in Southwark.

The deal for me training as a draughtsman meant one day a week, a Friday, at a college, but I didn't want to sit behind a classroom desk and rarely turned up; if I did it was to make a noise. They turfed me out of college but I stuck it with Durrants for it was an easy life – I was in the cashiers' department. I took cheques to the bank and in my little office briefcase I brought back the deposit slips and other bits of paperwork. Much more intriguing was the cash job when money for the weekly payroll was collected. The boss did that job, and it got him all wound up he was so scared of being robbed and kicked about a bit. It never crossed my mind to try, it wasn't my thing, but it shows how it all was in those days, in the Fifties.

Britain, and especially London, was truly only waking up after the war. When you feel lucky to be alive, it's natural to be casual about the day to day. I was too young to take any of it seriously – I wanted to get on, make a go of things, get some cash in my pocket, so off I went and met my pal Whippet at Waterloo Station to do some heavy lifting.

CHAPTER TWO

THE HARDER THEY FALL

Whippet Tear was a good friend, always on the lookout for you – as well, of course, as himself. And that's fair. He was making good money as a porter at Waterloo Station where lots of international travellers arrived in London. He said we could do well as a team, especially working the boat trains which came up from Southampton and through Clapham Junction to us. We'd be on the trains chatting to the passengers before they'd stopped at their platform. Soon, I was able to spot the elite Goyard luggage, which I learned was a big step up from the Louis Vuitton stuff, and a guarantee of good strong tips. These people move around with half a dozen cases, sometimes twice that, and they'd drop you a thick fold of cash for each bag.

We made sure we were first in line to be of well-paid service. I learned to read people' s characters, the men who wanted to show off their money to their women, those that were grateful for me easing their luggage burden, and those who felt entitled to walk off with their head in the air with me trotting behind.

I was happy to play the game – I was being paid for it. And the weight training with the luggage was good for my boxing. There's no question fighting was in our blood, and round our way that was a huge plus. A 'straightener', a man-to-man fight, was the method of choice to settle any argument, any outstanding score. I was always up for a straightener and so were lots of others. That meant regular punch-ups inside and out of the pubs around Wyndham Road.

There was nothing lyrical about these, but well-oiled tough guys battering each other like fish cakes around closing time was more entertaining than the telly. It was like watching *Tom and Jerry* cartoons because the fighters always got up and walked away, sometimes to become friends again over yet more drink. I was only beginning to understand the full significance of violence and having a reputation for it. If you were feared you didn't have to fight, your name was enough, but as time went on I liked to regularly endorse my credentials. It was professional boxers who were our sporting heroes and boxing was part of everyday life. Like youngsters who want to score the winning goal at a Cup Final or be the batsman to snatch victory from defeat at the Test Match, I wanted to be a boxing champion. Charlie and I were good in the ring, the old man had seen to that. He'd take us down on a Saturday morning to the Lynn club on the Walworth Road and show us how to handle ourselves. Charlie was always roughing up and giving off verbal mayhem. He took on a guy who was bigger and heavier than he was in the Evening Institute Championships. My dad missed the guy hitting the deck – he was in the office complaining about the weigh-in scales when Charlie knocked the other fighter out.

Still, Charlie wasn't that interested in boxing as a sport. I loved it, always have, always will. There were boxing clubs all around and that's where I wanted to be. The only thing the youth clubs and their table tennis had over them were the girls that went to them; for the girls I went to the espresso bars with their cups of froth and the new gimmick from America, juke boxes.

I was keen on girls and on having a good time. I was a teenager and it didn't take much to please me. Of course, enjoying both meant having cash and I was happy to work for it and also make use of opportunities. Not having cash was a trauma.

There was always some way you could do better.

I moved on from Waterloo to scale high buildings as part of a cleaning crew operating from outside cradles to wash down the outsides of the premises. I liked being there up in the sky, there was a great freedom about it. I used Charlie's insurance cards, him being a couple of years older, so I got a full man's wage – a little extra – and he got his cards stamped, which allowed him to be in more than one place at the same time.

We were living by then in a council flat with five bedrooms not much of a walk from Wyndham Road at a place called Champion Hill. I stuck mostly around Camberwell and Streatham, the West End was an out of towner, and we'd go a bit further afield – maybe to New Cross! – if we had boxing organised. Charlie and I sometimes were on the same amateur bill – just like Ronnie, Reggie and Charlie Kray once were – but he let it go and I was unlucky. Or, rather, I didn't push myself forward. I was a welterweight fighter after I left school but grew into an eighteen-year-old middleweight and trained in the gym on the top floor of the Thomas A Becket pub on the Old

Kent Road. I had sparring matches there with Bobby Callaghan who was a professional; his brother Henry was going to be my manager when I went professional. It was a fabulous venue, an inspiring place. A younger guy called Henry Cooper was about. [Muhammad Ali, Joe Frazier and Sugar Ray Leonard sparred at the Thomas A Becket when they were preparing for bouts in Britain. Sir Henry Cooper, the former British, European and Commonwealth heavyweight champion, trained at the pub's gym six days a week for fourteen years from 1956.] It was a boxing tragedy that stopped my professional career in the ring. Bobby Callaghan was severely hurt in a fight and died. His brother's death knocked the will out of Henry Callaghan and I stepped back. I was a teenager, and there was lots to do.

Truly, I believe my commitment wasn't strong enough or I would have kept at it, worked with some other trainers and managers. With everything you have to be enthusiastic. Another excellent reason was I was having success wrestling with girls. I was very active, chasing up buildings all day, dating girls and enjoying Saturday nights at the local dances halls where you could always find someone to enjoy a 'straightener' with if the evening needed livening up. Boring was the last thing my life ever became.

But possibly the most important fight in my life was with Charlie. As I got stronger and tougher and more single-minded our relationship began to strain.

I'd saved up cash for a coat and I was going to wear it out on a date but when I got home to Champion Hill it was gone – it was on Charlie's shoulders and he was out for the night. When Charlie got back wearing my coat I let off with the verbals; it wasn't polite:

'What you doing with my fucking coat? Fucking thief – stealing my coat.

'You fucking bastard, taking my things...'

Then he charged me head first, nutting me, his little party trick.

I retaliated in a frenzy. He was shocked. I could see it in his eyes: they stood out as if they were spring loaded. He landed flat out on his back.

We weren't boxing, there were no rules. He clipped me under the right eye and I gave him a good left hook and then we were grabbing and punching at each other, having a proper tear-up that was going to end in serious damage. Then, we were saved by a familiar and shrill scream. The only referee who had a chance of stopping this fight appeared – our mum. She'd heard the commotion, the whole street had, and she pulled us apart and stood there an arm on each of our shoulders shouting at us to calm down, to stop fighting. We weren't going to turn on her.

I stood still. Charlie was breathless but managed a snarl, turned and stormed out of the house.

I was eighteen years old and, that day, I was also my own man, a confident man and not beholden to my brother. Charlie knew then I would never play follow-the-leader with him. I had always been willing to go along with him, keep him happy, keep the peace, but he knew after that fight he could never intimidate me. Fighting had been the unofficial school sport and I won honours in it, I was never beaten, hit a few times but never hurt badly. I believe that was because I always thought ahead, worked out how the other bloke would react.

Charlie, of course, never gave up. Now, it was always stories of great prospects and deals, he was only ever truly happy if he was doing one dodgy deal or another. And he could talk a deal, oh, he could talk and spin and spin again. Despite our aggravations with each other there was always a place for me in his business adventures and, in time, I started working with him at weekends.

One day our dad and he took off for Canada with Elizabeth, a Scottish nurse. [My half-brother Charlie – yes, another Charlie – was born there and at the time of writing lives in Spain.]

We hated Dad for scarpering and had always taken Mum's side. Dad blamed Charlie and me for driving him away but he was the nuisance. Mum was always furious with Dad, but, rascal that he was, she loved him. The problem was that so did a lot of other women over the years.

I'd been working with Charlie at the scrapyard he rented at Peckford Place in Brixton, but then Mum heard – she was working with gran in the family sweet shop by then and picked up and broadcast more news than the BBC Radio Home Service – there was an end-of-terrace building and a yard up for sale at 33a, Addington Square, London SE5. It was a two-storey building off Camberwell Road and it stuck out; it looked like they'd forgotten to finish it as the rest of the houses in the Georgian square were three-storey.

The Peckford Scrap Metal Company Ltd was established on Addington Square. [Because of the Eddie Richardson family connection, 33a Addington Square appears in London history books, a prime example is *The London Compendium* by Ed Glinert, Penguin, 2012.]

I felt obliged to help out this family business. I could see it had a future but it wasn't easy money; there was a lot of hard graft and it was lucky I was a big, strong lad, for when I was doing it part time we hefted about great tons of material. They said they didn't need a crane when I was on duty and I could pick up most about anything including car engines. I'd have to cut the metals we picked up – and paid for – to make them manageable for transport. 'I was racing around in lorries, working cranes, and I enjoyed it for it was hard work for hard cash. I always liked having a thick wad of cash in my pocket. The business turnover was healthy and I was persuaded to join full time and Mum came on as the book-keeper.

I enjoyed setting down our business roots in Addington Square, which had a lot going for us in our particular line of work. There was plenty of space around the big old houses, real period buildings, room to move about although the yard itself wasn't as big as some. There was a lot of thieving and dodgy stuff going on all around me, always an opportunity being offered by friends. One led to me being nicked proper for the first time when I was eighteen: on reflection it was quite an achievement for me that it took that long given all the ducking and diving I did throughout my teens. A couple of friends I used to mooch about the Elephant and Castle with specialised in 'the plank' used to burst into shops. They needed a driver and that was me: we stole a scaffolding plank off a building site and the plan this time was to secure the plank to a car bumper and ram into a tobacconist shop, rush in and out with as many packets of cigarettes – as good as cash they were – as we could carry and not be nabbed. Before we even got to that piece of work we were spotted by the cops – the plank stuck out...

I tried to escape them like a racing driver but around all the twists and turns I drove into a dead end. I got my first experience of being banged up by being put on remand for a week at Wormwood Scrubs. It was like taking a university class, an honours degree. I learned more in that week than I had in years, more about being your own man and not taking any shit from anyone. It toughened me even more for it emphasised the lesson that you have to be seen to prove yourself, to face down or beat down those who stand against you.

That little touch of being locked up showed me the prison system is a breeding ground for first-class villainy; I'd seen how Charlie had learned many a lesson. I found myself in the Magistrates' Court with the police claiming we were out to rob a jewellery shop. I followed my golden rule and said nothing, admitted to nothing. The other two lads, who were a couple of years older than me – I always looked older because of my size, my boxer's walk – pleaded guilty and got nine and six months apiece. I got probation. It was a shaker for I was then seriously involved with Maureen and we planned to get married. I wanted a proper wedding, the full works. I have always wanted and to the best of my ability done things as properly and as special as I can. For Maureen it had to be the best wedding ever.

Many of the dealings at Addington Square were on the level, accounts-book legal, but there were regular off-books operations. It made me wonder about the security of the nation when we were told about torpedoes from the Royal Navy's submarines stacked in barges around local docks. The copper cones of torpedoes had great value but each one weighed a hundred pounds. I learned that the back-breaking way, lifting them into our lorries. The dockers, who we rewarded handsomely, made it easy for us to to get in, but undoing padlocks or cutting wire fences in advance with such 'hot' goods we had to be careful and turn the metal into gold, as it were, as fast as possible.

By then we were looking after enough people to be safe but it did no harm to be extra careful. We'd learned the lesson. I didn't want to pay but we had to.

Charlie had been cheap: he didn't see the point of lashing out more cash to the police if we were only dealing in legal scrap. He didn't realise that the cops wanted to be paid, no matter what we were up to, just to stay out of the way. It was a tax on us, a tax on our criminal potential. The more the potential, the more and more the penalty percentage. The police began making themselves 'seen' around Addington Square and it was bad for business. The totters didn't want to be seen around and even those with legitimate stuff didn't want to call round and show their faces to the watchers. The police finally got fed up with not being paid and Charlie was charged with dealing in a fiver's worth of stolen scaffolding. Charlie did his chat: he didn't know it was nicked, someone he didn't know had brought it in to him and rabbit, rabbit, but it did no good. He got two years' probation, but, like I was to be, got nabbed about National Service. I said I could look after the yard with Mum as Charlie went off to Blenheim Barracks at Aldershot, but he wasn't having two years away.

He played merry hell with the system, he acted crazy, complained of 'brainstorms' and had endless fainting fits. The result was a court martial for punching an officer and a dishonourable discharge: instead of two years he got six months inside the supposedly haunted Shepton Mallet prison in Somerset. Haunted? It depends how you define it: when Charlie was there it was alongside the Twins, Ronnie and Reggie Kray, and Johnny Nash of the six North London brothers. [The other five: Billy, Jimmy, Ronnie, George and Roy.]

NO HANDCUFFS

Of course, success can bring trouble. I'd never lost a fight and Charlie wasn't shy in nutting someone if they upset him. We took offence easily and I had a hell of a short fuse. I would blow up and lash out and that would be it. Charlie was quick to anger too but he also brooded about people who he felt weren't onside. I liked to confront the problem and deal with it right off. I also always put the word out if I was looking for someone to sort out. It made them jumpy, nervous and was part of the punishment for getting out of line. It also put me at an advantage.

With the business we were in there was an ever-increasing need for that special sort of unpleasantness. When people know you will respond in kind they tend to take less liberties. But, oh, that human nature again, some toe-rags enjoyed trying to chance their arm, to take those liberties.

CHAPTER THREE

TOP GEAR

Charlie knew when I wasn't happy and it was usually to do with some crafty deal of his or another. Still, irritating as he was, he was my brother and business was booming.

I was twenty, he was twenty-two, and in 1956 we were making plenty of cash. We were only ever interested in making money.

I'd kept the business thriving while Charlie was away and I'd learned to do things my own way, steady and careful but aware of opportunities. In his rush, Charlie took more risks with stolen stuff.

Yet, he followed what would be regarded as a formal business plan. He may never have used all the fancy business lingo but was dedicated to good practice, value for money, profit margins and even time and motion.

And we had cash in our pockets, wads of it. I spent it.

I was going out all the time and had a wide circle of friends, both long-time pals and guys from work, and couples Maureen and I would go to the cinema or out to dinner with. I worked hard all day and kept going at night. I never seemed to need too much sleep. Charlie had married Margaret Cheyney in 1955 when she was expecting her first child and they lived with all of us at Champion Hill. It was never ideal. I always wanted the best, and Maureen was that for me, absolutely fantastic and strong and loyal, and we went together for about twenty months before our big day at St Giles Church in Camberwell Church Street the following year. It was a fanfare of a day, a big white wedding with all the trimmings and without the punch-ups; then we were off on honeymoon to the seaside at Herne Bay in Kent. We got our own place in Eltham, a four-grand, semi-detached house on Sidcup Road, which, even if not up to nearby Henry VIII's Eltham Palace, was a fine starter home.

From the day we move into that house in Eltham, I financially looked after Maureen and our girls. It took all my time, for by then the Richardsons had become a big noise in the scrap-metal business. We bought and sold huge amounts of scrap. On a Friday the yard would be packed, stacked high with all manner of material. The turnover was quick and around £250,000 a year, £3 million in 2019.

I thrived at the legitimate side of it but all around us was the other side: cutting corners, paying the police to look or even glance the other way, was going on from breakfast until the stragglers were thrown out of illegal drinking dens in the early hours. Temptation was everywhere. That's because there were deals everywhere. If you had cash you could go along to a high street bank, deposit a few quid, have a glass of sherry with the bank manager, and walk out with a cheque book that was a powerful weapon in the fraud game.

Near Addington Square we found bigger premises at 50 New

Church Road, and that became the Richardson HQ. It had a weigh-bridge and it was perfect for us and I made sure we got it. New Church Road was where all the official and unofficial action took place for nearly a decade.

I was determined to get the premises as it was such a choice spot and we had room; you need space for stock if you're going to do the big deals. It was our depot. We had a about thirty blokes working for us, the most trusted running the yards, for there were half a dozen across South London, in Camberwell, at Battersea and Tulse Hill; Morley Street at Waterloo was run by Roy Hall, who had joined up with us when he was just a kid and Charlie caught hanging around the yard. We kinda adopted him. He was still a teenager, about fifteen years old, when he took over at Waterloo: he was on twenty-five pounds a week, a big whack. You could buy a new car for a monkey [five hundred pounds sterling] and a family's weekly shopping bill was less than one pound a week in 1956. It was a world where central heating was the luxury of choice.

Roy Hall was doing OK. We all were.

The black-and-white life – we'd watched the Queen's Coronation on a purloined 12-inch black-and-white television set on 2 June 1953 – we'd barged into after the war was now brightening up, life was more colourful.

Rock 'n' Roll had arrived and with it the juke boxes from America, which were in all the mock espresso coffee bars. Some blokes called me the king of the Teddy Boys but I was never a Ted. I didn't put brilliantine in my hair and fuck about like them. I liked to turn myself out well and the fashion at the time was drainpipe trousers and longer jackets. That's what people wore to the dance halls. The girls all wore tight sweaters with those circular skirts that swung out from the waist when they jived.

Life wasn't just good, it was easy on the eye.

And there were always opportunities. I worked hard for the profits, I put my heart into it. I really believed we, the family, the Richardsons, could turn it into a brilliant business success story.

I never thought I was taking chances. We were paying our way so everyone was getting their bung. Charlie was always quick to be upset and go after someone, take his revenge. He always wanted to proved he was the boss, he was hard and tough and in control. My idea was that unless you had to thump someone for taking liberties you might as well live and let live. Still, I was never slow to get involved when needed.

We were both twenty-something but, of course, we were getting a name, getting a reputation. And that means others get to know about you. I accepted the reputation for it was good for business and protected us from bother – but not all the time. The success of the yard at New Church Road meant we weren't getting the best use out of Addington Square. The dealers were a load of roustabouts and would be in and out of there and hang about. People had trouble going somewhere with their mates for a drink after the pubs closed at 3 p.m. in the afternoon or early at night.

I liked the idea of running a club in the upstairs of the yard's offices, running my own place, being *mine host*, so I went for it. I turned downstairs into a reception area and although upstairs wasn't the American Bar at the Savoy, it was built for purpose and serving the best liquor. We opened in the afternoons when the pubs were shut, and it was a success straight off with a solid crowd. We all loved having a go working behind the bar but I knew the necessity of barmaids too as an added attraction. Our dad was back from Canada and it was a lovely number for him working the bar. He was a scoundrel and his chat went down well with the metal men who used the club, which was called The Addington. He was a natural landlord, always ready to fill up a glass 'and have one yourself...'

He also looked and carried himself like a man who would take no nonsense, for the place attracted wild characters. It became a gathering spot for a bunch of people, bookies who worked the streets, the scrap dealers and their crowd of hangers-on, and would-be and professional villains. It was a safe place for all to have a quiet drink. And these boys lashed it down. The drinks, lorry loads of it, were consumed. Customers would order a crate of beer at a time and camp out at a table as if they were at home. The Totters, worked weekends, so business was big on a Monday when they'd sold off what they'd sorted out over the weekend; it was their day off, their day to get pissed up. Of course, drink and tough lads brings trouble: there's always someone wanting to prove how hard they are. Some of them who'd been away in prison had no idea about the Richardsons and would take liberties. I'd usually be around the New Church Road yard, about 100 yards away, and I'd be called in to sort out trouble. Usually it was straightforward. I'd flatten the guy and when he came round we'd give him a drink and it would be sorted. People understood that way of dealing with trouble. But there were always real chancers.

One South London lot of heavies who hadn't done their homework minced round looking for 'a drink' and cash to protect the club. There were five of them. I went round from the yard with Charlie and Roy Hall. There was lots of broken furniture and bones and the three of us went back to work fully fit leaving the toe-rags unconscious in the street. We had sent out the message that this was Richardson territory and liberties were dealt with severely. Still, there are always one or two idiots.

We had our regulars and there were a bunch of them in one afternoon when Dad was behind the bar. A man who had a cowboy name like Buck was making noise. He was threatening drinkers and being an arse. He was the hard man of Peckham but it turned out he wasn't the toughest guy in Peckham. I'd been loading a lorry, so I was warmed up and frisky and when I got to the club and rushed up the stairs and saw him mouthing off I shoved an arm over the bannister and cherry-picked him up by the scruff of his neck.

I dragged him downstairs.

I waited till he got to his feet, and as he went on shouting I chinned him, knocked him out with a punch on the jaw. Good, that was that dealt with. But we wanted him off the premises and Ken, one of the barmen, came and helped me lift him up and take him out of the door. But bullyboy Buck came round.

He kicked out and landed a boot right in my stomach.

Well, I came down on him with all my weight and I heard a bone or two snap in his legs. There was some squelching too. We heaved him outside and left him on the pavement. He was out of the game for months.

In hospital, where his injuries were reported to the police, he never said anything about what had really happened to him. That was the way, you never did. It wasn't worth it. If someone ended up in an ambulance or in hospital they'd always had a car accident or fallen down the stairs.

I enjoyed having the club, which was making money and having a social life,. I had, and still have, a lot of friends around me. Believe me, there is indeed strength in numbers, knowing that there are those who will look after you or yours if the need be. It was that kind of fellowship which made me part of the Westminster Boys Football Club when I heard it was in trouble. Arthur Barron, who worked in the yard with us, encouraged me, and we took over what was a Sunday league side. We got the team up from blokes from the yard and a few real good players, including a onetime Queens Park Rangers forward, and played the in the Metropolitan Sunday League. After one season we were in the First Division. I got us fitted out in a full red strip and I used to race around in it as centre forward. Charlie never played but he'd turn out to watch the games. It was fun and relaxing and it brought the lads together at weekends.

The Casbar, upstairs from the New Church Road office space, was just the job and a big step up from The Addington. For a start we could measure out the liquor: we had optics and the beer came in bottles. There were several seating areas and you could sit as well as stand at the bar. I wanted a comfortable atmosphere, so I got in good carpeting and had the club professionally decorated. It was just for us and our friends, the football lads and all the boys from the yards. I wasn't going to socialise, let my guard down, with people I didn't trust. I used to wheel in nurses from local hospitals who were always up for a lark and we'd have parties, a good time. It was nice to let off steam, for we worked hard in the yards. On Friday nights we'd have music and invite girls back to the club.

NO HANDCUFFS

Nights at the Casbar could get hot and heavy. I was nightclubbing it and all that but I never failed to open up on time in the morning. Some of the others weren't so careful and loads of booze made some of the blokes fail to get to work the next day. Then, it was just another Friday night of innocent fun in South London where we'd opened a string of clubs.

I was young and so was Charlie. We were in a new world with its own set of rules.

The difference, as I saw it, was that we were making the rules.

We'd dealt with Bill Slack and our name was getting around. We weren't going around fucking beating people up for no reason. It was out of principle. There were few incidents but it was nothing to do with getting money. We didn't go in there to get a reputation, but you do get a reputation when you do things like that. We were to be reckoned with but we were also loyal to our friends and workers. If they got into trouble we were there for them.

It happened with one of our drivers, Pete Hagen, who got in bother with some hard nut who turned up at Addington Square with a bunch of his mates including [Great Train Robber] Charlie Wilson to sort Pete out. They'd met up down the road from the yard and there were a load of looky-loos who just wanted to watch but also a bunch of them really looking for a scrap. It was serious, they had guns and bayonets. There were twenty to thirty heavies.

When we got the word at New Church Road, I leaped into a lorry and swung it round there with my foot on the pedal. I screamed right up on the pavement at them and that got them a bit ragged. They fucked off but turned up at New Church Road. One bloke thought he was Mr Big and was waving a shotgun around. The police got called by an onlooker but Charlie gave these raiders the shivers before the cops arrived. He walked out with a bottle of acid and good old Arthur Barron screamed: 'Charlie, not the acid! Not the acid!'

That scared the wankers.

They ran for it, but at the same time the police showed up. I got the blokes who hadn't escaped into the yard, told them to hide their guns and bits of nasty metal in with our scrap. I told the coppers they were customers. I didn't want to see anyone get nicked. It was just being reasonable. When the cops went I told these lads to get lost and they did, something rapid.

Just as rapidly my nightclub enterprises were prospering. We'd opened the Cavern in East Dulwich, which did alright but was a bit off-base for us and we let it go. Getting a licence to sell booze was a doddle; you bunged in a small fee and you were now the proud owner of a private members' club.

We had cafés out front and drinking clubs behind the scenes. We'd get nicked for serving after hours but that was part of the business. It never hurt business or us. We also had the Orange Club in Walworth Road and it was a big success. People could come to dinner in the restaurant and we had the drinking club above with gambling. The green baize was provided by a second-hand snooker table where dice were rolled and cards dealt. It got lively and I reckon we invented karaoke in London by having punters get up and sing with our microphone. It got a bit lively and we lost the licence after one too many after-hours antics. We simply flipped it about a bit, called it The Rainbow, switched the drinking club with the restaurant, and got a new licence. It was all fun for me and extra cash over and above the real money coming from the metal yards.

I had no idea the traps that were being set when we started up the Shirley Anne Club, which was at the back of a garage just behind the Queen's Road in Peckham. In time, there were more spooky characters through there than there is in Harry Potter. Of course, you couldn't tell – they looked like young men out for a good time, just like me. We opened up at around 11 p.m. when the pubs were closing, and groups used to come to us from all over London. There was always someone you knew having a drink, but it was an illegal set-up as we were often serving through the night. The cops would raid us and impound the booze but that was a flea bite; we'd close for a couple of days, re-stock and be off again.

One copper we dealt with was Ken Drury [later Commander of Scotland Yard's Flying Squad, 'The Sweeney', the most senior policeman ever convicted of corruption, jailed for twelve years in 1977] who was the local police sergeant at the Peckham station. When the cops wanted to close down the Shirley Anne they could never find the owner to serve notice. That was handy. Drury was great pals with a man who called himself John West when he ran the Shirley Anne for us. He was the tall, dark and handsome type but a villain, if a successful Casanova, always up to something, and he had a couple of lorries so was useful to Charlie for moving metal about. I didn't know it but Charlie used him for other little jobs too. John West was certainly fishy.

But if someone wasn't doing me harm, getting in my way, I was happy to live and let live.

That was similar to the thinking of a friend of mine, Albert Dimes, who for many years was a powerful player. 'Italian' Albert – he was a crackerjack mix: Scottish mother, Italian father, born in Lanarkshire, how tough can you get? – was a couple of decades older than me and knew the ropes. Our world was changing, expanding, and so was his with the grandeur of his and associates' activities fading – and being threatened. So, sensibly, he and his mentors were happy to be kind to people like us who were stepping up the ladder. Albert Dimes was a good-looking man and a couple of inches upwards of 6 foot tall. By the time I knew him he was something of a legend: he'd been in prison a few times, once for busting a copper's jaw. Just before the start of World War Two, all the faces [criminals] said he'd dealt with an East End gangster called 'Chick' Lawrence who'd taken too much of a liberty. He was never arrested for the murder. 'Italian' Albert was serious muscle as was his onetime employer, Pasquale Papa, who'd been a terrific bantamweight boxer long before I was born.

These were people who you were invited to visit or were introduced to and were content to give respect to. Although only newcomers in their terms, we were known as reliable operators and the compliment was returned. Pasquale Papa boxed and robbed gold bullion and got up to all manner of venality under the name of Bert Marsh.

He wanted to take over the riches of the racing track point-to-point racket – there were no legal betting shops in the Fifties and all [legal] wagers were made at the tracks – where the best venues naturally returned the most lavish profits. 'Italian' Albert was sent in the summer of 1955 to suggest that the onetime king of it all, Jack Spot [Jack Cromer], should voluntarily give up his control. The tension began. Spotty had a West End club, the Galahad in Charlotte Street, and a bit of a walk away Italian Albert had his little premises across the road from Ronnie

Scott's Jazz Club on Frith Street and there the two men agreed to meet on 11 August 1955. Spotty saw Albert in the street and they began pushing and shoving and then cantered into a shop. Albert and Spotty cut themselves to bits with a stiletto and splattered a great deal of blood about trying to chiv [stab] each other to death in the greengrocer's shop.

It was a nasty tear-up but farcical too, when Mrs Sophie Hyams, the greengrocer's wife and a big, burly woman, picked up a large metal scoop and bashed both of them on the heads. Bert Marsh rescued Albert, and Spotty got taken off to hospital. They were both in a mess. Albert had stab wounds all over him including a six-inch job right into the bone in the left side of his head. Spotty had been stabbed in the chest and all over his body. When the coppers caught up with them they said nothing and it became 'the fight that didn't happen'. But this phantom knife battle signalled the all-change that was happening in London.

Spot knew he was finished but still couldn't or wouldn't convince himself that was the way it had to be. Ageing dinosaurs can be trouble even outside Jurassic Park.

Albert Dimes, as well as being with Bert Marsh, was a loyal associate of Billy Hill, who in the 1950s was the *godfather* of the London underworld, a canny, clever and rich man. Billy Hill was remarkable in his influence, which ranged from back-door spielers [gambling dens] in Soho, to Scotland Yard to the aristocracy. [Lady Docker, who was extremely fond of Billy Hill, went to the party at Gennaro's Rendezvous in Dean Street, now the Groucho Club, in 1955, when Billy Hill celebrated the publication of his ghosted, by crime reporter Duncan Webb, autobiography, *Boss of the Underworld*.] For years, if anyone wanted anything fixed they first went to Bill's flat on Moscow Road in Bayswater. But they trod lightly if not invited. Bill always had a cigarette on the go and it was the fags that finally got him. [He died of cancer on 1 January 1984, 'the richest man in the graveyard'.] When Gordon Richards, at that time the only jockey to be knighted, was robbed in 1953 of the golden spurs presented to him by the present Queen's father, King George VI, Scotland Yard were doing their pieces. One of the senior coppers was friendly with Billy – he had some very heavy contacts at Scotland Yard – and asked him to get the prized spurs back. He did, without much trouble. As one of Billy's boys, and as a respected operator, Albert Dimes was well connected. He knew every policeman who mattered, top to bottom. My friendship with Albert enabled much of my business in the changing times, It was also the beginning of a gloves-off wild and violent era.

As Jack Spot's empire expired – Ron and Reg Kray were making a noise in the East End –Billy Hill wanted done with Spot, who'd once been his partner. When they'd fallen out, Spot had taken liberties and now there were hassles for everyone. All the in-fighting, jostling to be the boss or the hardest man in town, was complicated by government pressure on the coppers.

It got even worse for the law when Albert and Spotty escaped punishment for cutting each other up. Albert didn't even go to trial. At the Old Bailey in September 1955, Jack Spot got off for inflicting grievous bodily harm on Albert when his clever lawyer Rosie Heilbron produced the Reverend Basil Claude Hudson Andrews, eighty-eight, who said he had seen the encounter: 'I had read an account of the fight in a newspaper and was surprised to see the fair man [Spot] described as the aggressor. It astonished me, I thought: "Dear me!" because the darker man [Dimes] was the aggressor.' Spot was acquitted and when

Albert was rolled in for his separate trial they dropped all the charges. Of course, the old boy, the vicar, was a plant. He liked his whisky and women and didn't pay his gambling debts. Sony the Yank found Rev. Basil wandering about the Cumberland Hotel, living on nothing but 'continental breakfasts'. He and Moisha Blueball [called 'Bluebell' in the newspapers to avoid the 'embarrassing reference' to his discoloured right testicle] bunged him sixty-three quid to tell his story in court.

That should have been that but Spot was a silly bugger. He got himself an after-Christmas present at the start of 1956, paying the tough character Joe Cannon to shoot and wipe out Albert and Billy Hill. Three younger lads were to back up Joe, and Spotty supplied the weapons. I don't know if Joe did shoot at Albert and Bill but he said he did; the other story was that the young lads talked too much before anything could happen and Spot was given his guns back without them being fired.

They might as well have blasted bullets all over the place. The intention to do so was enough. Billy Hill could never lose face with a nonsense like this – it was something I understood only too well. And Albert wasn't going to let it roll over, either. Of course, the two of them played cat and mouse with Jack Spot. He asked for protection from the cops.

They were puzzled. Why? He couldn't say bad men were out for revenge because they know I, Jack Spot, tried to murder them, could he?

He knew, and that was part of his punishment, that a very bad moment for him was on the way. It happened in time [2 May 1956] outside his flat at Hyde Park Mansions when, arriving home with his wife Rita, he was jumped by about a dozen men. They left him bleeding in the gutter. He had been thoroughly kicked and punched and worked over with a cosh, a shillelagh – one Rita said had been a gift from her to Billy Hill – and a knife and open razor. He was patched up like Frankenstein's monster. [Spot received seventy-eight stitches in his face and left hand, two pints of blood, half a pint of plasma, a pint of plasma substitute, and his body was wrapped like an entombed Egyptian mummy in bandages which when removed showed a livid scar running down his forehead, over his left eye, along his nose to his top lip.]

Spotty and his wife, who was badly bashed about, survived. Spotty did the terrible thing of naming his attackers – Billy Hill, Albert Dimes and several others. Bill and Albert, naturally enough, and some others, had unbreakable alibis. Of all the names he gave only Bobby Warren and Frankie Fraser appeared at the Old Bailey on 15 June 1956. They were convicted. Frankie Fraser had fifteen previous convictions, including a razor attack and a bottling. It was announced in court that he had twice been certified as insane. [Frankie Fraser boasted he had three insanity certificates but lost one amid his paperwork.] Bobby Warren got seven years in jail and so did Frank, who was forever after known as 'Mad' Frankie Fraser. He'd served that sentence when we met for the first time.

CHAPTER FOUR

THE PRODIGAL SON

When Frankie Fraser came round to see me for the first time it was with a big smile and to thank me for helping Jimmy Brindle, who was married to his older sister Eva. Frank had got the story of our motivation a little wrong but not the circumstances. It was our Friday night blast-out and we'd been drinking at the Masons Arms on East Street off the Walworth Road and were as usual going on to the Casbar to carry on having fun. One of our drivers, Reggie Jones, stayed back with the car to load up on booze, a few crates of beer and a few bottles of vodka and whiskey.

The booze was always boxed out the side door after closing time and Reggie was twiddling his thumbs waiting for the order when Jimmy Brindle came racing out the pub and jumped into the passenger seat. Behind him were a mob of blokes who grabbed them both out of the car and gave them a proper going over. Jimmy Brindle's problem that night was a big bastard called Jackie Rosa who wasn't long out of the nick. To top it off, Jimmy had been helping Rosa out with a bed to sleep in, but now he'd turned on him. Rosa had wanted a drive up to town, to the West End, but Jimmy refused. He was no tough guy, so when Rosa and his mates jumped on him they did a lot of damage, broke his jaw and ripped off half an ear. When he got away and back to the Casbar his face was black and blue and his eyes puffed out.

We were furious. I tracked Rosa and his lot to the Reform Club at the Elephant and Castle. We took off, about eight of us in two cars, and when we got to the Reform Club I saw the group standing, preening themselves, big, tough guys in the middle of the dance floor. Charlie nutted one. I chinned the one next to him. I picked up a big bottle full of champagne and cracked it open all over Jackie Rosa's head.

He lazily, in a sort of slow-motion parody, grasped out trying to support himself by holding the bar, but he slumped along it causing a waterfall of smashed glasses and drink.

But by then I was punching out some other chancer. Charlie and Roy Hall had a couple more on the floor. It was South London's big Friday night out and they'd seen some action. One bloke came up to me: 'They'll be after you with shooters...' I didn't care about that.

Back at the Casbar, Charlie and I toasted each other. I don't think there were many more moments like that when we seemed to have the world at our feet. We were people to be reckoned with. I was young and ambitious and I thought we could conquer everything and anything ahead of us. We were making plenty of money.

Some of the metal we received was stolen but how could we tell? Well, one wanker brought us a load of lead piping he'd nicked from a housing estate and the cops matched them to the homes they'd once been attached to.

The cops were on the payroll and they wanted paying but Charlie chased them off'. It was fine for him but I was in the frame, too. He said he was innocent – and we didn't know the lead was stolen – and would fight it all the way. He was fined £80, I got away with half that, and then Charlie appealed and lost; that cost him another £800, which was a huge bill.

But we were making good money. We'd be having nights out in the West End and the Astor Club owned by my friend Bertie Green, who was a good man to know. It was just around the corner from Berkeley Square in Mayfair and was, as it turned out, a costly favourite: doormen, tips, cigarette girls and glamour girls and good time girls and famous names. Champagne was cheap and the girls were all over you to buy it – they got £1 a pop. It attracted a mixed bunch. The Princess Margaret set went there, a proper mix of gamblers and gangsters, deals were done and there were all sorts of European and Arab big shots – or supposed big shots. They only thing for certain about anyone there was that they were spending money and ours was as good as anyone's.

The doormen would park my pale blue Bentley for me. They knew they would get a fiver so as soon as I pulled up they were on me; when I wanted to get my motor it would be parked right outside. We were certainly getting around and meeting new people. Johnny Nash's brother Jimmy was the doorman there before he got put away for five years for GBH [Grievous Bodily Harm] in 1959 – he was lucky, for a year earlier they were trying to hang him for shooting dead a bloke at a club in Notting Hill. He was acquitted at the Old Bailey.

Billy Hill was behind the scenes. He ran the show, ran London, and wanted to show Bertie Green the Astor needed protection and that his particular talents were worth paying for. He gave one of his lads a monkey [£500] for being open-razored across the face at the Astor. He also paid to have the guy's face fixed with plastic surgery. It displayed that without protection nasty things could happen to frighten the rich patrons and keep them away.

The cops were always under control in the West End. But not so the cops who Charlie had shown contempt for who were now after us: they didn't like us policing our clubs and protecting ourselves without giving them more and more money. The biggest protection racket in Britain was run by the Metropolitan Police and they didn't want us muscling in. They wanted it all. Human nature: everyone gets greedy. All they wanted was their bung. They'd make life difficult and Charlie would telephone their boss, arrange a payoff – and this was a top cop – and life would be easy-going again. Until the next time. It was a barter system and the cops were all give and take, to them and from us. It makes me smile about law and order. They were a dreadful bunch of thieves and swaggering around shining on about protecting the public.

There had been a little business to nobble a character called Mickey Roff who ran of with one of our employees' girlfriends, which was fine, shag who you like, but he'd nicked the bloke's furniture as well. I went along with Charlie and a couple of our lads to sort it out and we retrieved his stuff but Mickey Roff wasn't about. When we did find him, he drove and said bullets were fired at him. I kept out the way and escaped being arrested; Charlie was nicked which was a liberty because he didn't have a gun but he sorted out the charge.' I wouldn't carry a gun; it was absolutely fucking stupid. Possession of a gun put you right in the slammer for a long time.

I was only twenty-four years old, and I was really getting into my stride. I had no fear of anything or anyone. I was big and strong and guns and knives were neither here nor there to me. I'd bash a rival with whatever was lying about.

Not all the cops were getting a whack and after Charlie got away with the Mickey Roff shooting charge some of the hungry ones went after him. All over some big lumps of bacon. The coppers set him up from the start through someone who knew someone who had six sides of bacon to sell on the quiet. Charlie was up for that, added his mark-up, and was caught bang to rights. They sent him off to jail for six months for receiving in 1959 and I was left running the yard, which I must say allowed me some peace and quiet to get on with it. Charlie was looked after in prison, where he stayed for four months and kept in touch with the business.

By then he had five kids with Margaret, but that was all that was holding them together, the only reason they talked to each other. Even then our mum was the one who looked after the kids most of the time. Charlie had tucked himself up with Jean Goodman who none of us around the yard liked. He had her working in the office. Roy Hall thought she was a right pain but Charlie was all over her.

I didn't think he was paying enough attention to the business and sure enough Charlie got nicked again, this time for receiving metal. He'd been arrested delivering to a yard in East London, caught with all the stuff on him. It was in May 1960 that he got bailed for a couple of grand, which was a lot of dough. I remember the date, it's stuck in my mind. Charlie was freed on two bonds of £1,000: one from Reggie Rumble who ran a profitable demolition business and the other from Reggie the Milkman, Reggie Saunders who'd been our milk deliveryman before we gave him a job on the yard.

This total of £2,000 was loads of money for these boys. But it got Charlie out of jail. With his new bird, this Jeannie, he had fucked off. Where'd he gone? No one knew. He had just fucking disappeared. Two people had stood bail for him and he'd scarpered. Jumped bail.

I was fucking livid. Typical Charlie.

Then, I checked the yard. All the stock had gone during the weekend; he'd sold it off. There was nothing in the yard. Sweet FA.

I looked at the Monday morning accounts. Bugger all left.

I got in touch with a couple of our metal suppliers to try and get something on account off them. Charlie had already been in and had fucking loads off them. All the suppliers had given him cash on account. And he'd taken off with this bird Jean Goodman and gone to Canada. 'He pissed off with this bird and about £40,000 from Peckford Metal Ltd.

The one good thing I discovered was what grand friends I had, people like Arthur Baron, who were so loyal to us from when we lived on Wyndham Road. I borrowed here and there on my good word and was able to get some cash around me to keep trading. The business began to build up again. I felt honour bound to get the two Reggies back their bail bond money and I did in fairly quick time. I raised more backing by selling off half of The Rainbow club to my friend Patsy Callaghan, which freed up more cash and more time for me as I was juggling all the businesses – and winning. I felt good, able to move the work around, to divide myself into different boxes and deal with each problem or opportunity. Good management, I suppose.

For Charlie it had gone the other way in Canada. He'd bought a scrap metal company and after about eight months he'd gone skint, the company was skint. He spent all our money and he came back to London. In the meantime, we'd got the business thriving again. Everything was fine, and I'd paid off the fucking people that had looked out for him. I welcomed him back like the fucking prodigal son. We made a fuss but I'd changed. Charlie never understood that, couldn't see past himself. He kept himself out of the way, in Norwich for a while, until we got the charges outstanding against him dropped. Then he was back to being Charlie.

He was even tighter with Jean Goodman. Margaret had scarpered with the kids but Charlie had hauled the children back, and our mum was taking care of them. He never saw Margaret again.

Our brother Alan also vanished from our lives in a dreadful tragedy in 1961. Alan was only eighteen years old, loved a kick about at football and was chirpy enough to have had a try out at Crystal Palace; I always thought Charlie and I had got our dad's naughty gene that took you off the straight and narrow but that Alan had escaped that. He was a nice lad and I mean *nice*. He was pleasant and helpful. He got on with people and they with him. He'd work at the yard and knew there were consignments going back and forth, but he always nagged about us being straight in business; that's what he wanted. Alan was a lovely, sweet kid. He wouldn't have gone the same way as Charlie and me. I still well up when I think of it.

NO HANDCUFFS

Charlie was being flash. He had a Sunbeam Alpine sports car, very natty and nippy, and he'd bought a speedboat which he kept on the river, not far to drive from our yards. He fancied this as the leisure life of a big deal businessman. He talked Alan on going on a boat ride down the Thames with him and Jean. He needed Alan to launch the boat. Alan didn't fancy it but Charlie could convince people of anything. He could even talk himself into believing he knew what he was doing.

They'd gone under Waterloo Bridge and were about to go under Blackfriars Bridge when Charlie wasn't able to control the speedboat and it hit the wash of one of those pleasure cruise boats and flipped. The timing was tragic. The three of them were thrown into the water as a barge sailed past and the pull of that wash dragged them under the water. Charlie and Jean Goodman surfaced and were rescued by the crew of the pleasure boat.

There was no sign of Alan. Not a trace, not a clue or hint what had happened to him. He was lost somewhere in the waters of the Thames. Later, when Alan's body was recovered, they found that he'd been trapped under the water, snarled down there by a rope from the boat around his leg. He had no chance. Until the day our mother died and we buried her in the same grave as Alan, she never truly got over it. We dealt with it by putting our heads in the sand. We didn't talk about it and that makes it eat away at you more. When it happened there were no grief counsellors and bereavement centres and looking back I wish there had been, for our mum at least. It crippled the family and Arthur Baron had to identify the body because none of us were capable of doing that.

I still dwell on it and it haunted Charlie too. It was a depressing time. Work didn't help.

THE PRODIGAL SON

I was getting more and more fed up with the business. Charlie's kids didn't get on with Jean and neither did most of the lads. She just didn't click.

I'd had enough. I was all for family but I wasn't going to be bossed about by Charlie or second-guessed by anyone else. I didn't let go but started working part time and doing my own work as well.

I had cash in my pocket and I backed a bookie called Patsy Hogan and it was fun and different, for about three months tops, going round the racetracks taking bets and laying them off. I made cash but the return was miserable compared to what I was used to. I never got into horse doping, but when I got the word on some races that's when I made a few quid.

Billy Hill was the brain behind it all for years. They paid out-of-work actors at a tenner a time, a shift really, to provide different faces to make the bets at racetracks around London on the dog races that were fixed. Tony Armstrong-Jones, before he married Princess Margaret and became Lord Snowdon, was another fresh face and did the job happily and got a few bob in return. He lost that job when he became the Queen's brother-in-law.

I was getting more out of the scrap game with Charlie, although there was always an edge when we got together. He was very much into the long-firm business with various warehouses all over London. He nearly got himself very badly burned with one which didn't help the atmosphere at the Peckford Metal yard which was already unpleasant. Jean Goodman was running around the place and was living in a little flat she and Charlie had created above the premises. Then, she and Charlie moved to a nice house near Camberwell, in

Denmark Hill, a smart little street called Acland Crescent. Crescent Avenue. They were a bit like Lord and Lady of the Manor. I was keeping as calm as I could for business was good. But I knew my patience wouldn't last for ever.

The Mitre Street blast was the limit. Charlie and a pack of his pals had filled this rented warehouse in Aldgate with a huge amount of long-firm goods, in particular a batch of Italian silk stockings. With the suppliers needing to be paid, all the stock had been offloaded to be sold at bargain prices. Normally that was that and the 'owners' of the company would simply vanish. This time Charlie and his lot decided to burn the place down, say the stock had burned up – and claim insurance. He had a former Scotland Yard copper in charge of the building. Some character called Gerry the Sparky was recruited.

This Sparky, a professional electrician, was supposed to fix the wiring so that it appeared a fire had started by accident, set off by an electrical fault. He got there at night when the City was quiet but couldn't get in because there were a few people hanging about the building. He decided to use his initiative, soaked some rags with petrol and shoved them through a window. He then fired a fireworks rocket – it was November 1962 – through the window. *Whoosh*. The place went up. You know when they say it 'was like the Blitz', well, I know it was. The London skyline was aflame. Bits of metal and blazing debris were flying all over the place, twisted in the heat, and the television crews were filming; it was all over the news. There were twenty-seven proper fire engines involved and whole squads of rescue, gas and Electricity Board vans. Other buildings were damaged, windows blown in and most of the street was a mess. This was Charlie's 'quiet little fire'.

THE PRODIGAL SON

Gerry the Sparky only lost his eyebrows and they were lucky no one was hurt, not one person. The fire people knew the fire was dodgy but Charlie and his mates were smart enough to simply stay quiet, shake their heads in apparent shock. The suppliers of the stockings were told they were not insured. Of course they were, and that bundle of cash added to sales of the stockings, turning a profit in that swindle.

I didn't see Charlie as being evil towards me then; he had some demons he couldn't control and he was always jealous of me in that I could quietly get on with business and have a good time. We argued and shouted and that was that for the time. We weren't at each other's throats, but I sensed there was every chance of that happening. And ending badly.

I'd kept the business going and I'd worked hard at it. I now know what had happened – I'd grown up. I was my own man. I just walked out. I walked out with nothing. I didn't ask for anything. It was over, over and out for me, out of Peckford Metal and all my business dealings with Charlie.

I got a shop down Deptford High Street and, being who I was, I got a little bit of free rent there to do it up and decorate it. It was the Walk Around Bargain Store – and everything was a bargain.

I enjoyed this working on my own, but I soon had some interesting and unique new friends. With them came more opportunities.

CHAPTER FIVE

THE JACKPOT

Partnerships can be trouble but there was never any between me and Frankie Fraser. I never heard him make an idle threat.

In 2013, he was eighty-nine, he got an ASBO [Antisocial Behaviour Order] after some bother at his at his care home in Peckham. His attitude and actions were black and white, the timing unpredictable. He had his code and that made him a constant aggravation during his long years in prison. If he felt badly done to, he'd attack whoever was going, a guard serving tea or the top man. He didn't care, but, of course, when he went off on one the system crashed down on him. He'd been flogged, fed on bread and water and kept in chokey [solitary]. He was, they ruled, insane: he was certified so in the Army during the war, another time at a hospital [the now closed, in 2008, Cane Hill Psychiatric Hospital, Coulsdon, Surrey] and he scored a hat trick when they sent him to Broadmoor.

NO HANDCUFFS

Ronnie and Reggie Kray found Frank quite normal. They had been kind to him while he was inside for the attack on Jack Spot and ferried his sister Eva around the prison system to visit him. Every time there was trouble in a jail where Frank was they moved him. He was taken on such *holidays* more than a hundred times. He saw the inside of every penal institution going, so Eva was driven all over the place by the Twins. If they couldn't take her by motor they laid on train tickets for her, first class. They wanted Frank as a friend not an enemy when he got out. With Frank, that was always the sensible choice. Their indulgence of Frank didn't reward them.

I had no qualms about befriending him when he walked into my Walk Around Bargain Store in downtown Deptford. He knew of the Richardsons and had been told about the revenge on Rosa and his lads for them messing up Jimmy Brindle. Of course, we'd been looking out for one of our own, for Reggie Jones, but what with one thing and another, we got on. Frank was even more of a football fan than me [later the two would take Frankie Fraser's favourite team, Arsenal, including the players Don Howe and Terry Neill, for a long, long 'no strings attached' lunch] and we had lots of mutual friends. Frank loved the Gunners. There and then I agreed to help Frank with cash to help pay the legal defence of one of his pals, Jimmy Essex. Jimmy had a reputation, he was a heavy-set tough guy, the sort the coppers called 'notorious', and had been charged with the murder of a seventeen-year-old lad called James Harvey during the war. He ended up doing three years for manslaughter; it was a messy thing, a robbery in a no-go area because of the Blitz blackout, which ended badly. Yet, what I liked most about Frankie was his attitude, *his* code.

THE JACKPOT

If you were nicked for something you said nothing, went all *Tutankhamen* – kept shtum.

Frankie was a dozen years or more older than me and even when we met that first time in Deptford he had spent much of his life in jail, most of it in chokey. Frank hated the system and it hated him back. He was beaten and bashed about severely by prison officers but he never complained; he simply tried to eat their faces off when he got a chance. He, like Billy Hill before him, had suffered the cat o' nine tails, been flogged by the whip, but the Establishment never beat his spirit. As I said, he forfeited almost every day of remission and that was truly because he wouldn't take any of their bollocks. [Frankie Fraser first got eighteen strokes of the cat in 1945 when, aged twenty-one, he attacked the governor of Shrewsbury Prison with an ebony ruler he grabbed from the governor's desk. In Wandsworth Prison on 28 January 1953, the day of nineteen-year-old Derek Bentley's hanging for the murder of police constable Sidney Miles, he was punished for spitting at and attacking the executioner Albert Pierrepoint. He was moved during his 42 years of incarceration 123 times from one prison to another on security grounds; sometimes spending only 48 hours in one penitentiary.]

Frankie was a professional; if he said he'd get it done it was as good as. What made us click so quickly was that we were both looking for a new business. I was doing OK but wanted more of a challenge. Frank, just out, and like many people in his line of business not one with a bankroll, wanted to earn. There were new gambling laws [The Gaming Act, 29 July 1960] and smart casinos were coming into play, but it also meant that one-armed bandits, good ol' fruit machines, were legal.

If ever there was a glorious moneymaker in gambling it's the fruit machine. They are truly addictive, and in 1962 I set-up the Atlantic Machines Company.

Then, the punters were gambling pennies while now it's thousands of pounds. Frank had shares in one-armed bandits with Joey Wilkins and I said we should go and see Joey and get back the shares. I knew Joey's uncle, Bert Wilkins, who was a onetime partner of Bert Marsh [aka Pasquale Papa the mentor of Albert Dimes] and had worked with Billy Hill. Bert had been a regular at our yards and I knew him well enough. Frank was partnered with Joe Wilkins but it was clear he wasn't thrilled with it. Thing is, Frank had no idea about business, about how to run things outside a prison. He couldn't cash a cheque. If he wanted money, he'd go and stick someone up. He said he had half the takings from the fruit machines, but he couldn't run it, he let Joey run it. He didn't like that.

I asked him why he didn't get his half back. He didn't have an answer. I said: 'I'll come up with you, and we'll get your half back.'

Joey Wilkins was not keen to give Frank back his share of the machines but he reluctantly agreed. I suggested him that he didn't want to stand in the way of progress.

Which is very much what it was as I moved into the West End of London. Soho still seemed lost in time but for all the shambling 'characters' there were lots of hard businessmen moving every manner of entertainment around for a price. It's always seen as if Soho, this wicked den of a place, was the perfect spot for fruit machines, but they work to a huge profit in a pub or a golf club. Put one in a saloon bar and it will make more than the beer. This was big business. With big boys involved. The pressure was always on: more machines, more venues. It got so we had more customers than we had machines for them.

I was operating out of Windmill Street where we'd set up offices for Atlantic Machines, so being at that end of Tottenham Court Road we were a wander into Soho. We had cream-coloured notepaper and letterheads compiled to match, and my friend Leslie McCarthy became a director. As the front man for the company we had Sir Noel Dryden who enjoyed drinking cocktails and, for the money to quench his thirst and a little extra, he became the CEO. He was a nice enough bloke, in his early fifties, had been an actor and was now an irregular television announcer. He had the right title and voice and no interest in our business other than his stipend. Other than the odd hiccup he was our silent partner.

Albert Dimes had much more to say. He was as knowledgeable, and influential, about underworld activity in London as anyone. Albert had done his share of working on the streets, of being muscle and a strong-arm man, but had matured into something of a gangland ombudsman. If you had a problem, Albert usually had a solution. He still worked closely with Billy Hill and had warm relations with the Mafia in America and Europe. Albert Dimes was properly connected. As now so was I, in person and reputation, in the West End. We prospered getting the [one-armed] bandits into scores of places all over London. We had not one problem getting sites for these money-making machines.

I had all the boxing contacts and the clubs and pubs; the demand didn't surprise me but it did overwhelm me, for the supply was my problem. I'd put out what cash I could to buy the machines from the best makers and suppliers in England, Ruffler & Walker, who had their headquarters on Lavender Hill on our side of the water. They turned out truly genius machines. They cost about four hundred nicker a time but they'd wash the face of that investment in no time. I had chucked in a few grand and there was money coming in from the Deptford 'poundland' operation but not enough to truly take advantage of the opportunity.

The market was endless. I helped it along as well for, of course, there were other people in the business and they might have machines in a particular place, a club or premise we fancied doing business with. I'd go and see Albert Dimes and he always got the site for me. If the other suppliers, local villains, complained, we told them to fuck off. The pubs and clubs liked us around rather than those nasties as people wouldn't kick off if they knew it was Eddie Richardson's machines that were in the place. Making trouble and interrupting business would have been very stupid, and all but the cracked in the head knew it.

The Soho clubs and the others wanted our machines in their places, they kept control of local villains who would come into them. Doing business with Atlantic meant people were getting protection too. I'd go for a drink around the clubs – I always paid my way – and be seen about. It stopped people trying to hold them up for protection money.

Word of the success of Atlantic Machines – I arranged a twenty-four-hour repair service, regular servicing of the machines and I was straight with all our customers and stuck to whatever split we agreed to – got out. There is nothing easier than legal money. Getting more to invest was the difficulty. I knew from

Albert Dimes that there were 'investors' interested, but I wasn't.
I didn't want partners; I wanted cash to use as I wished with no
outside interference. Billy Hill was the man for that. He was boss
of London, the Chief Executive Officer, officially 'retired'. But
he had the finger in everything, all the big pies, and wanted his
helping at all times. He was quiet and subtle about it. There were
no fanfares; he planned everything.

Just as he planned the [officially] still unsolved 1952 Post
Office robbery in Eastcastle Street just off Oxford Street, right
smack in the middle of the West End. An actual 'daylight' robbery
without doubt. They'd rehearsed the raid and explained their
movements by saying it was part of a crime movie they were
making. On the day there were seven of Bill's boys all masked
up and they snatched what in modern cash would be around
eight million quid. They boxed in the PO van with two cars,
took off with about thirty mailbags before any alarm went off,
and stashed the money at a pre-arranged drop. It was smooth
as can be. There was hell to pay. Churchill was Prime Minister
and was furious; they offered rewards, there were questions in
Parliament and coppers everywhere: they said more than 1,000
of 'em. Never got a whiff of anyone. Or the money. Billy Hill, of
course, had most of that.

When Billy Hill wanted to see me I was pleased. Frank knew
him better than me and told his story:

'Bill doesn't know the meaning of the word fear. That's why
he is special. If fear had come anywhere near him, he would
already be plotting away how to go around it. Or he'd get in
first and wipe them out before they could have him. At certain
times, he had every cop that mattered in London in his pocket.
He could pick up the phone to the top men. I reckon at one

time he had a hot line to the commissioner. They knew they could trust him. They knew he wouldn't shop them. They'd all come to Bill for their bit of dropsy or for help. There has never been another man like him before or since. If you wanted to pull a bank job, rob a post office or make chalk drawings on and of the pavements of London, you had to have Bill's OK.

'I first met him when I was very young and getting a name for myself – not Bill's standards but always in plenty of trouble in prison. Your name went around. I done a call for Bert Rogers, him and his brother. They were in Chelmsford Prison with Bill before the war, when Chelmsford Prison was a Young Penal Service institution for those around twenty-one to about twenty-eight. Bert Rogers knew Bill well and he introduced us to him. Some years later, 1947 or beginning of 1948, I was in Wandsworth Prison with Bert Rogers and who come on the exercise but Billy Hill. He had just got three years for a warehouse job. Bill didn't want to hang around that long.

'That's when he tapped up Jack Rose. Jack Rose had the caps done three times, he'd been birched for punching screws and he wasn't getting out early.

'Bill said to me: "Do you think he'd stand for it?"

'I said: "What do you mean Bill?"

'"Well, get him to attack a screw – he's lost all his remission; I jump up and save the screw... Do you think he'd stand for it?"

'I said: "Provided he's going to get some dough out of it, of course he would Bill. He'd love it."

'We approached Jack and did he love it. He got a monkey which was a lot of money in 1947. A lot of money.

'A day or two later, all of a sudden, Jack jumped up and shouted at a particular screw: "What do you keep looking at me for you bastard?" The screw hadn't looked at him at all! But Jack goes for him, starts attacking him.

'Bill's rushed in there and pulled Jack off the screw and calmed it all down. For his good deed Bill got a few extra months on remission. Everybody was happy. Including the screw.

'What I didn't know then is that Bill had the screw in his pocket 'n all! Bill always covered all the angles.'

So I was on alert when I went to 4 Moscow Road, Bayswater for my meeting with Billy Hill. I get over there and it's a fabulous ground floor flat with two big bedrooms, a huge lounge, plush fitted carpets throughout and trimmings. There's a chandelier in every room, even one in each of the two bathrooms, and at the end of the lounge, although Bill was teetotal, a Formica bar stacked with every drink going. The wallpaper was that red flocked stuff you see in Indian restaurants, the furniture all red leather and walnut. All he had was top dollar but, of course, he had the choice of the best of everything. All the shoplifters would visit him one time or another: his sister Maggie ran the most extensive shoplifting operation in Britain for decades. Bill had wardrobes packed with Sulka shirts and cashmere jackets, and racks and racks of suits. Billy's hair was all smoothed back with hair cream and he was wrapped in a silk dressing gown over navy cashmere trousers and highly polished shoes. He was a gent, one of the richest gents in Europe. He'd got a pot of tea on the go and we sat down and had a cup.

He asked about everything except the machines. We talked about the metal yard business and this and that and then to how Frankie and I were getting on. In time, we got to why we were there. How much did I get out of the machines a week? He was astute, numerate – number of machines times cash out and he had his sums done – and said it sounded a good business but involved a lot of work. He looked me in the eye and I explained how profitable they were and how I thought we could expand. He never rushed and kept holding me with his eyes. He knew the score but said: 'Well if you've got enough machines...'

Which was my cue: 'We've got sites, many, many of them, but we can't fill them because we can't afford more machines. People are asking for our machines but we can't supply. It's a straightforward cash flow problem. They are not cheap.'

He didn't say anything but sat looking out, above my head, and then pushed himself out of his chair.

Casual as you like, he wandered over to a desk and pulled out a drawer and picked up a stack of cash. He didn't count it, didn't look at it, held it for a moment in his hand and the next thing *I* had a handful of cash.

He gave me £5,000, which was a lot of money, a lump in the early 1960s. It was good. I'd passed my test. He was helping me but he was also helping himself. He was looking ahead to the next year and the one after that. Like Frankie and Albert Dimes and many others I was indebted to Bill – I was on his side. From then on I was looking out for his interests as well as my own. It was good business for all concerned. Especially me: Billy Hill, the most successful criminal in twentieth-century Britain, *the* boss, had endorsed me – and backed it with his money, with five grand. I was pleased but I was also shocked at the amount of cash. It was a lot of faith. I was going to justify it.

———

[Billy Hill was a charismatic man addicted to taking every criminal opportunity, who from a boyhood thief emerged as the instigator and planner of some of the most 'perfect' robberies of post-war Britain. When the Great Train Robbers of 1963 first hatched their plan they took it to Billy Hill. He gave them advice but saw too many loose ends, too many crooks, and did not get involved.

He wasn't going back to jail, something he'd vowed on his release from Wandsworth Prison in 1949. On that rather cold October early morning he had his plans made: to spend the evening alone with his wife Aggie (a rare event and usually only when he'd just left jail) and to expand the criminal empire he'd been running from behind bars for the past three years.

One of the prison guards was his 'clerk', being paid four pounds a week (tax-free) on top of his straight wage of four pounds a week (before tax) and made daily phone calls on behalf of Britain's most debonair convict. Inside, Billy Hill lived better than the majority of post-war Britain as he didn't have to deal with the nonsense of ration books or poor supply. Yet his taste didn't run to the gourmet, but to fare no more elaborate than corned beef and potatoes, a taste developed over seventeen years in prison. Hill was no champagne Charlie – it was pots of tea, not buckets of wine – and it was his clear thinking, opportunity taking, intricate planning and later life risk aversion which allowed him to fill his boots and die in 1984 with them on and, legend says, 'the richest man in the graveyard'. In the decades before, he'd been one of the liveliest gangsters ever.

As world war and the 1940s began he was the boss, very much the leader, of teams of crooks, safe-crackers, smash and grab artists, burglars, hard men, clever men, forgers and fraudsters, who played the advantage of air-raid blackouts, the policing vacuum left by the best policemen being drafted into the armed services. For some in this London, it *was* the best of times, if for others the worst. By the end of World War Two, that spot of international bother, Billy Hill was wearing 40-guinea suits; hand-made shoes (with trees), 30 guineas; hand-made silk shirts, 10 guineas; and ties from Sulka of Bond Street, 6 guineas. He was gifting his wife Aggie 'straight tom' (bought) jewellery ('tomfoolery') rather than stolen.

The mishap in judgement which got him three years in Wandsworth did not prevent Billy Hill from enriching his empire. From inside prison he 'managed' what became his total control of London's West End, the clubs, the gambling dens (spielers), and the rackets; Wandsworth was an easy visit for his lieutenants. Society, upstairs and downstairs, was fluent in the language of despair and Billy Hill offered nylons, cigarettes and opportunity.

As buildings, businesses and lives were rebuilt, these calculating opportunists, young men, sometimes not even needing to shave, were killing and scheming and creating criminal enterprise in London and paying a tithe to Billy Hill for being allowed to do so. He was a modern Moriarty. His mission was to allow anyone to make 'a bent sixpence' – Hill himself had lads collecting the coins from Tube stations and melting the sixpences down into silver which was worth more than the face value – as long as he was given his due. He was a hands-on Emperor.

Billy Hill was as ruthless and vicious as he was successful. And cognitive: 'I was always careful to draw my knife down on the face, never across or upwards. Always down. So that if the knife slips you don't cut an artery. After all, chivving is chivving, but cutting an artery is usually murder. Only mugs do murder.' He'd seized control from ferocious gangland toughs and made it clear, several times, that he'd personally 'cut up' any upstart who reached for his crown. Yet, the awful anomaly was the he was straight in his own particular way, even in his errant dealings. Everybody liked Billy Hill, even some of the people he murdered. Through 1950 and into 1951 there was a profitable peace throughout gangland London. It had been won by Hill's attitude: he personally dealt with threats to his rule: 'In our business it is it is too easy to find minders to do your work for you, but if it gets known you need such characters you never stand a chance if a bunch of tearaways came across you on your jack one night. All the time you've got to do your own work. If someone fancies you it's got to be on him. It's out with the chiv, a few stripes here and there, and that's his lot. If it's not, then it's your lot. And after that you can say bye-bye to it all. For once you've been done up you needn't call again. The bloke who does you up is the new guv'nor. That's how it is in the jungle of Mayfair and Soho, London's West End, where the underworld lives and dies. It's the law of the chiv that counts, and once your knife is slow on its way to work you can go back home from where you came from, because the mob just don't want to know any more.'

He never lost control. Someone told him he looked like Humphrey Bogart in *Casablanca*, and knowingly or subliminally he played to that, in trench coat and trilby. He dressed to kill.]

———

I took every opportunity I could and some of them came from Billy Hill's connections. One was a neat operation raking in thousands from the car parks at London [Heathrow] Airport.

Still, the big payer was Atlantic Machines. It all seemed so simple and, of course, I was still in my twenties. I got the machines into the Astor through Bertie Green, into Al Burnett's The Stork Room ['The food's very good even with six gorillas working in the kitchen with the chef,' was Al Burnett's joke about his Stork restaurant]. Al Burnett also had The Pigalle in Swallow Street. It wasn't always *nice-nice* at the Pigalle or any of the other clubs and you could always count the increase in aggravation in relation to the number of rounds of drinks. One evening at the Pigalle there was a charity evening and a row broke; the police arrived in a rush of cars.

They leaped out and asked the doorman: 'Who's in there?'

He told them. There was Billy Hill and his crowd at one table. At the next table was Albert Dimes and his pals. Beside him was the Twins' table. Billy Hill, Albert and the Krays. The police wouldn't come in. If they had everybody would have united against the police for a straightener. It wasn't a terrible row. It was only a fellow, Tony Mellor, who got killed afterwards in Soho. The row had begun when Mellor, who was into girls and pornography, upset Billy Hill. Hill made no fuss, just got up and knocked Mellor over the head with a big glass carafe of water, knocked him clean out and then poured the chilled water over him. I think Mellor might have had his throat cut. Or he was shot. One way or another he was killed. He was that sort of person, not going to be around long.

For me, I had bundles of cash in my pocket and the chance to do and be anywhere I wanted. I was having the time of my life. I was running the shop at Deptford, ducking and diving around on other projects, operating Atlantic Machines and finding some time to spend with the family.

THE JACKPOT

I must admit it was often only an hour here and there: I wasn't the perfect husband but I was an earner. If I saw an opportunity I'd work hard at it. And you got plenty of chances around Soho and the West End: it was jumping every night. I'd wander into the Stork Room and you could see anybody, there was a real freedom to go anywhere you wanted. I reckon they could squeeze a couple of hundred people in the Stork Club – and what a mix: any evening you might see Harold Macmillan, John Profumo, Frank Sinatra, Ava Gardner, Lana Turner, Bette Davis or Elizabeth Taylor.

[In 1955, Al Burnett with his business partner Bill Ofner, bought the Pigalle Club at 196 Piccadilly opposite the Piccadilly Hotel for £75,000. It became the place to go, to be seen, with lavish floor shows; one involved eighteen chorus girls in £6,000 white fox furs bought outright for a thirty-second appearance. There was a little-known private exit from the Pigalle that could take guests discreetly into the anonymity of Jermyn Street. When he bought the Pigalle, Al Burnett also completed a £25,000 arrangement to reopen The Society, a club on Jermyn Street that had closed down a year earlier. It had a concealed door to a passageway through the kitchens, dressing and store rooms and then straight on for a few yards into the Pigalle. Halfway along there was a private elevator which could whisk the coy and their special guests into the night. Or luxury surroundings. Berkeley Square was on the corner and the Mayfair Hotel met it at Stratton Street. The Pigalle was a playground for London society, European and Arabian royalty and Hollywood movie stars, where Princess Margaret might meet Peter Sellers or Richard Burton, Audrey Hepburn, Marlene Dietrich and Gary Cooper, or greet the Maharaja of Baroda, Sir Pratapsinhrao Gaikwad. Everywhere you turned you were following money. Or girls. Some guests would have bedroom entertainment sent into the Pigalle and if they were acceptable the next stop was a suite at the Mayfair.]

Al Burnett gloried in all the celebrity. He'd tell anyone: 'King Hussein of Jordan is here when he's in London. He jumps on stage and takes over the drums. Jean Simmons always takes off her shoes and dances with me in her stockinged feet, but that's nothing compared with what some of my customers do...'

Funny, he wasn't happy when me and my mate Tommy Clark [aka Fitzgerald] paid a visit to the Society, which was like the crown in his nightlife empire. I'd convinced Al, who had a very American manner – he went to Florida for weeks every year – that all I wanted was a quiet few drinks at the club. Tommy Clark was an elegant ballroom dancer and a tough guy who worked for Charlie, but he was fun to have around. That night Tommy vanished off to the toilet and at the same time the floor show began, which involved a chorus line of gorgeous dancers. As I watched them from left to right there on the end was Tommy high-kicking with the best of them. Al Burnett was not amused but luckily the crowd were. Still, I don't think Al ever forgave me that.

Nights like that might not sound it but they were part of my work. I did my rounds of the clubs and pubs and if I noticed a venue where machines were making money but were not Atlantic Machines I'd make arrangements, maybe have a word with Albert Dimes, or visit the place again myself or with Frankie Fraser, to introduce ourselves – and our machines.

If there was action, it was usually at the Astor. Bertie Green's

place was a magnet for chancers, for troublemakers, and ı
stars like Diana Dors went there.

They desperately wanted to be in the West End but th
weren't having any of it. Bullshit and myth has overtaken t
Krays, overwhelmed who they really were; for me at the tin
they were just a couple of lads wanting to muscle in on m
manor, no more than that. Oh, they had lads carrying guns fc
them and swaggered about, but anybody could do that. The
regarded Charlie and me as 'straight' businessmen and, yes, w
were running businesses. The Krays, certainly Ronnie, couldn'
run round the corner by then. At that time they regarded us
as competition but they weren't a concern for me. I was only
interested in business.

I had gambling machines all over London and Albert Dimes,
who the actor Stanley Baker called 'Dimsey', made many of
the introductions. Stan Baker was close to Albert and based
much of his 1960 film *The Criminal* [Baker and director
Joseph Losey collaborated on the script] on their friendship
and the inside track Albert gave him on gangster and priso
life. He was a big, big box-office star and when he had th
huge hit with *Zulu* (1964) he was an even bigger mate. I
always said that as the son of a Welsh miner he'd been luc
[Stanley Baker's luck did not last: he was knighted in Pri
Minister Harold Wilson's resignation Honour's List in J
1976, but was suffering from an aggressive lung cancer
aged forty-nine, died in Spain that month. As he did no
to receive his knighthood officially he cannot be calle
Stanley, but the Queen agreed that his widow, Ellen N
could style herself Lady Baker, which in 2019 at her h
Belgravia she continued to do.]

NO HANDCUFFS

Stan was a generous man and willing to live and let live. He made no judgements and he got me out of trouble a couple of times – the first time by simply looking the other way when he'd come round to see me on a Friday, 9 July 1965. And by staying shtum.

I remember the day exactly because it was twenty-four hours after Ronnie Biggs went over the wall at Wandsworth Prison. God, the headlines over that, a Great Train Robber escaping. There was hell to pay. Three blokes escaped with Biggsy [all of them 'special watch' inmates] but only Eric Flowers who was in for a dozen years for armed robbery was meant to go out with Biggs. Another man, [Robert] 'Andy' Anderson, doing twelve years for a post office robbery, and another robber, Tony Jenkins, who was doing four years, went along on a chance. Anderson was a stocky Scottish bloke and he'd been inside with a friend of ours called Patsy Fleming. Patsy was at school with Frankie Fraser and we had him on the Atlantic Machines payroll as one of our growing teams of mechanics servicing our one-armed bandits. The machines were played with a sixpence bet, and coins often stuck in the mechanism – getting them unstuck fast helped the profit margins.

So, here is Frankie Fraser wandering back to the office when he sees this bloke' wearing prison overalls – Patsy had given Anderson our Windmill Street contact. Frankie rushed him into our offices. Well, I'm there with Ronnie Jeffrey having a nice drink. The Biggs escape is all over the news and the evening papers – we all know what this is about. And how big a deal and dangerous for all of us it is having Anderson on the premises. But all everyone wants to do is keep Anderson on his toes [on the run], to look after him. It's risky. Very, very risky.

THE JACKPOT

Now Biggsy was on his toes – less than a year after another of the Train men, Charlie Wilson, had been sprung from Winson Green Prison in Birmingham – and the police and the politicians were jumping up and down over it. Especially as all the embarrassing details of the prison break were coming out about how Biggsy and the others all leapfrogged over a 30-foot wall: a ladder was thrown over the wall from the outside during the their afternoon exercise session and up and over they went on to the top of a van. They'd taken off in three cars. It was all over the wireless:

> Every police car in London has been notified and all ports and airports have been alerted. At 3.05 p.m. one of the four officers on duty in the yard saw a man's head appear above the outside wall. The officer immediately rang the alarm bell and at the same time the man on the wall threw over a rope and tubular ladder. The four prisoners immediately made for the ladder and climbed over the top. The prison officers tried to stop them, but were stopped by some of the others in the exercise yard. The officers went outside and discovered a van with a platform on top parked against the wall and the ladders secured to the top of the van. Police also found a loaded shotgun and a set of overalls inside. Scotland Yard has warned members of the public not to approach any of the men as they may be armed and dangerous.

I looked around the room, watched the faces. No names were mentioned. Ronnie Jeffrey was about the same size suit as Anderson, so he gave him his clothes. I got him about four hundred quid in cash. Frank said he'd take him to hide out with his mother, who he called Lady Margaret, in Camberwell.

He stayed with Frank's mother for a little while, for a few days, and then we arranged for him to go to Manchester. We knew a guy there who ran all the market stalls. He looked after him for a little while, and then he went back to Scotland. My friend Arthur Thompson who ran things in Glasgow [he was called 'The Godfather' and he and his family mirrored and suffered that story with many murders and revenge killings] made sure he was looked after. Later, he returned to work for Bobby McDermott on the markets in Manchester but got nicked again on his way back to Glasgow for a weekend. He'd been on his toes for nearly a year – Biggsy stayed on them for decades. Stan Baker's involvement in that was never mentioned when he was alive. Or his help when the cops wanted to do me and Frank over a stash of thunderflashes at Atlantic Machines.

We had busy premises and lots of the mechanics were ex-cons who loved being able to get some cash in hand. I believe one of those rascals, Jimmy Andrews, was planning some job or other hid the thunderflashes in the cellar of our building. There was a lot of thieving going on with the gambling machines – a valuable commodity – but we never had to nick them. Still, someone suggested to the cops that we had a pile of stolen machines. When they raided us all they found was the thunderflashes. I say 'all', but it was a serious crime to have such stuff, explosives. They were sanctioned for the War Office [the Ministry of Defence] or movie-makers to produce special effects while filming. That was our out – the movies, Stan Baker. He found a friend to say he was keeping them there before shipping them abroad, to Spain for some action scenes.

THE JACKPOT

Stan Baker wasn't one of those fair-weather friends who liked to hang around the underworld but disappeared when things turned a little awkward. He truly got on with us and enjoyed our company, as did we his. There's a photograph at the Astor of Stan with his arms around Frankie Fraser and me that has become iconic of the era –famous like the photograph of Christine Keeler on the chair – and it sums up the strange camaraderie of the time, of the 1960s.

CHAPTER SIX

LIVE NOW, PAY LATER

Parking charges are the biggest crime going. We all know that. So the airport car park swindle was rewarding, not just for making us huge amounts of loot but for giving the finger to these rip-off artists. It was the best of its kind and that came from [Jack] Ruby Sparks, He was a friend of mine and this was his gift. Ruby was a generous sort. Once, more than he ever intended.

He'd become notorious, before the war, along with his partner Lillian Goldstein, as 'motorised' thieves. Lillian wore a red motoring coat and a red beret and was known as 'The Bob-Haired Bandit'. She did the getaway driving while Ruby did the smashing and grabbing.

When he came to see us, Ruby was getting on but still had his eye for an opportunity. I liked him. He was quite retiring. He was a robber from the start but became a clever cat burglar. One of his early jobs in 1936 was knocking over a house in Park Lane in Mayfair. He nabbed a box of big, uncut red stones. He immediately rushed off to a fence [dealer in stolen goods] with them but was told they were too perfect to be real. They were worth nothing. He went for a drink and, after one or two, gave the stones away to anyone who wanted one.

The newspapers the next day explained he'd robbed some maharajah or other and that £40,000 of uncut rubies had been nicked. Jack Sparks became 'Ruby' Sparks from then on.

By the time he told us about the goings-on at London airport he'd personally nicked a fortune. He was a true professional. Yet, to me, this one sounded too good to be true. I was wrong. It was a licence to make money. The swindle had begun at the airport in 1962 when a group of attendants, all disabled or former servicemen, at the car park found a safe way of boosting their weekly pay packets. By altering the time stamp – and, remember, there's no computers, no clever electronic systems – after a driver had gone through the exit kiosk they could make the parking period appear shorter than it was. The motorist paid the full whack; the attendant pocketed the rest. It was a cash cow with more than £100,000 a year, somewhere around £1 million annually in modern money, being taken out of the multi-storey car park. I wanted some of that. And it was the silliness of this lot that gave us our chance. They were rolling in money. At first the ringleaders handed out their shares in envelopes but then got cocky – the tickets were never checked after they'd been through the machine – and told everyone to help themselves from the cash tills. They all were having a spend up, buying houses and cars, going on cruises and – their mistake – going on nights out in the West End where they did too much drinking and talking. Which is how Ruby Sparks learned of the opportunity.

Ruby would get his cut for introducing us to one of the gang heading up the scam. We wanted our own man on site as car park supervisor. We chose William Charles, who'd worked the airport car park but was now a croupier at 'The Vic' [the Victoria Sporting Club on the Edgware Road, London], and he had no choice. We invited him to meet 'the Guv'nor of the West End', which was us. We told Charles his old job [with Airpark Garages Ltd who operated the car parks for the British Airports Authority] was available and a perfect opportunity for him. He got the message from us to do what he was told. And he did.

It was sweet. It was 1964 and my life was sweet, too. I liked being around Soho, the nightspots, the girls and the drinks with the blokes. I'd drive up to the clubs and they'd park the motor for me, right out the front. For a young terrier it was a grand life. I was getting on really well with Stan Baker: he'd had a tough time growing up in Wales; he was a Valley boy and they don't come much more determined than that. We had good talks and lots of fun and he managed our football team, the Soho Rangers.

There was plenty of intrigue in Soho and you had to watchful, careful and, as always, check someone out before you entrusted them with even your thoughts. I had a three-month driving ban for jumping a red light but I got around in my Bentley, the pale-blue one, with a chauffeur, Alan Tear, the brother of my pal Whippet. Alan, who was useful and discreet, drove me over to a café near the airport to pick up our money, usually about a grand at a time, a monkey each.

'I was fed up hanging about on payday, and to save us the trouble got Willie Charles to bring the cash to Atlantic Machines at Windmill Street. We also had a 'cash drop' at Draper House, a block of flats in Southwark.

I wasn't being lazy, I've never been that, but we were expanding the gambling-machine business and as it played out we did ourselves a favour. We were never nicked for the airport swindle but we might have been had we kept personally collecting our money. Unknown to me, there was a copper who thought he was James Bond investigating the scam. This bloke [Detective Sergeant Peter Boorman] was buying a newspaper at the airport when he saw a 'Be A Secret Agent' child's kit for sale.

It contained invisible ink. So, this copper starts marking up the car park tickets he's issued with. It was good – illuminating – evidence, for when the attendants did get done the tickets nailed them. The cop stood in the witness stand at the Old Bailey and used a cigarette lighter to heat the tickets and the writing in 'invisible' ink appeared and proved the time stamps had been falsified. A dozen or so of those involved all went away, one or two got seven years.

———

I had other things to worry about then, but for the moment I was getting busy with the porn merchant, Jimmy Humphreys. He was in with 'Big Frank' Mifsud who'd come over from Malta; he'd been a traffic policemen there, and was now directing girls in strip clubs and brothels. Frank – he weighed eighteen stone – joined up with Eastender Bernie Silver in the 1950s and had taken over from the Italians, the Messina Brothers running vice in London. They ran what was known as 'The Syndicate'.

It was a tough outfit and Frank [he died, aged ninety-one,

back home in Sliema in Malta in December 2017] was heavy with anyone who tried to muscle in. I got on well with him and he was an easy character to get to know. He was what he was: a businessman running girls. He started off with one strip club in Bower Street and, by the time I got to know them, Frank and Bernie controlled nineteen of Soho's strip-clubs and were in with Jimmy Humphreys. The girls working for them ran about Soho and Mayfair and earned between £200 and £500 a week. The Syndicate bought property in Soho, running strip clubs in the basement or ground floors. In the floors above, prostitutes operated full-time in separate flats, paying £100-a-week rent. The Syndicate would collect over £100,000 in rents from prostitutes every week.

It was a huge business, a tremendous moneymaker. And Big Frank and the others had no intention of sharing it. With handfuls of cash and fear, they insured they never had to. The West End, was run by Bernie Silver, Maltese Frank and Jim Humphreys. It was their kingdom. They almost never dealt directly with girls, leaving the collection to their frontmen, who deducted their own fees then passed the remainder on to the main men. Cop shops were on retainer and loads and loads of money was paid over every week. They all got a little cut out of it. They let The Syndicate reign. If you went to open a porn shop or something like that there, you'd get shut down, and the cops would call all in all your dirty books and all your stock and everything, sell it cheap to the other three, and that was it. You couldn't open. When I was doing my rounds of the clubs in Soho and checking on our machines and picking up cash, I noticed that film clubs were opening up showing porno films, all manner of stuff. There were touts roaming about cajoling anyone they could, men and women, into the clubs.

But Frank and his friends were letting it happen. It didn't make sense. I went to see Maltese Frank.

I said: 'Look Frank, what's happening with the film clubs? Is it any interest to you?'

He said: 'No interest to us whatsoever.'

That was it. Once he said that, we took over.. The blokes running the clubs – we did about a dozen in all – got a fucking backhander and were told not to open again. We nicked all their equipment and took over. The important part was getting the touts. If the touts could work for no one else they had to work for you, didn't they? So, while there were other firms about, the touts who wanted to earn sent the punters our way.

We had approaches, a visit from Freddie Foreman [the Krays' runner] and another kid, asking if they could open a film club. They had someone to run it and this and that: the usual bullshit. We assumed they were acting for Ronnie and Reggie who wanted to get into the West End but didn't know how to go about it. Sending Freddie Foreman! We said no. Foreman got angry when we said no. But the Twins weren't going to poke their snouts into the West End with Frankie Fraser and I walking around. We had complete control of the film clubs, the blue film racket. For people who wanted to see blue films in the West End, we were the place they would go for that action. People could watch and they could buy the films. It was a good business.

There was no shortage of money. We had the airport too. Nothing to do with Charlie – he was messing about with South Africa. He had the money off the Train Robbers and at least another two hundred grand, a million quid or so today, off his *associate* Alfie Berman ['a wholesaler'] who he sold lots of long-firm goods to on the cheap. He had grand after grand after grand off Alfie Berman, who was a cute business bloke but had no chance with Charlie. As I explained, a fucking very good salesman was Charlie. George Cornell would often do that for him. George was on the firm with Charlie. If there were problems with the long firms, trouble with supplies or people not paying up, George was the man to sort it out for Charlie. Funny, as it turned out, he'd grown up in the East End with Ronnie and Reggie and knew the Krays' MO but he didn't rate them. George also dealt in puff [cannabis]. He liked a toot himself and that's not always so clever in that company. He was noisy, he liked to be heard and didn't think through what he was saying. He'd say out loud what he thought, but he was a useful bloke.

We knew how to buy up the cops but Jimmy Humphreys had a special knack. He'd corrupt an angel. When the friendly police raided porn shops in Soho they would call up Jimmy Humphreys and offer him the confiscated magazines. He would drive over, hand over the cash, and fill up his Rolls-Royce with the porn magazines. When I knew him he'd think nothing of dropping coppers three grand a time. He owned a big farmhouse in Kent with twenty-eight rooms, and a smart Soho apartment. He was perfect symbol for the time – a world of vintage Champagne and no knickers.

Not strong foundations.

[It all came crashing down in 1973 when the self-styled Emperor of Porn, convinced he had been framed by police in an assault case, made public the diaries in which he had recorded all his corrupt dealings. By the time he had given evidence against all the policemen he had paid and wined and dined, 74 had been arrested, 12 had resigned, 28 retired and 13 were jailed. It was the biggest police scandal in a century and, two years into his eight-year sentence for wounding, Humphreys was rewarded with a royal pardon. He died, aged seventy-three, in Hastings, Sussex, 22 September 2003.]

Yet Jimmy Humphreys was getting as good as it got in Soho. Like the blue film largely featuring 'Dick' Whittington, we used to say that the streets of Soho were paved with gold. I was becoming a familiar figure about the place, with Frank Fraser, and we were always being offered opportunities. Often, it was to help a friend out and if you did so there was usually something in return. It's what friends are for. I was oblivious to any possible problem. I took great precautions to watch my back and all that was going on around me.

They talk about *a chain of events* and that is what was starting, but it was invisible to me. If it had been spelled out in a storybook I don't think I would have got it, seen how tangled and entrapped I'd be, what I was getting into to. If there's a starting point I blame 'Cheerful' Charlie Chester, the much beloved radio comedian who was a fixture on the wireless for every national event when I was growing up. He'd sold his name to be picked out in neon on a casino in Archer Street: what was The Contessa Club was rebranded the *Charlie Chester Casino*.

The club, in the huddle of buildings covering Brewer Street and Atlantic Machines in Windmill Street, all west of Wardour Street, never mirrored the glamour of the performer Charlie Chester's Royal Variety appearances.

It was not a glittering casino – never could be on Archer

Street, which was always a bit of a walk on the wild side with lots of doorways and alleys busy with girls – but it was popular. The betting limits were low so you got lots of tourist types, but it also attracted proper gamblers like the artist Francis Bacon. He was a regular. David Bowie and his mates ran about there with music people but that meant nothing to me. What did was an American gambler who was regularly cheating in Charlie Chester's. That wasn't in the least funny.

A good man called George James, a Welsh guy, owned Charlie Chester's and he'd done the deal direct with Charlie Chester to get what was a household name. The whole country knew his catch phrase: 'This is Cheerful Charlie your Chin-up Boy Chester.'

The idea was having a strong 'family' name which broadcast honesty and reliability. Marked cards were not on.

This Yank doing the cheating had to go. He was part of a group who'd sold packs of fixed cards into casinos and he was 'reading' the cards and walking out a big winner almost every night. I brought Albert Dimes in on the action and we lured the American into some back rooms with the promise of a pay-off. Frankie Fraser and I got around the guy and warned him off while Albert was physically persuasive. No one ever saw the Yank again. It was the beginning for me of a profitable association with George James. I was on a retainer, as was Frank. Of course, Frank, being Frank, was always easing in to get some extra cash for himself. Frank was never ever shy of having his handout. One time George came up to me in a club:

'You know that money what Frankie had off me?'

I said I didn't know anything about the money.

'You know, the ten grand he needed...'

NO HANDCUFFS

In a moment, George knew that I never knew. I would never have stood for it.

Frankie slipped in private and got this fucking money off George, his little tricky number to get a big backhander for himself. When Frank took any money on, that went and you would never, ever see that money again. Me, I was out fucking spending. But I made Frank pay the money back.

Still, for George we were *his boys*. He was opening clubs all over and we were supplying him with machines, but he also liked us to be around. I was full of aggression and very quick to get into a fight, but it was also over quickly. If I'm perfectly honest I did enjoy it, giving someone a good thumping, inflicting pain. I won't say I loved hurting people. It was more about proving my manhood. And when I was in a room I knew I radiated aggression. I was confident. I'd never truly lost a fight. I revelled in my own reputation as a hard man; I liked being feared. Frank and I, together we scared off trouble – and there was always the chance of that when you had money, and lots of it, around the place – by simply being at the bar having a drink. When Frankie joined up with me some clever clog said it was like China getting the atom bomb. Of course, there was always some fella willing to try his luck. They were usually pissed and nothing more than a nuisance. A slap would sort them out. Our job for George James was keeping out the competition, the heavy boys who wanted a slice of his action. George also knew the value of promoting his clubs. In his Swansea place he'd give us a load of money and tell us play loudly and make big bets. He put it around that big-time London gamblers fancied their chances at his tables. And, yes, it brought in the punters. If we won, we kept the cash and, if we lost, it didn't matter – George had provided the stake money. Some nights he asked me to work at losing. When you try to lose it isn't always easy. Every time he opened a new casino he invited us. We supplied the machines and a bit of London gangster glamour for George. And we were looking after the place for him, protecting his investment.

Which is why Frank and I found ourselves up in Southport where all the Manchester crowd went to gamble at George's casino, the King's Head, which was on the seafront. It was exclusive: there was nowhere else in Lancashire to gamble but Southport. The night started off with a fight as we arrived at the doors of the King's Head. A bunch of toe-rag tearaways were inside kicking off with the croupiers and staff. We went in to sort it out and I wrenched a big bit of metal off one of the tables and set about cracking a few heads. Between Frank and me and another lad we had them all busted and on the ground; there was a lot of screaming and yelling but that was over and out fast.

It got a little more heated at the Horseshoe Club. We were putting our machines in there but this character, Peter 'the Greek' Joannides who managed the gambling tables, objected. In a very bad way. Frank and I were putting on a show to apply the pressure and I suggested this Peter the Greek bloke come outside. He didn't seem inclined. The Greek went over to the bar and got himself a drink but he started making remarks, being the clever bugger and slagging me off.

I glassed him. I'd delivered the message but all hell broke out. It looked like every big man in the world wanted to jump on me and Frank. We heaved it for the door with them all yelling and swearing and waving clubs at us. A big Alsatian dog was chasing us, too, and before Frank could slam the passenger door shut the dog jumped in too and was on the run with us. It was the friendliest dog I ever met, even as we were losing rubber screeching away in the motor. We'd got clear of the mob before we let it go and it legged it back to the club safely. The blokes there were more worried about the dog than me glassing Peter the Greek. Frank and I went back to George James's place where we'd been staying.

We thought it would blow over, nobody would grass up. But this Peter the Greek complained to the local rozzers. It made their day to be after Eddie Richardson – I never knew what a star I was up north. The Southport police gathered all their evidence, issued an arrest warrant for GBH and sent their lads on a nice out-of-towner to pick me up in London.

When they got me back to Lancashire and locked up in a cosy cell they asked me what I wanted to eat. I was a celebrity. I was given restaurant menus and landed up with a medium done steak and chips and a half-bottle of red wine to wash it down.'

I got out on bail of fifteen grand, which was a lot, on the nod there would be no 'intimidation of witnesses'. But I had to be ready for [committal to trial proceedings] when they got me up in the Magistrates' Court. We didn't have the advantage in Southport of dropping the coppers extra cash to lose the evidence. Special measures were called for and boys on the firm came good and circulated themselves, some cash and some menace about Southport. One of the main witnesses got a monkey, some of the others got visits or phone calls suggesting they forget what they'd seen. My friend Bobby McDermott, who had a good hold in Manchester, was good at getting a positive message out.

In court, it turned out that Peter the Greek didn't recognise me. When asked, he looked around the court, his eyes sweeping past me, and announced: 'I am rather vague, I was under the influence of drink.'

His mate said he saw the fight but didn't recognise me. No one, it turned out, did. One even said Peter the Greek attacked me. The charges were dropped, no case to answer. Some MPs made a noise but the Home Secretary [Henry Brooke] was a nice fella and there was no nonsense. Peter the Greek got paid a decent sum of money.

They would not do a deal because they thought we'd killed their dog, but when the dog turned up two weeks later they were on with Atlantic Machines. We were going for gold. And, after all the nonsense up north, I was heading south – to South Africa.

I needed a holiday. Even, as it turned out, a busman's.

CHAPTER SEVEN

THE VULTURES

All of our group on that twelve-hour flight on 24 August 1964, from London Airport [renamed Heathrow Airport, London, 1966], were on tickets provided by one of Charlie's new associates, Jack Duval.

I'm asked, and I've asked myself, how a clever schemer with no conscience like my brother Charlie could get conned? And get conned rotten? Sometimes we want to believe something so badly that we allow ourselves to be taken. Charlie was never shy about his ambitions. Or slow in asking questions.

Jack Duval had all the answers.

I was still about for Charlie at that time, happy to support him in any trouble, any battle, which is how I encountered Duval. I didn't like him. He was one of those people who told you their life history, tried to impress you from the off. One of those who congratulated themselves before patting you on the back like a dog. He'd been in the French Foreign Legion, the RAF during the war, run nightclubs and was the all-around genius of the day. He *had* flown Spitfires in the war but the rest was here or there or nowhere. Jack Duval was awas a superb fraudster and at times operated in Italy and across the border in Lugano, Switzerland. Next door to Lugano is the tiny 'independent' principality, Campione d'Italia, which is legally part of Italy and has a huge casino [Casinò di Campione, the largest casino in Europe, takes advantage of its status as gambling laws are less strict than in either Italy proper or Switzerland]. Duval didn't deliver a paid-for batch of nylon stockings, which even in the early 1960s were a bit of a luxury. Charlie asked me to investigate.

Duval was a roly-poly man who talked loudly and all the time in a strange accent [Russian-born, he was brought up in France]. I'd no idea, and didn't remember him, but he'd been to the Addington Club in Camberwell.

When I got to him in Italy nothing was too much trouble. His hospitality was as generous as his belly. I didn't trust him. All my instincts told me he was a right little fucker. Which he was. He took me over the border to Campione, to the Casinò di Campione, a few times. He was always scuttling about and meeting people for his business interests.

I was furious, because I was there to sort out why Duval hadn't made good on his delivery. The twisty road on the hill sneaks down very steeply from the Casinò di Campione to the main road across to Milan. I grabbed hold of Duval's neck and made him stop the car. Out the car, I all but had him hanging up by his feet as he told the truth for once.'

Back in London, things were getting serious too. Charlie was mixed in with all sorts of fraudsters but by the nature of their trade you couldn't trust them.

THE VULTURES

Since our visit from Freddie Foreman, I don't think Frankie Fraser and I had even talked about the Twins. They weren't a concern for us. Ronnie and Reggie talked themselves up and Ron Kray was clearly off his head. He thought he and Reg had such a place in London that they could drive tanks down Pall Mall and blow up Buckingham Palace. And still have immunity.

'It's just a question of paying the right cops,' was Ron Kray's view of the world. Reggie was more sensible, but together they were a right fucking nuisance. They brought attention trying to be celebrities. They'd seen too many Jimmy Cagney films, 'You dirty rat!' and all that stuff. Billy Hill used them as messenger boys. Yet, if you give a stick of dynamite to... The Twins were trouble because they hadn't the brains to be otherwise. They read gangster comics. They believed that they were invincible.

I felt the same. What do they call it – hubris? Fucks you every time. I was content with what I had but happy to try for more, but without aggravation. Charlie was trying to create his own overseas empire and we were a powerful force in London, south of the river and in the West End. I had a lot of power and people around me who I trusted, relied upon much more than I ever would characters like Jack Duval.

———

But that hot August day in 1964, after I landed in Johannesburg, I was to get to know men – and women – who were much more complex than Jack Duval.

One of them was on that flight: Richard Aubrey who, like Jack Duval, was an overachiever. He was a film-maker, a scriptwriter and a businessman. He was also an annoying Welshman, so he was probably a prize-winning baritone too. I never asked.

Charlie had met Richard Aubrey in Cardiff when Charlie was pursuing one of his schemes, getting usable-sellable coal from a slagheap at Ruabon [near Wrexham, North Wales].

It was another of Charlie's bubble dreams that went bust. Yet, through Aubrey's chatter and his own gullibility, Charlie became fixated with what was, from then on his lifetime obsession.

He was going to dig up diamonds bigger than the Ritz.

The tease, the come-on, from Aubrey to Charlie was the mining rights to four million acres in Namaqualand, South Africa, land extraordinarily rich in minerals and precious stones. Funny, another one of the areas involved was around Ghost Mountain in Zululand, near Lake Jozini where wild elephants go swimming, which inspired the location for H. Rider Haggard's diamond fantasy story, *King Solomon's Mines*.

Charlie never saw the irony.

By then Aubrey had linked him up with Thomas Waldeck, the owner of the prospecting rights, and introduced him to his shady pal Gordon Winter, a crime reporter turned fulltime spook for the South African Bureau of State Security (BOSS). Charlie never had a chance. I only ever went to South Africa for the travel, the fun, the beer and girls, and to drop off some cash for Charlie. I was politically naive. I was there to have a good time, Charlie to follow his daft dream. Neither of us was up to speed with global politics. You didn't get much of that in scrapyards in Camberwell or, come to that, round the snazzies of Soho. Charlie was hooked in by a crock of second-class conmen, blokes who had more ideas at the bar than behind a desk; yet, slick men who were a trumpet warning of disaster because of their misplaced confidence. They believed they were geniuses. Waldeck, who styled himself as a qualified geologist, who had endless schemes and partners, convinced Charlie that his future was in mining. I never thought much of any of them, but they were presenting Charlie with everything he dreamed of. He met Jean Lagrange, Gordon Winter's wife, and was enchanted by her. When we were growing up I was the one who was comfortable getting the girls while Charlie held back. When he encountered Jean Lagrange he was out of the starting block like a starving whippet.

It was in 1964 at the Ambassador Hotel in Hillbrow, a pretty rundown white area of Johannesburg, that I first met Winter. I didn't like him being a crime reporter and said so. He explained his own crime background [he was a convicted jewel thief and a gigolo defrauding rich women and getting sexually involved with susceptible contacts. I still didn't like him, but when I acted up, and showed him he wasn't getting a free pass, he made a point of saying he would never write about us. Spying on us was another matter but I didn't know what a toe-rag bastard he was.

[Yorkshire-born Gordon Winter was one of seven 'journalists' in BOSS and was personally recruited by Hendrik Van den Bergh who created South Africa's Republican Intelligence (RI) which, in 1969 when he was General Van den Bergh, became the infamous South African Bureau of State Security (BOSS). Winter was also linked with *Broederbond* (aka Bond of Brothers, or Brotherhood), South Africa's equivalent of the Ku Klux Klan, of which Thomas Waldeck was a member. Winter, in his 1981 book *Inside Boss* (Penguin), says that when he became a reporter for the *Sunday Express* in South Africa he found the best way to help his career was to be a police informer: 'The only way to get police contacts is to shop people, which is what I did: provided the police with bodies and convictions. I spied on blacks, on visiting journalists, I used to set people up and do terrible things. People lost their lives, people hanged themselves, people committed suicide, people were tortured to death.']

Winter was part of the set-up. The pitch from his pal Waldeck to Charlie was simple. I have the mining rights, I need cash, I will sell you half the business. What Waldeck didn't say was he had three other partners, all members, as he was, in the secret society, *Broederbond*. He, truthfully, had government associates. Just as certainly he needed money. His company [Concordia Development (Propriety) Ltd] sounded as if it was on to something and Charlie went ahead with them, sunk in loads of cash.

Charlie was still thinking about diamonds – he talked to me about them – but he came round to believing the real money was in the mining rights, all legal, for semi-precious stones and perlite [uncommon, strong volcanic rock and hugely valuable in building and construction industries] around the Ghost Mountain. It was his dream, becoming Mr Big, a legitimate industrialist. A very rich one.

I was able to enjoy myself in Johannesburg. It was such a nice place to be that even that irritating Richard Aubrey sometimes didn't piss me off. I'm having little holidays out there, and I'm so pleased to fuck off over there for a trip.

On a flight there that August in 1964, we had a few drinks, and decided we were going to make a movie called *Jungle Girl*. Aubrey got in touch with Barnaby B. Smith who was a film agent at the time in Johannesburg. We went to see him and said, 'Look, we're making this film – *Jungle Girl* – and we need a couple of girls...' We had a load of birds lined up for interviews for parts in the film. We took them out; I was playing the part of the financier at the time and they were all over me. It was great. It was very good. Aubrey had the patter and when he broadcast our needs for attractive girls to audition for the title role and for parts as her 'handmaidens' plenty of girls turned up time and time again. We had a lot of fun with them, but the cameras never rolled on our action. I never felt guilty about these adventures. I worked hard to provide money for Maureen and the kids and I was, and am, devoted to them, but I never had a conventional life – and that covered my love life too. I had girlfriends, I had girls I saw once or twice, and I had my family. That was the way I was and I was never going to change. I liked girls.

In South Africa, especially Johannesburg, I was given a royal welcome; Waldeck, Winter, they wanted to keep Charlie sweet to get his money. And he was sticking tons and tons of it in. If he ever had a doubt, it would be trumped by Waldeck with another opportunity knocks card. And I got the same VIP treatment. Charlie was also getting lots of Jean Lagrange'. For the first time in our lives I saw Charlie being all wobbly over a woman. She really had Charlie coming and going. [Jean Lagrange claimed she was born in 1948 but her birth certificate, with her surname named spelled *Lagrange,* not *La Grange* as often given, gives her being born on 13 August 1941, in Cape Province where her father John Lagrange was the town clerk; he was also a friend of John Vorster, Prime Minister of South Africa from 1966 to 1978.]

For me, I was just there for a laugh, out on holiday. Jean Lagrange told me I was caught in a sex trap. Wrong verb. Being honey-trapped was nothing but a pleasure for me. A great pleasure. I'd been drinking in the hotel bar with Gordon Winter, who was easy-going about his wife making eyes at Charlie as she fondled her cigarette holder, when this tall, dark-haired girl became very interested in everything I was saying. She seemed to be very turned on by my pearls of wisdom while I was equally excited by the look of her. We talked and talked ourselves up to my bedroom. I have no idea what I told her, I could have recited the telephone book, but it was of no consequence as I neither knew nor cared about the politics. Of course, the secret police could have turned it into high treason if they wanted to set me up. I knew what circumstantial evidence could do. They could have fixed it that I was doing something against the State. They could have had me in a frame anytime.

Earlier, Gordon Winter had taken me to meet Winnie Mandela. They had not long locked up Nelson Mandela on Robben Island and thrown away the key and his wife was living in a nice house in Soweto. I'd expected a shanty town, and there was plenty of that, but she was in a comfortable place. Gordon Winter said his journalistic contacts had got him permits to visit the township and I didn't question it.

Winnie Mandela [she died on 2 April 2018] wondered what it was all about; she was icily polite but was given no reason for me, with my white face, being there. Gordon Winter also took Charlie to visit Winnie Mandela [herself a 'quiet' informant for South African Intelligence]. We'd both been to see a woman married to a man the South African government had tried for treason, convicted and locked up for ever. If I had known all the implications [amid the sinister world of apartheid-era South Africa] I'd never have gone back to South Africa on another trip but for my friend Stanley Baker saying to me: 'We're flying half empty, if you want to come on the plane it will cost you nothing.' Stan offering me a free ride on his chartered Boeing 707 was an offer I couldn't refuse.

My brother told me: 'Do us a favour and go and give this geezer this bunch of money because he's got to pay the workers.'

For me, bon voyage; for Stan, to make another classic film; for Charlie, to make his fortune. What do they say? God listens to your plans and has a laugh? Well, it was a laugh going out to watch Stan make his movie *Sands of the Kalahari*. My best mate, Harry Rawlins, came along with me and we flew out with the cast and crew. Coming off the success of *Zulu*, Stan was able to attract a lot of attention. He was starring in the film and he'd got his childhood mate Richard Burton to agree to co-star. Burton's wife [for the first time in 1964] Elizabeth Taylor was to provide the glamour. Burton was well up for it but his missus didn't like the idea of filming in Africa.

American Stuart Whitman, a nice fella, and Susannah York, the British actress, had taken their roles when I got there. It was a good story. Whitman is a big-game hunter and a survivalist. Shortly after a plane crashes he risks his life going into the burning wreck and recovering supplies including a hunting rifle. He's no good guy – knowing his own chances will be improved alone he plans to kill his fellow survivors, one by one, except Susannah York for obvious reasons. It doesn't go his way. The others escape, he's out of ammunition and a bunch of belligerent baboons are heading towards him.

I can't tell you how many fucking millions went into this madcap mining adventure of Charlie's. It was dafter than any movie script. It was like kindling the fire with pound notes. The problem was that so many of those pound notes belonged to other people. Yes, Charlie put his money where his mouth was

– 250 grand and more – but when he ran out of his stash he was after other people's. He had 100 grand off Alf Berman. He had all the money going out of six scrap yards. All that went out there; apart from expenses and payroll all the fucking money was going out there. I remain annoyed at myself for even letting him talk to Danny Pembroke, who invested £25,000. I knew of others, but how many others there were in total I do not know.

We had to visit a bloke called Jimmy Collins who was a good-natured type, the ones Charlie took advantage of, a large Liverpool-Irishman, who was on the firm in South London.

Now, he was out in the middle of nowhere overseeing exploratory drilling by geologists on the land co-owned by Charlie and Tom Waldeck. He was in charge of the workers – the poor folk digging the holes for the geologists to poke around in. Charlie is paying for all this, of course. It never stopped, the digging or the paying out. That was part of his deal with Waldeck. That tosser split the land rights with Charlie who paid for investigations. Charlie had his life in this enterprise and Waldeck never understood what that meant. If he had, he'd have been a great deal smarter in his dealings with Charlie. If Charlie wondered about progress then suddenly the news was good, signs of 'rich deposits' of perlite. Which was another reason Jimmy Collins was there. He was armed and charged with 'protecting' Charlie's interests. Waldeck, a classic catch-me-if-you-can operator, had his hand out all the time but he knew how to put a greedy sparkle in his mark's eye.

I'd told Stan Baker we'd join him up in the Kalahari Desert – they'd settled in a place called Windhoek in Namibia [South West Africa in 1964] – when we'd finished our rounds which began when we bounced down in a tiny chartered plane onto an airstrip in Mkuze in the Natal. I thought we'd only be a couple of days and then on our way. Jimmy Collins would have kept us there for ever if he could. He was 'talking' in sign language to his workers, some of whom wore tribal chief headdresses. He wanted to gossip about London, about Soho, but he was fond as well of his workers. They were getting a pittance, four shillings a day, and Jimmy Collins felt sorry for them.

We were sitting with him under a tree and he pointed out the guys working: 'That one is only fourteen, so he don't get so much. I give that guy a little more for he's got kids.' The chief's son was on our side – he was the one to say what everyone was owed. The workers' food came from sacks of oats which were mixed with sugar and water. They called this mealy rice. In their unique way they were doing porridge.

Jimmy had also got the bug off Charlie, that gold madness, crazy ideas and such, and was chasing diamonds, convinced he was going to dig up a up at any moment. Like so many of this lot dragged into the great fortune hunt, they could not put their minds to a bigger enterprise: the value of the perlite, of these deposits of a high-value commodity. To them this perlite, worth ten pounds sterling a ton, and supposedly there were a million tons of it, was the stuff that dreams are made of. Yet thieves want to be able to pick something up and flog it on. If it's a diamond, all the better. They don't have much imagination – to them a load of perlite might as well be a load of manure. It's a bore. I was under no obligation to Charlie. When I went to South Africa I always paid for myself, never had any money off Charlie. I'm fed up with it and I'm not by nature a patient man. I'm on holiday, and I'm enjoying myself. I don't need any more prattle about diamonds. We up sticks and Harry Rawlins and I go back to Johannesburg, back to the action, but our plans do go up in smoke. It's the piston of this car we've got hold of to drive up to Windhoek to see Stan and enjoy the filming. It dropped dead on us after about two hours on the road to the film set. It was completely buggered. After finding somewhere to stay we also located a farmer who agreed to fly us on our way after we agreed a price with him of £10 per flying hour. I felt like a real adventurer. While we were getting there I told Harry Rawlins about a shooting lodge up near where Stan was making *Sands of the Kalahari*.

Again, it was all to do with friends, this time those I'd made on my South Africa trips. This was Harry's first trip and I wanted it to be special. After the car fuck-up, I wanted to make sure we had some real fun. I told him we were going on safari and he was all for it. I look at the photographs now and we certainly look as though we're on the warpath. The hunting lodge was in the middle of about a hundred square miles of wild, wild land. It was equipped for World War Three.

When they opened up the gun cupboards they were kitted out with high-powered rifles, shorter range rifles, shotguns, pistols and all manner of knives and hatchets for butchering the animals after they'd been shot. There were first aid kits – for the hunters. We were warned how swiftly the animals could react. We were told the check our boots and to carry snake serum. I looked at Harry with some awe. We had everything. We weren't going to be short of anything. We got into the van and fastened our seat belts. I had handguns on my belt and a couple of hatchets. I was ready for action. Which was just as well when the vultures turned up.

The flying variety. It's their kind of wasteland, home to a lot of death and carcasses to feed on. Our guide tugged at my sleeve: 'Look, out there, up and to your right.' There it was: a great evil-looking thing I swear was looking down right into my face. I got off a round and shot it and it flapped to the floor. The guide he's off the back of the fucking van. We both had our handguns out and got fucking eighteen rounds in it. It was a release pumping all these bullets into the vulture. You would pick up the wing, and you would still have a load of wing on the floor: they were big birds, a wing span of 10 feet. I was happy and ready to take aim at anything that moved. It was the Big Country. And it took time to get about, and often the weather was against you.

Harry and I spent so much time playing our White Hunter roles and simply roaming the land, horseback riding and sightseeing that I messed up getting to the film set. We were delayed getting out of Mkuze to get to Johannesburg and it left no time. I was furious but luckily the pilot paid no attention to me and we waited for the weather to settle before take off. When we did we had to divert when the storms came in. When we finally made it back to Johannesburg the thought of another eight hours in a tiny plane was too much. Harry and I got on a nice big jet back to London.

In London there was as much double-dealing and double-crossing as in South Africa. And almost as much shooting, although, as far as I know, only of people.

Atlantic Machines had transformed into a highly profitable business and, as such, it attracted some people, who should have known better, to try and edge in. Charlie was flying high and flying solo. He had his team of blokes around him and they were unquestioningly loyal. I got on with most of them, some more than others, but I had my own crowd that I kept close, blokes like Harry Rawlins and and old mate of ours, Ronnie Jeffreys. Charlie was the big cheese with offices in Mayfair, on Park Lane, and with all his payoffs he seemed impregnable. [Charlie Richardson boasted: 'I benefit from the most extensive protection racket ever to exist which is administered by the Metropolitan Police; sometimes we would pay people to be "found" committing small crimes so that our friendly local protection racketeer in blue could have somebody to arrest and look like he had been busy'.]

I certainly felt safe. I'd spent out seventeen grand on a house in Chislehurst in Kent: it had its own name, *Randalls*, and was on Mead Road where the neighbours were bankers, businessmen, and there were a few doctors who worked up in Harley Street. I had a big chandelier in the front hall and the whole place, six bedrooms, was done out wonderfully by Maureen. We had a sprawling garden, plenty of space. I wasn't there a lot but when I was, there was always a drink in my local, the Gordon Arms. Charlie had his place, a big house, in Camberwell, and Jean Goodman was still living there if not in domestic bliss. I think she felt safer down the offices of Peckford Scrap Metal Ltd of New Church Road, Camberwell.

CHAPTER EIGHT

ON THE WARPATH

It was that splendid time in my life when the way ahead looked all clear.

The giant chemist's, Revvon, in Deptford, was paying me solid dividends and the blue movies and one-armed-bandits were doing good business. Boxing was still my passion and I wanted to organise professional boxing in Ireland. I had good contacts, Albert Dimes set up drinks for me with Angelo Dundee who managed Cassius Clay/Muhammad Ali, and I knew Henry Cooper from the South London gyms. I was personally friendly with the boxing manager Bert McCarthy and an Irish bookie called Barney Eastwood. I met them when I went over there to support English boxers who were pals. I'd get a gang of us fans to go over.

I needed a figurehead in Ireland, for the sport, and I approached Eamonn Andrews who was big on our TV presenting *This is Your Life*, but more importantly to me had been a boxer himself and a sports broadcaster in Ireland. He'd just started his own talk show [Britain's first 'chat show', *The Eamonn Andrews Show*, 1964–9], so he was a great choice.

Eamonn was all for being chairman of the Boxing Board of Control of Ireland, and the Irish promoters and fighters supported him as there was no existing professional organisation. A sports writer on the London *Daily Telegraph*, Terry Goodwin, was going to help with public relations with his contacts in the sport and on the other newspapers and television. I saw it as a truly grand affair and we'd picked out a venue, the Intercontinental Hotel in Dublin, for the fights, with the fans sitting all dressed up at tables around the ring.

It was on the way to becoming reality when events – and Eric Mason – got in the way.

[Mason had been a thief since he was a kid in the war, bursting into a Home Guard station and nicking hand grenades and rifle ammunition, and had started his education in remand schools – the Nicholas House home in Enfield in North London, and the St Vincent's approved school in Dartford, Kent. He was out in 1945 when he was sixteen years old and his neighbourhood hangout was Soho, before he graduated to borstal at (Wormwood) Scrubs and Portland Prison when he was seventeen. Just like our family did with Charlie, an uncle of Eric's got him into the gym and boxing to try and straighten him out. He was using a boxing club in Lambeth, Kline's in Fitzroy Square, when a moment that had consequences for many, many people took place. Call it happenstance, for in the early 1950s at Kline's, Eric Mason met another young boxer called Reg Kray. From then on he was part of the Kray Firm, running about for them like a yappy terrier.]

I was on my evening tour of Soho with Frank Fraser and, as

usual, we called into the Astor Club. It was a good night and we'd had few drinks when trouble broke out near the bar with some Scottish blokes having a self-inflicted tear-up. It was nothing to do with Frank or me, but Bertie Green the owner came over and gave us the nod that he was going to call the police.

We paid our bill, made our excuses, not wanting to entertain the men in blue, went out to the back door and walked right into Eric Mason. He'd been in the mob that roughed up Frank's brother-in-law Jimmy Brindle but that was all dealt with. Now, he behaved liked a fucking idiot.

'The Twins won't like this,' he said of the fight going on.

I said: 'What do I care what the fucking Twins like?'

Frank grabbed him as well and we bundled him into my motor.

'I think we need to have a chat, Eric,' I told him.

He was squealing and struggling but he got an elbow in the ear from Frank and that quietened him down.

We drove him to the basement at Atlantic Machines on Windmill Street and started giving him very strong verbals: 'What have the fucking Twins to do with anything? We called him all sorts of a cunt and then Frank went off on one and pulled out his hatchet and buried a blow in Eric's head shouting: 'Take this back to Vallance Road.' He gave him a real going over with the hatchet. There was blood splashing about all over the three of us.

It all happened in a frenzy once Frank kicked off, but it wasn't worth killing Eric for what he'd said. I stopped Frank and we got Eric in a blanket and bundled him back into the boot of my car. We dropped him off, shoved him onto the steps of the London Hospital across the river on Whitechapel Road. It was on my way home. Mason survived but took some weeks being patched up and recovering. He never went near the police but as soon as he could he moaned to Ronnie and Reg about us. They didn't want to know. They 'retired' Eric, his redundancy payment was a lump sum, forty quid.

All the Twins did was talk big down their mum's in Vallance Road in Bethnal Green. Gert and Daisy were real mummy's boys. The thought of taking on Frank and me upset them. But it also annoyed them and that, soon enough, made 'Colonel' Ron even more paranoid, and dangerous, to himself as much as anyone. Ron brooded and kicked around those weaker and smaller than him. Still, you'd have to be special to face him down as he had madness dancing across his eyes. His eyes told you he was capable of any atrocity.

The problem for him – and for me, which it should never have been – was all the squabbling toe-rags he had around him. They were the kind of people who believed their own bullshit and some of them tried to take Charlie for a fool. He was blinded by dreams of diamond mines and the allure of Jean Lagrange but Charlie was not forgiving. It wouldn't have bothered me a bit, any of his escapades, but I was very much perceived as part of the package and would prosper or be hung out to dry along with him. I never knew the full extent of Charlie's fraud schemes, not because he didn't want to tell me but because I believed I was better off without being in any way involved.

But, but... what can I say? Charlie had been caught up – very willingly – in all manner of long-firm schemes with Jack *The Rat* Duval and Duval's unpleasant cabal of helpers. And all the business – especially the nasty part of it – happened at the Peckford Scrap Metal Company on New Church Road. That was Charlie's kingdom and where Bunny Bridges, who'd harboured

Jack Duval with him in Brighton, and Duval's smooth-talking associate, Lucien Harris [Derek John], were called to dance attendance on him. Roy Hall and Johnny Bradbury and George Cornell were usually around to help Charlie with his *negotiations*.

Now, Charlie, until the day he died, never admitted to torturing anybody. Charlie never coughed to anything in his life. He'd swear black was white and vice versa, whatever worked. He also denied things so well and with an oath, swearing on his kids' lives or the the like, that sort of nonsense. As if that made him any more truthful.

BOOK TWO

CRIME AND PUNISHMENT

CHAPTER NINE

THE WILD BUNCH

Ron Kray delighted in telling of when he killed George Cornell. Mentally disturbed, Ron broke the rules and carried his own weapon, a 9mm Mauser automatic when he murdered the man who'd called him 'a fat poof'.

There was, of course, more history to it than that, although it was quite enough for Ron Kray for the murder of George Cornell, thirty-nine, in the Blind Beggar pub on the Whitechapel Road on 9 March 1966. In the moment, Ron Kray said he relished his warped sense of justice, explaining to one of his inner voices that his killing of Cornell was revenge for one of his own men being shot dead. He was also repaying Cornell for belittling him and Reg when they were kids in the school playground, beating him in a fight and poofing them off in company.

All Ron, thirty-three, really wanted was to play soldiers, to have a war with the Richardsons, for, no matter how we had gone about our separate business endeavours, in the eyes of the law and the Krays, Charlie and I were a double act. We would stand or fall together.

The bad blood that had been simmering went on the boil. To me, the Krays were a nuisance; to them, we were a threat. Truthfully, we weren't. Leave us alone, and it's live and let live, but Ron's paranoia had him preaching live and let die.

I was living my own way. I'd enjoyed my trips to South Africa but how deep Charlie was in with their Secret Service I had no idea; he never said anything to me about it, about spying. I didn't know that MI5 and MI6 were dancing around. I don't think I'd have cared – and that ignorance of the conspiracy of events cost me – for what I was up to was of no interest to them. I was always able to make good money, just by having our machines in a club often was enough, and that bought my family security. I was and am a money getter. My family never went short or any of my friends if they were in need of help. Maureen was a superb mother and home-maker for Melanie and Donna and that was good, for it was going to be difficult for me to be around much. As I said, I never reckoned on chance in my life – I believed I made my own luck – but how else to explain what kicked off?

An old pal of mine had an interest in a club in Catford called Mr Smith's and the Witchdoctor's Club [before that it was named The Savoy Ballroom and was the nightspot for the Metropolitan Police's Blackheath Road Section House], but was always known as Mr Smith's after the actress Diana Dors had opened it in October 1965.

Now, six months later, in March 1966, the place was having trouble with rowdy customers. The owner, who was from Blackpool, got in touch with Billy Hill and asked him to sort

Left: My mother, Eileen, never complained, and she had my dad Charlie to put up with.

Below right: Dad with his brother Jim Richardson (right). Uncle Jimmy was the one who made it possible for Charlie to get his own scrapyard.

Below: My school football team photo, with me sitting far left. From my schooldays I always loved playing football and watching it – especially Millwall in action.

Left: The young bride and groom — Maureen and me on our wedding day outside the church in Camberwell Church Street. A wonderful wife and mother, she always stood by me.

Right: I've had my ups and downs but always enjoyed great friendships, and here I am with my good mates in our younger days on a night out at the boxing. Left to right: Harry Rawlins, me, Leslie McCarthy, Ronnie Jeffreys and Martin O'Day.

Left: Me in my late twenties, at the time when I was working in the family scrap-metal business in Camberwell – there was a lot of hard graft and it was lucky I was a big, strong lad, for we hefted about tons of metal.

Left: Me on holiday in Morocco. Out in Africa I saw so many remarkable things. It was an amazing continent to explore.

Right: With some of the young mates I made out in Africa.

Left: In the saddle on a camel. It might have been like the Wild West at times in London but out in Africa they do things differently.

Above left: After being inside I got hooked on skiing and would take every chance I had to take a holiday on the slopes. Here I am in Austria about ready for a day on the mountain.

Above right: Me (far left) at Harry Rawlins's wedding: my great friend Harry and his bride-to-be, Della, set their wedding date for when I was freed from prison and could be Harry's best man.

Below: With my longtime friend Joan Harris. When, in 2001, I was released from prison after serving thirteen years of my sentence, it was Joan who collected me from the Isle of Sheppey and drove me back to South London.

Right: Me in a 'white hunter' hat during one of my trips to South Africa.

Left: 'We weren't going to be short of anything ... I had handguns on my belt and a couple of hatchets ...'

Right: '... Which was just as well when the vultures turned up ... they were big birds, a wing span of 10 feet.'

Left: Bruce Reynolds, the mastermind behind the Great Train Robbery, who was finally arrested in 1968, five years after the robbery. We used to refer to him as 'Napoleon', and Charlie and I got to know him well in prison. *(© Popperfoto/Getty Images)*

Right: Me (left) with an acquaintance in South Africa – I enjoyed my trips there, but Charlie's attempted involvement in the mining business proved disastrous.

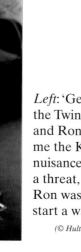

Left: 'Gert and Daisy' – the Twins, Reggie (left) and Ronnie Kray. To me the Krays were a nuisance; to them we were a threat, and 'Colonel' Ron was determined to start a war.

(© Hulton Deutsch/William Lovelace/ Getty Images)

Left: A night out with the lads, including Joe Pyle (second left), Alan Lake (Diana Dors's husband, centre, with cravat) with the actor George Sewell, all, sadly, now gone; on my right is the boxing promoter Alex Steene.

Right: 'Mad' Frankie Fraser (left) and me sharing drinks with the actor and film producer Stanley Baker, who was a good and generous friend. Both Baker and George Sewell appeared in the 1967 film *Robbery*, loosely based on the Great Train Robbery.

(© Fleet Street New Agency)

Left: Gangland dinner: I am in the centre, leaning in to the table to speak to someone; Charlie is third from right, behind the seated woman with the cigarette, with Alfie Berman to his left. The photograph perfectly reflects both the time and the indulgent lifestyle of 1960s gangland.

Top left: My prison visitor, Lord Longford, with the portrait of him that I painted and which he liked. He visited me in prison and rather 'adopted' me, and we became friends.

Top right: Me with the former undisputed World Middleweight Champion, Alan Minter, at my eightieth birthday party in 2016.

Middle: With actor, playwright and theatre director Steven Berkoff, who has created some of the screen's most memorable villains.

Right: I've made many good friends through boxing, and still receive invitations to high-class events – here I am with Frank Bruno. It was professional boxers who were our sporting heroes and boxing was part of everyday life.

it out. Bill asked me and that's why we were there. The owners wanted to maintain a gaming licence, so had to keep an orderly establishment with gambling and dancing and drinking over and the place closed by 2 a.m. The deal was that I would organise the 'security' inside and on the door of Mr Smith's. In return we'd get to place our slot machines in the club; we were double dipping with more than one dog in the race.

It was a neat, lucrative deal for us and there was no haggling; in fact they were really glad of such an arrangement. It was such a good prospect that we went over to the place on Monday, 7 March 1966 for a look round. Bertie Green from the Astor Club provided the entertainment and the girls. It was a lovely place, the club. A raised dining area, dance floor and a place, a stage, for entertainment. It had the makings of a nice earner. Everyone was interested in there not being any trouble at Mr Smith's and, of course, there was no need for there to be. Nice grub, nice drink and nice girls to look at. Where's the problem?

We were well welcomed but did not stay for lunch, saying we'd come back in the evening and sign off on our deal. The snag was a group of local hard men who had decided they were in charge of the club's protection in return for free drinks and whatever else they could get were there when we returned. Another of the locals, Billy Haward, was having it off with the wife of one of our mechanics at Atlantic Machines, and he thought it was personal. We couldn't give a fuck who he was shagging – unless it got in the way of our business – but it had him on edge. There was Frank and I, Harry Rawlins, Ronnie Jeffreys and Billy Staynton, in our little drinks party. I saw the other blokes, they were familiar but on nodding terms: Billy Haward, Billy Gardiner, Henry Botton, and Peter Hennessy. At that point, around 10 p.m., I never imagined it was going to turn out like the Gunfight at the O.K. Corral, but it did. Maybe not in so many dead, but in the legend of London gangland it was the beginning of the end of an era. I'll try and do it justice but it happened quickly. I got the shotgun treatment. I've got a load of pellets in my leg half a century and more later. I've had a knee replacement, and when they X-rayed my knee, the technician asked: 'What's all that?' It's still there. As is my memory.

The atmosphere was tense and I tried to lighten the evening up, kept the drinks coming. I'd talked to the management and our deal was done. We were in charge of security and good order in the club. And, then, Jimmy Moody, who I knew but who was a friend of Harry Rawlins, came in and joined us for a drink. The paranoid Billy Haward panicked, for he knew Moody was someone who could make problems vanish, in a puff of smoke, as it were. [Jimmy Moody became a multiple killer and IRA hitman and was himself assassinated on 1 June 1993 at the Royal Hotel, by Victoria Park, Hackney East London. That Tuesday evening the pub, Moody's 'local', was quiet at 10 p.m. when his killer (6ft tall, aged around thirty-five, long haired) wandered in, ordered a pint of Foster's lager, and put two one-pound coins on the bar. Without touching his drink, he stood away from the bar, turned and shot four bullets from a Webley .38 revolver into the 18-stone body of Moody. The execution over, the gunman calmly left the pub and drove off in a white Ford Fiesta. He was never caught.]

Haward was joined by his other mate, Dickie Hart, just out of jail for GBH, and they sent out for tools, for guns. Hart got a .45 pistol and Haward a sawn-off .410 double-barrelled shotgun, cut down to the size of a big handgun. He believed he was the boss being tooled up in the place he thought of as his HQ. It never had been anything to do with him, and with us on a nice retainer it was startlingly out of his league now. When it came to the off, I had no idea about Haward's love life or that they were armed – that Haward was better dressed than he looked with a sawn-off shotgun under his jacket, and Dickie Hart also had an accessory, an automatic in a shoulder holster. These guys thought they were Jimmy Cagney. In Catford. Although, the way things went down, it was the Wild West.

To keep within the law the drinks had to be over by 2 a.m. and the management guys told me that Haward and his lot were refusing to go. It was 3 a.m. I was being paid to sort that. I was restless and getting edgy. There just wasn't any reason for trouble.

As good as I could be, I leaned over, no verbals, and suggested it was time to call it a night, the staff wanted to clean up and shut.

Haward stared at me: 'What the fuck is it to do with you?'

I stayed calm.

I told him: 'I'm running the door here from now on; it will be my blokes on the door.'

Peter Hennessy was a big fellow and he went wild, he went off on one, and I could see Haward bringing up the shotgun. Dickie Hart had pulled his gun out. Harry Rawlins grabbed at the shotgun and hit Haward over the head with it but Dickie Hart shot him with the pistol, puncturing an artery in Harry's left arm which spurted blood showering into the air.

Hennessy yelled at me: 'You, I'm gonna have a fucking straightener with you.'

'You want a straightener, you can have one,' I told him.

We went out to the dance floor and went at it.

There were guns about and I expected a bullet in the back at any moment. Hennessy was a big bloke and he was relentless. He was landing them on me – good, solid punches – but the more he connected, the more he hurt me, the more I gave him back.

I thumped him and he went down. I got astride him and I wanted to punch his head through the floorboards but he was shouting: 'I've had enough, I've had enough.'

I was on a no-win with the guns but I won the fight. Hennessy was out of the game and I was breathless. When I turned around it was a bloody circus, the fighting had burst over into the back of the room. Frankie Fraser had leaped on Hart right after Harry Rawlins was wounded. They were fighting with Frank and a couple of others struggling to get the gun off Hart. Frank took a bullet in his side from Hart's .45, right through, smashing his thigh bone. He was crippled by it but still trying to get at the gun. Hart's gun was turned on him and he was shot. I know who did it but I won't say.

Haward was smashed over the head and wounded with an iron railing. Ronnie Jeffreys got a shotgun blast in the groin and stomach. I didn't feel it at the time but I also suffered a shotgun blast, all across my buttocks and the back of my leg. Frankie Fraser had made it outside but only to a next-door garden, where he'd collapsed. It was Harry Rawlins who was in true trouble. Jimmy Moody came good and got a tourniquet on Harry's arm and I think that probably stopped him bleeding out fatally. The street was lighting up like a Christmas tree and we had to get out of there. Jimmy's Jaguar was nearest and I helped him get Harry into it and we were off. Jimmy got out of the area and when we thought we were a decent distance from the trouble, he dropped us at East Dulwich Hospital. Jimmy scarpered when he knew the doctors had got to Harry and me. It didn't look good for Harry who couldn't speak and the doctor said was 'in danger of dying'. He was on a drip right away. I told them I was George Ward, first name I could think of. I said I had no idea who Harry was.

The police had collected Frankie and Ronnie Jeffreys from outside Mr Smith's and taken them to Lewisham Hospital. They'd found Dickie Hart comatose, lying under a lilac tree, and taken him there, too, and that's where he died. As I saw it we were the victims. We'd gone to the club unarmed and not looking for trouble and now we were shot up. Frankie's leg had been shattered by the .45 bullet and my leg had ballooned up with lead poisoning. Harry Rawlins was all but dying in the hospital bed next to me. But, of course, the police appeared like bad weather when you don't need it.

Neither Harry or I were able to move far, but two coppers were put on duty to guard the side ward we were in put in. I was saying nothing, and announced that in front of the hospital staff as I didn't want some copper making up statements for me.

For the cops the total was four seriously wounded, one dead: it was the start and the end all at once. I was charged with 'making an affray' and Frankie was charged with the murder of Dickie Hart and stashed in the hospital wing of Wandsworth Prison. The others on our side of the trouble were remanded with me in Brixton.

Charlie was in South Africa with Jean Lagrange, fucking

her and, unbeknown to him or me, the rest of our lives. Still, when he heard of my trouble he got the first flight back to start fixing whatever was necessary. Yet, in the moment, that geography made Ronnie Kray very brave. I was in jail. Frankie Fraser was in a hospital bed in a high security prison. Charlie was in South Africa. Ron Kray couldn't believe his luck. On 9 March 1966, two nights after the gunfight at Mr Smith's, Ronnie Kray shot George Cornell dead.

George Cornell was more of a Charlie man than a friend of mine. He never worked with me. He worked for Charlie running a long firm and sorting out business for him. He was alright, George. He wasn't the Brain of Britain but he was OK and earned a few quid. He was brought up with the Krays. He had run-ins with Ronnie Kray. He used to slag 'em off when he'd see them. All the time. George Cornell was hard man and could be irritating and loud when he'd had a drink, but his killing was way out of order. He had been on a Good Samaritan mission, gone to Stepney to visit our mate Jimmy Andrews who'd been shot up over some fucking love triangle. Cornell was banned from driving so he'd blagged a lift to the hospital off Albert Woods, a long-time pal of mine.

The Twins were all ready for action. 'Colonel' Ron had them fitted up with machine guns and grenades and pistols and bayonets because they were so excited that we all got knocked out of the game. Ron Kray had tabs on George Cornell so, when he and Albie Woods went for a drink in the Blind Beggar after visiting Jimmy Andrews, he knew all about it. Ron Kray had sworn to sort out George. [Ron Kray wrote in *My Story* (Pan Books, 1994): 'In front of a table full of villains, George Cornell called me "a fat poof". He signed his death warrant.']

It worked out that way. 'Scotch Jack' Dickson drove Ronnie Kray and his 'minder' Ian Barrie to the Blind Beggar, while George, Albie and a bloke called Johnny Dale were going easy and sipping light ales at the corner of the bar. George was on a stool and Albie had his back to the door. The barmaid had put 'The Sun Ain't Gonna Shine Anymore' on her record player behind the bar [there was no juke box at the Blind Beggar in 1966] and was talking over the music to George. Albie Woods, who officially saw nothing, said that the girl had gone along the bar to wash some glasses when George's eye looked past him and with a big grin he said: 'Well, just look who's here...'

Ian Barrie pulled a gun and fired off shots into the ceiling. That made Albie and Johnny Dale abandoned their light ales; the bar girl ran down into the cellar. It was 8.30 p.m. There was an older man idling time with a pint of Guinness in the public bar, and a courting couple in the saloon bar.

It's all happening in seconds, in that slow motion of movements that come with all violence. It's difficult to put into words. There's something you realise is about to happen – you haven't a clue what. Danger is in the air, floating about you, a pre-warning of catastrophe.

Ron Kray pointed his pistol at George Cornell's head and pulled the trigger. It was quick, simple, brutal and fatal. Ron turned and he and Ian Barrie walked out to the street where 'Scotch Jack' was already revving up their Cortina. He slowly let out the clutch and drove off. When the police arrived no one had seen anything, but before the evening was out most people who knew anything knew that George Cornell was gone. And Ronnie Kray had sent him on his way.

When I heard the detail I was still in hospital and suddenly quite chuffed there were coppers guarding Harry and me. Albie Woods saved his own life by saying nothing. Same with Johnny Dale. The old boy with the Guinness insisted to the Old Bill that he saw nothing. The pressed him but he said: 'I hate the sight of blood, especially my own.'

It's all legend now. Part of that reports that a bullet ricocheted and hit the barmaid's record player and the Walker Brothers' record jumped on 'The sun ain't gonna shine anymore, anymore, anymore, anymore... anymore, anymore...' while George Cornell lay bleeding on the floor.

There was nothing could be done for him when he was taken across the road from the Blind Beggar to the London Hospital. They took him off to see a brain specialist the Maida Vale Hospital but he died before they could even take a proper look at him. It was on the wireless about midnight that George Cornell had died, and the underworld word throughout the night was that the Krays were celebrating. They'd gone to the Chequers, a pub on the High Street in Walthamstow, and had a drink-up – and a burn-up. They set fire to all of Ronnie's clothes and sent off the little burglar Charlie Clark to get rid of the gun. He did a fucking useless job and the gun turned up again. [The German Mauser was found in the River Lee much later and in 2018 was in Scotland Yard's Black Museum].

The Twins thought they owned the world – or at least London. I understand how they thought that for a time. [In the book *Rough Justice* (Fontana Paperback, 1981) Albie Woods said: 'The Krays respected them (the Richardsons) and didn't come nowhere near. When Eddie and Frank was about they never came in the West End. Whether they fancied themselves, I don't know. But as soon as that happened at Mr Smith's and

Frank and Eddie all got done, all of a sudden they want George out of the way, no doubt about it. You see, when Frank and Eddie got done, the Krays had a licence to go into the West End and take over.']

The Twins didn't know the half of it, the pincer movement coming around me as I was facing a trial for the business at Mr Smith's.

———

Yet I wasn't just getting grief from the law and the newspapers, who loved all this shoot 'em up gangland stuff, I was writing their fucking headlines for them, from the Krays, daft Gert and Daisy, but from Charlie too. He'd ordered the assassination of one of his South African partners and that was coming back to haunt us all that spring of 1966. The shooter was Lawrence Johnny Bradbury. Bradbury was a nuisance and lover boy in London, and he'd been up to much of the same in South Africa. He'd had an affair with Corris, a lovely bird, and the wife of Tom Waldeck, the 'prospector' who'd hooked Charlie into pumping a fortune in cash into South African mining. Charlie couldn't care less about Waldeck's wife being given one or two by Bradbury but he didn't want Waldeck or any serious 'investors' to be upset by any scandal. He officially 'fired' Bradbury, who nevertheless stayed on in South Africa.

About five months later, in June 1965, when he convinced himself that Waldeck was having him over, he arranged for West/Bradbury to take care of his swindling partner. It's bizarre what they said about Charlie and Waldeck's feud, that as shareholders in the mining company they fell out because of a 'friction over voting rights'. It would be hilarious if it hadn't brought Charlie's house down, all our houses. The guy, Waldeck, had a small fortune off Charlie, Charlie got ripped right off. We can talk about it and that's why he was done. 'Johnny' Bradbury was a Peckham boy and a Charlie mate from when he chose to attend school. He had been humiliated by Charlie, his arm cut about with a broken bottle as a straightener. I could see that happening, for Bradbury was annoying, loud and arrogant, but, like others he remained loyal through gullibility. Or fear.

Waldeck's wife Corris was serving supper on Tuesday, 29 June when Bradbury turned up at their house [7, Arran House, Melrose, Johannesburg, which they'd bought with Charlie Richardson's 'investment' money] and rang the front door bell. Waldeck answered. Four shots were fired and two killed him outright. Of course, there was a lot, lot more to all that than I ever knew then or now. There was all the spy intrigue through Gordon Winter – Bradbury used Winter's Beretta to kill Tom Waldeck – and Charlie doing favours for the South African Secret Service to help his mining business and his other business with Jean Lagrange. Of course, trouble never arrives alone. Investigations had begun into our travel arrangements. All our junketeering, our commuting back and forth to South Africa – it became as casual as a London bus ride for me – was free. The now disappeared Jack Duval had started the travel business scam and Charlie had forced him out and taken it over: it was like a long firm, buying tickets through travel agencies, booking them in the name of his 'companies' and then never paying the travel agencies. When they totalled it all up [in 1967] a few quid more than £900,000 had been thieved in all. Although the scaffolding around the scheme was getting shaky: Charlie was using the tickets.

There was more discomfort back in London from January 1966, when fact and some horrendous allegations began to be splattered all over the newspapers in South Africa and Britain. Like a snowball rolling down Everest, the problems were getting bigger and bigger and the stories more outrageous.

What I didn't know then was how sensitive a spot I was in by being a *Richardson*. Following the shooting of Waldeck, the South African secret police put the strong arm on Charlie. They knew how much he had invested in cash and, truly, his life, in digging up his fortune there. When he got a promise from Jean Lagrange's uncle, Hendrik van den Bergh, that he'd be protected in return for some 'favours', my brother was thrilled. Why wouldn't he be? Now, the truth or fantasy of exactly what went on between Charlie and that tall, nasty South African spy, I don't know. I went to South Africa to have a good time. I wasn't even interested enough to be accused of political naivety. Charlie? I understand now he didn't have a clue how determined and downright dangerous these people were. Whatever your game you never think you can be had. A thief never believes he can be stolen from. An arrogant villain like Charlie never for a moment thought anyone would be able to have him over. That's bollocks, but those up their own arse never grasp that.

The trouble Charlie was in was more tricky than all that had gone before; I was also up that creek without a paddle and in a leaking boat. For me as well as Charlie were under the cosh of the British security services because of whatever deal Charlie made with the South Africa spies. He said he tapped the phones of Harold Wilson who was our prime minister for much of the 1960s and burgled and infiltrated British organisations opposed to the South Africans [Amnesty, the Zimbabwe African People's Union (ZAPU) and Anti-Apartheid]. Now, Harold Wilson was paranoid enough about spies and South Africa so how's he going to feel about his phones being bugged by a South London villain called Richardson?

You've got to remember the Cold War was going on and all these political types were in a frenzy about the world going up in a puff of smoke. And here was my brother burgling about on behalf of foreign spies. Harold Wilson was convinced Jeremy Thorpe [then leader of the Liberal Party] was also a South African target: Thorpe did keep banging on, criticising apartheid in speech after speech. But, of course, Wilson knew the truth – that Thorpe was homosexual and had a gay lover and was therefore open for blackmail. There were papers [UK Government files on this period remain 'protected' and many documents have been redacted] on Thorpe in one of the anti-apartheid offices Charlie had a go at, but whatever that was about got lost later when Thorpe turned up at, for us, a more familiar hunting ground – the Old Bailey. He got a better deal than we ever did, the toffs always do. [Thorpe and three others were acquitted, on 22 June 1979, of conspiracy to murder Thorpe's lover Norman Scott.] On behalf of Hendrik van den Bergh, Charlie had documents stolen from organisations who were seen as enemies of South Africa and he said he would supply ground-to-air missiles for them. Typical Charlie – helping to start a fucking war. [UK Government files on the murder of Thomas Waldeck and associated events are 'protected', sealed until 1 January 2041.]

There was just so much the British Government was going to tolerate. It all seemed so incredible, chaotic, complicated, for it was so illogical, but however illogical it was and is and will always be, it was the reality of the increasingly towering pile of shite Charlie was in. I was a bullseye in the middle of all this, but I was simply trying to stay out of trouble following the fall-out from the shoot-out at Mr Smith's. The trial proper was pending but there was more aggravation than that heading my way.

As deadly for us as Charlie's spookery and missile dealing was, another sort of incoming – reports from Johannesburg of the arrest of 'Johnny' Bradbury for the murder of Tom Waldeck. 'He'd been nabbed on 7 January 1966, and was babbling about the gangland world of South London, of 'torture' and 'a real-life Chamber of Horrors'.

It was all kicking off, the madness of the South Africa expeditions and the kingdom of fraudsters who'd done business with Charlie at Peckford Scrap Metal Ltd, New Church Road, Camberwell.

CHAPTER TEN

DIRTY TRICKS

The reporting of the trial for Bradbury for the killing of Tom Waldeck allowed newspapers in South Africa and in Britain to print all the allegations being made by him as he fought for his life in court in Johannesburg. He said Charlie had ordered him to kill Waldeck and that if he did not his own family would be murdered. He said his lorries had been used by Peckford Scrap Metals yard to transport stolen stuff. That was as mild as it got.

The grisly tales in the dirty tricks campaign against us – stapling victims to the floor using six-inch nails, cutting off fingers and toes with bolt cutters – were rolled out.

Bradbury brought me into his testimony going back to when he was known as 'John West' and working in a club of ours. He said he'd wanted to quit working at the club but was *persuaded* to stay in the job. He said he was held with his arm straight out and was cut with a razor from elbow to wrist.

He said the razor was then drawn up and down his wound. He said that I 'straightened' him out when he didn't pay off a debt. Bradbury could say what he liked in the South African court, and what he did say had Scotland Yard blokes getting a nice trip, 'a silver bird' jolly – good expenses on these ones – out to Johannesburg.

What I didn't know is that the coppers had more than Bradbury's evidence to investigate and corroborate. A nasty little geezer called Jimmy Taggart had endured a run-in with Charlie. As I recall it had to do with money owed to Alfie Berman who Charlie wanted to keep sweet and pumping cash into the mining. I believe with the help of Tommy Clark ['Tommy the Torturer'] they did give him something of a belting.

Taggart was upset by the roughing-up. He said he was stripped naked and horribly beaten by Charlie, so much so that his head had swollen into giant proportions. He said he was made to mop up his own blood with his underpants. Taggart lost the plot and went to the cops.

The problem was he didn't go to anyone we knew. He avoided Scotland Yard and visited Welwyn Garden City [No 5, Regional Crime Squad, Hertfordshire] and one of the head coppers, Gerald McArthur, who was known as 'Mr Mac'. He certainly wasn't like that 'Uncle Mac' off the kids' wireless. This one was a right menace. He'd help get the Train Robbers. And as an assistant chief constable he had clout. [The Metropolitan Police was thought so corrupt in 1966 that Labour Government Home Secretary, Roy Jenkins, considered replacing 70 per cent of the CID and other specialist branches with CID officers outside London.]

Taggart was so frightened he'd have jumped over his own

shadow. The more McArthur told him he would look after him, protect him, the more he told stories. He also supplied names. After he began squealing, McArthur, who'd got some straight bunch of Old Bill around him, fucking 'Untouchables' if you like, started investigating. And now, with Bradbury shouting his head off in Johannesburg, the horror stories and names were matching up in the early months of 1966. It was overwhelming and I see now the manipulation of events that went on behind the scenes. The retribution which was going to crash down on me was as over the top as some of stories became. It was, they said, the Richardsons' – me included – 'trademark' to crucify and cripple people.

Now, I've always been one for cracking heads and shaking hands: after the liberties that have been taken have, in turn, been avenged, there's no need to go further. I was always aggressive and ready to get into a fight but it was also over quickly. Charlie liked to stretch things out, to toy with people, eat his fish and chips with the boys, while his victims were tied up or hooked up and squirming. Punishments, they said, included whippings, cigarette burning and teeth being pulled out by Frankie Fraser. I never saw Frank pull a tooth. Still, he loved being called 'The Dentist' and later he made a lot of loot with a pair of gold pliers and stories. Charlie admitted nothing and, as usual, blagged: 'If you can find anyone who says they got nailed to the floor by us or got their toes cut off I will give you £10,000 for each one.'

No one, and I include myself, believed the Richardsons couldn't get themselves out of this.

Jack 'The Rat' Duval had been revelling in pursuing his talents, swindling anything that walked. He'd squirrelled himself away in Leeds, well out of the South London manor, but got nabbed for passport fraud.

Duval lived up to his nickname. He did a plea bargain deal and talked and talked in return for a reduced sentence [from three years to one]. I knew nothing of any of this and all my concern was for the upcoming problem of what would go down at my upcoming trial at the Bailey for what happened at Mr Smith's. As if to focus my mind on trials and verdicts, on 2 May 1966, Bradbury was found 'guilty of the gangland killing' of Tom Waldeck. He was sentenced to death.

That was a shocker and, of course, made huge headlines, with the Richardson name once again like a carnival in the newspapers. Bradbury [his death sentence was commuted to life imprisonment in return for his evidence] had made it impossible for *anyone* called Richardson to get a fair trial. Still, I saw myself as a victim that night: I hadn't gone looking for trouble and I hadn't gone armed. We'd had a problem and I'd have been glad to sort it out with a straightener. The others brought guns to the party.

Frankie Fraser saw it the same way. He'd been charged with the murder of Dickie Hart but his only comment – and I think the only thing he said throughout the whole business – was: 'I'm completely innocent of this. It's perfectly ridiculous. I was at the club. I had no gun. I took no part but I finished up a victim. I do not know who caused my injuries.' He said nothing during his trial at the Bailey and the jury was told to find him not guilty [no one has ever been convicted for the murder of Dickie Hart] but he got five years for affray. A week later, on 28 June 1966, I was facing the same charge at the Old Bailey along with some of the others from that bad night at Mr Smith's. As soon as the jury was set, Charlie tried to do something.

Whatever they planned was fucked up when a bottle was chucked through a juror's home window with a note warning them to find me and the others guilty. It was a reverse ferret and dirty trick from the cops. The judge told the jury to ignore the nonsense and then he marked their card. They would have twenty-four-hour protection during the trial.

Mr Justice Griffith-Jones might have waved a flag announcing this as a wild bunch of villains who needed putting away, but it shows how thin the case against us was that Ronnie Jeffreys and Harry Rawlins were acquitted. Quite rightly, Billy Haward was done for having the sawn-off, as was Henry Botton who talked to much and convicted himself. They both got a five for affray and Haward had another three added on for the shotgun. I found myself in Neverland. On 26 July 1966, Jimmy Moody, Billy Staynton, and I, after nearly a month in court, were given another roll of the dice.

In 1966, a jury verdict had to be unanimous and in our case all twelve couldn't agree. We were remanded in custody at Brixton Prison for a retrial and I was a happy man. There was no case. And the new trial was set for some time in September. I was confident of bail and confident that this time I would be found not guilty.

Four days later, on 30 July 1966, England beat West Germany 4–2 to win the World Cup. That victory didn't help my day. *'They think it's all over... it is, now!'* shouted the BBC commentator Kenneth Wolstenholme and that turned out to be the most accurate news report on the Richardsons for years to follow.

Charlie and a dozen or more people I knew were arrested

by Gerald McArthur's band of policemen, at dawn when most were still in bed. They turned over many of the friends I've mentioned before and some toe-rags too; they found drugs, puff, at Charlie's, and a gun at Roy Hall's and a lot of people in every sort of denial. They denied they'd done anything, but they also couldn't believe it was happening. How could it? I was in Brixton Prison and I heard news of mass arrests on the radio but it was short of detail. It couldn't be Charlie, could it? Everybody was paid off, everything was sorted, was fixed, how was this happening? Well, it was, and from then on I didn't stand a chance of a fair hearing, of a fair trial, a fair anything. I was going to get it big for having the surname Richardson.

The newspapers that had been filling pages with the Bradbury trial in South Africa, with the gunplay at Mr Smith's, now had the greater sensation of this criminal empire round-up. They boasted it was the most carefully planned operation in police history. It was certainly quiet, no one had heard a whisper of it. Charlie said he got a tip about it, but that was bravado; he wouldn't have hung about. There wasn't much I could have done being banged up but even then, inside myself, I knew it was a stacked deck. From the off the Establishment – the sort of people who couldn't believe Jeremy Thorpe could attempt murder – established a circus with Charlie and I as the prime attractions. With us in the Big Top were Frankie Fraser and Roy Hall, Tommy Clark, Jimmy Moody, Johnny Longman and Alfred Berman. Jean Goodman also made a short appearance and I had to feel some sympathy for her – well turned over by Charlie, done all the work he demanded and more, and then dumped for a bit of Mata Hari.

This was something you could sell tickets to. As the steam

built up in the newspapers, it was announced that the first court appearances we'd make would be in Clerkenwell Magistrates' Court. That was because one of the most historic courts in the land, Bow Street Court, was being *refurbished* to accommodate the Richardsons. They were making the dock bigger so we could all fit in. To add to the cavalcade of hysteria about us we all had court escorts, marked police cars, motorcycle outriders, all monitored by a police helicopter hovering over us as we sped through the streets of London with sirens screaming like banshees. The world was being told we were on trial – and what we were accused of.

There was no escaping the charges and the lurid allegations around them.

As far as the public were concerned, we were the most deadly villains who'd ever lived. And some of these people would the ones to judge us. It was open season. There was nothing I or anyone else could do about it. The case brought a change in the law, on what could and could not be reported, but long after the event to be of help to us. During our committal, day after day, the newspapers were ripe with the prosecution's case against us. I wasn't named in most of the charges but I was on the list and I was in the crowded dock. And I was the other *Mr Richardson*: we were all in the same frame.

The powers that ruled the land wanted me and Charlie and all things associated with the Richardsons stuck away, out of sight, out of mind, for as long as was possible. All our 'friends' appeared desperate to ingratiate themselves with the law and get a better deal for themselves; almost all of the witnesses were in the shit themselves.

Jimmy Moody was one who didn't give anything away. He

nutted a police-custody sergeant after he'd been beaten about on his way into court. They had him handcuffed in the dock for a couple of days, which didn't help our collective public relations, which wasn't up to much anyway for they'd got twenty-five coppers, all in uniform and polished shoes, surrounding the dock. There were seventeen men and Jean Goodman in the dock listening to the horror stories being broadcast.

Jack 'The Rat' Duval and his pals, the conmen who were never short of a story to tell, spilled out what was required in return for saving their sorry arses. It was effective evidence: the protection money collector who was skimming money and was nailed to Tower Bridge warehouse floor. He was supposedly kept there for forty-eight hours and 'watered' – peed on. Johnny Bradbury, saving his life, had already confessed in another court to using torture, excusing himself by saying he had to do it or be hurt himself. He said we tortured our own friends to keep them in line and to stop them from talking.

Jack Duval was like a record spinning out the same old stuff. [Duval was known as 'The Prince of Fraud' and Charlie Richardson described him as 'a turd that floated down river to my part of London.'] He was the 'front' for the long-firm frauds but claimed he was told he was not working hard enough for the company and was summoned to Peckford Scrap Metal where he was punched and beaten by me with golf clubs. He said he saw Alfie Blore, another of Charlie's cohorts, being used as a bullseye, with Charlie throwing knives at him and hitting the target.

Benny Coulston made a good witness for them: he said he had been attacked outside a pub then driven to Camberwell where Charlie placed a gun on a table and ordered him to be stripped as Frankie Fraser appeared with a pair of pliers. Coulston testified: 'He put them into my mouth and started to try to pull out my teeth. He slipped and pulled a lump of my gum out. Then he tried again and pulled part of a top tooth out.' Coulston said he was punched about and then Charlie held an electric fire against his genitals. And that lighted cigarettes were put out on his arms and chest, before he was wrapped in tarpaulin and 'taken for a ride'. He said I dumped him and told him we got the wrong man and I was sorry. [Coulston had X-rays for a fractured skull, which also would have shown if his teeth were pulled by pliers. The X-rays were lost and not produced in evidence.]

A toe-rag called Cyril Green told the court that he had his toes broken with pliers. Afterwards, he could hear the screams of another man being tortured. This evidence went on day after day and there was little we could do to challenge it. And there were statements that couldn't be challenged; they were *stories*. One bloke said that when he heard 'the Richardsons' wanted to speak to him he drove to Heathrow Airport but was so terrified he couldn't form the words to buy a plane ticket. They didn't need evidence to paint us as monsters. It was like *Sunday Night at the London Palladium*, the variety of charges and characters against us they were producing. Our alleged victims were granted immunity from prosecution if they turned Queen's evidence; a complete lack of physical evidence wasn't allowed to spoil the party. I'd been brought up surrounded by villains and most of the people I dealt with were the old-fashioned sort in that you made your own rules and kept to them. That meant you dealt with your own problems, you policed your own manor and your affairs. Like that Bill Slack who'd we done over for his attack on me and Dickie Martin at the snooker club in Peckham. Bastard that he was, he never went to the police about that attack. That was the code. What Charlie had done was brought in a load of fraudsters with multiple names and passports who lived by the code of their bank accounts — money was all that mattered.

Charlie was lost in his own fantasy and never saw the reality of those he had surrounded himself with. We were seeing it now.

And with all this banging on, I was hauled off to the Old Bailey for my retrial on the night out at Mr Smith's. Jimmy Moody and Billy Staynton were up, too. The authorities hadn't got any new tricks up their sleeves so they played the same old dirty ones. There was a fanfare about the jury being under police protection and one juror had a cop sleeping overnight in their house. They confused it more by getting a 'tainted' juror dismissed, suggesting he'd been nobbled.

For three weeks of September 1966, I had been big-type headline news as part of 'The Torture Gang'. Now, in the last week of that month I was in front of an Old Bailey jury trying to defend myself against charges of violence. It was a ridiculous state of affairs. Justice? I complained about the unfairness of having the retrial after all the publicity, but it was pissing in the wind. I knew then it was hopeless, but your heart rules your head and you think it will work out OK. I hadn't carried any guns, I hadn't started the trouble, I had defended myself and my friends against an onslaught of violence. But the attitude was: OK, Eddie, so what?

On my side I had my barrister Jeremy Hutchinson. He was one of the most applauded legal eagles in the land who helped get victory for the publisher [Penguin] in the [1960] *'Lady Chatterley's Lover'* lawsuit. His clients included people who were in, or would be part of my life, one way or another, Christine Keeler, the spies George Blake and John Vassall, the Train Robber Charlie Wilson. Mr Hutchison [Lord Hutchinson of Lullington, QC, died on 13 November 2017, aged 102] was a charmer and revelled in the daftness of legal procedure.

What Mr Hutchinson, friend that he was to my absurd situation, was not, was a miracle worker. And I didn't help his defence. I was between Alcatraz and a hard place and young enough to believe that if I broadcast the stitch-up performed on me then it would be undone. Mr Hutchinson suggested it would be better if I stayed out of the witness box: there was no case to answer. I thought I knew better and wanted to tell my story of how we weren't tooled up and didn't start the trouble. I should have listened to my barrister. I did alright in the box but staying silent would, as he said, have been more effective. As it was I got an even harder deal. I was sentenced on 26 September 21966 to five years for affray.

It was a travesty.

My record [four convictions: stealing a torch, aged thirteen, 1949; taking a car and possessions of housebreaking implements, 1954; receiving £25 worth of waste piping, 1959; jumping a red light,1963] was Persil clean compared to Frankie Fraser and the others but I shared the same punishment. The opposition, who'd had guns, got the same five years, and Billy Haward who'd brandished the shotgun got eight years. That there were characters in court who looked as though they'd sneaked out of the back door of the Home Office, and Special Branch boys that Jimmy Moody – he and Billy Staynton did get justice and were acquitted – recognised, told me strings were being pulled. I felt personally persecuted and I felt alone. Yes, I'd stretched the limits, but their retribution twisted the law against me: the two trials, Mr Smith's and the Torture Trial, should never have run concurrently. Such injustice has never happened again.

I said I felt alone. Well, after the Mr Smith's conviction I *was* alone. I was shipped out to Wandsworth Prison where I felt like a caged animal. I was in solitary confinement for twenty-three hours every day I was there. It was just done, there was no reason given for me being in the *chokey.* I swore to myself that I wouldn't let the fucking system beat me. I was furious and that anger fuelled me, gave me the energy for a very long battle against our supposed betters. I believed, and I still do, that it was part of a class war in the 1960s, us against them. It wasn't easy for me going it solo and I dropped a lot of weight, but the biggest torture was mentally you feel so fucking impotent. There is nothing you can do to help yourself or your family, and thank God for them, for Maureen was on my side and, as ever, watching over our girls.

Life in the chokey at Wandsworth was an ongoing frustration. The only 'freedom' were days at the committal hearings, which went on and on and on. [The 'Torture Trial' committal proceedings concluded with legal submissions between 24 January and 27 January 2 1967, after 71 days of hearings in which 250 witnesses had appeared offering 1,500,00 words of evidence. The Richardsons and the other defendants were committed to the Old Bailey; only Jean Goodman was freed, having won bail on condition she stayed away from Charlie Richardson, at the end of 1966.]

The committal was simply a dress rehearsal for our star

turns as the world's most vicious gangsters at the Old Bailey. The charges were reduced to twenty-two counts including assault and GBH and fraud and extortion and lots of stuff involving menace. That was the only reduction – the atmosphere, the tension, was heightened by the authorities. Before the jury had been sworn in – and that took a lifetime with eighty-five prospective jurors being challenged by the prosecution and our team, which comprised twenty-five barristers [including ten QCs] – it was published that sixty hand-picked policemen would be on guard at the Bailey. Plainclothes police would guard and 'shadow' the jury. Streets were closed off, or made one-way, and we had a convoy with sirens going and everything flashing apart from Jumpin' Jack. I was brought to the Bailey from my hellhole in Wandsworth while the others arrived separately from Brixton. Still, we shared the daily attention-grabbing concert of welcome. As did our prospective jurors who had all been vetted by Scotland Yard's Special Branch, the big-footed soldiers for MI5. It was blatant *embracery* – influencing a jury – in this case by the entertainment falderol of portraying myself and the others as requiring maximum security for being a clear and present danger. And *embracery* is a criminal offence. I was livid about it but the men in wigs who were arguing about points of law, men who got to go home at 4.30 p.m. when Court 2 at the Old Bailey closed down for the day, did not argue this point.

Neither was Mr Justice Lawton [Sir Frederick Horace Lawton, Judge of the High Court of Justice from 1961] concerned. He always caught the 5.31p.m. train home to Purley, Surrey. Without a bodyguard. This wasn't thought necessary for this judge, the man in granny-glasses in charge of 'The Case of the Century'. Yet more than 100 police were involved in moving us back and forth from prison to court. Outriders, squealing sirens, a Black Maria convoy for us and vans stuffed with coppers following us.'

By the time we squeezed into the dock the charges had been trimmed to involve thirteen offences, with the Crown going for the kill and with all of them involving violence or extortion. I was up on four charges, Charlie on nine, Roy Hall was on five and Frankie Fraser faced four; the others were all on one. Mr Justice Lawton had a no-nonsense reputation and was also said to be a bit of a card. His offbeat comments may have been politically incorrect but his instincts and intentions were very much in line with the politics of our prosecution. Which involved allowing witnesses with fraud convictions scattered around them like confetti to not only be heard but for the evidence of these attack dogs to be recorded in court against us. He immediately rejected all our applications for separate trials on the different charges. The judge let the prosecuting counsel, Sebag Shaw QC, who off-duty was a likeable man to have a drink with, a great gambler, and a much sought-after *defence* barrister, off the leash first:

This case is about violence, not sudden violence committed on the spur of the moment but brutal violence, systematically carried out with utter and callous ruthlessness.

I imagine, members of the jury, when you have heard the evidence, if you accept but half of it, you will come to the conclusion that not one word I have just uttered to you is without ample justification. When the police finally intervened, the policy of the gang had been successful for some years, and Charles Richardson grew in power and influence in that particular fraternity over which he presided, and the policy was so successful that no person who became a victim of it dared to complain lest worse, if worse were possible, befall him or members of his family.

I was lumped in with this vividly painted picture. Sebag Shaw [in 1955 he was junior counsel for the defence of Ruth Ellis, the last woman hanged in Britain] understood how I felt about that and he theatrically turned to the jury and told them that when I was arrested I said: 'You are undermining the whole structure of the British justice system by bringing these charges against me when you know full well I am innocent.'

I bloody did, too. But this was Sebag Shaw's show and he went on: 'You will give that [Eddie Richardson] speech all the weight you think fit but we all know that British justice is safe in this court.'

As far as I was concerned it was not. It was a joke but not a funny one. Jack *The Rat* Duval repeated stuff from the committal that I played a round of golf all over his body, that I beat him about with golf clubs. It was a nonsense – he made it up as he went along – and that was one instance when the charge, GBH, was kicked down to ABH [Actual Bodily Harm]. It should never been left on the list against me. The whole thing was fixed up.

I was angry then and I'm angry now, which is why I wanted to explain, while I can, and when what I reveal can no longer cause problems for others.

I was off in the West End by 1963 and, yes, Charlie would always be on the phone to me or whatever. But when it came to taking care of problems he always used to get Frankie Fraser to come over when people were slapped about or whacked on the head. I got caught in it all. Bennie Coulston's stories about Frankie Fraser pulling his teeth out with pliers – they say 'print he legend' and they've been doing it ever since – I thought would be laughed out of court, down to Ludgate Circus and up Fleet Street, but the good judge let it all roll out and into the public record. M15 and M16 have certain people that are on retainers, judges and the like are on a retainer, and every now and again, they want to use them. The prosecutors had all of them. We had no one and absolutely no chance. And the jury were told what to do and what not to do. It was a fit-up. Anything to set us up. I was made a scapegoat. *Judge Lawton!* He came out about me having a Bentley. A Bentley! Right in my face, staring at me from the bench. He must have been fucking mad. I don't understand it: because I had a Bentley car he was giving me a hard time. He made it seem the biggest fucking crime I'd ever committed was having a Bentley. Strange, the legal profession. It's jealously.

I was paying myself a decent wage, obviously, out of my hard-earned from my chemist's selling natural stuff, which was part of my pharmaceutical company, Revvon. I had a business account and it was turning over huge sums of money. I was running a proper business. I was legitimate. I could afford a fucking Bentley.

But that was not viewed kindly through Mr Justice Lawton's granny glasses. It was, *I* was, I think, an affront to the status quo.

Instead, he was thankful to hear the full parade of lies from that fucking rat Bennie Coulston who was presented in court as an oracle come down to enlighten us all. He went round and sold crooked cigarettes to my mate Harry Rawlins's brother. (He sold Billy a parcel of cigarettes, got his money and there weren't any cigarettes in the boxes.) Remember, Billy Rawlins killed himself over it, and now this Brixton villain, with great form for violence, was in the dock ranting rubbish like a lunatic. Yes, I'd sorted him out, but that's what he deserved for taking such a liberty. In the right manner of our world it should have stayed there, sorted and over after Charlie had him over at the fucking yard and we went down there. Coulston linked me to all the rest of it, to these fucking fraudsters and Charlie's antics, the extent of which I knew nothing about.' I didn't know anything about that conspiracy or the implications, MI6 on our backs. That's why it was so heavy and we couldn't do anything about it.

Believe me, it was tried. We got some nonsense published by some gullible bastards at the *Daily Mirror* to try and discredit the prosecution; money was paid and offered to all sorts of witnesses, but there were other deals being done by the cops with Charlie's erstwhile 'friends' like Duval and Alfie Berman and Bunny Bridges. Charlie's credibility account with these people was bankrupt, and with offers of immunity, get out of jail cards, they were willing to say whatever was required. Yes, there had been violence and extreme acts of it. Yes, I'd been involved in violent acts but always on the nod that you gave it out and took it if you had to. That's the way we'd grown up. Clearly, the workings over at the Peckford Scrap Metal had got maniacal. It didn't take a lot of bullshit to make it look like a horror show. And with my brother believing he was some superspy and eavesdropping on the Prime Minister, I was royally fucked.

NO HANDCUFFS

[The so-called 'Torture Trial' concluded on 7 June 1967, after forty-five days, which included four days of Judge Lawton summing up. The jury – eleven men, one woman – returned their verdicts after nine and a half hours of deliberations.

Eddie Richardson was found guilty of just two charges, ABH (actual bodily harm) on Jack Duval and GBH (grievous bodily harm) on Bennie Coulston.

Charlie Richardson was convicted of nine charges, involving fraud, extortion, assault and GBH, and Frankie Fraser, Roy Hall and Tommy 'The Torturer' Clark on charges of violence and wounding. On public record – much has been redacted– six senior policemen 'retired' from Scotland Yard for 'associations' with the Richardsons.]

Judge Lawton weighed away Charlie for twenty-five years in concurrent arithmetic. There was nothing to smile about but I had to be amused that the good judge wondered how Charlie, with his 3 million quid in South African mining interests, got legal aid. I felt like telling him: 'The system, dear boy, the system.' There was not much chance of that for I was next in the dock and had Judge Lawton peering at me. He handed me ten years for the GBH and two years for ABH, but to run concurrently. That was still a decade in the slammer – on top of the five years I got for Mr Smith's. That took away any hint of amusement I might have felt. I was being punished for being a Richardson. I was not alone in being victimised, ostracised, for being around Charlie. Jean Goodman escaped the trouble [all the charges against her were dropped other than the possession of an illegal drug for which she received an absolute discharge], but a string of others were jailed for this or that but singularly for knowing Charlie Richardson. What chance did I ever have as his brother?

DIRTY TRICKS

Yet there was one place now where the name *Richardson* as an absolute asset – and that was inside the British prison system.

When I went to jail I was an angry man and intent on fucking that system as much as was humanly possible. And I was a tough guy. I was, I was to quickly find out, a man with a reputation.

CHAPTER ELEVEN

GRAND SLAM

Prison was an education. I made some amazing if sometimes eccentric friends. Somewhere, I hope, I've still got the postcard from Moscow from my pal Peter Kroger. We had a big party for him in 1969 when he left Parkhurst Prison in exchange for a British 'businessman' who'd been arrested by the Russians. Peter was really Morris Cohen, a top Soviet spy, but I knew him as a man who played a good hand of bridge and liked a nice piece of fish on a Friday. A little group of us – a couple of the Train Robbers, Dennis Stafford [the one-armed bandit killer] and Harry Roberts [in 1966, he instigated the Shepherd's Bush murders in which three policemen were shot dead] – laid on various bits of food and some homemade drinks for him in our special security wing. We made big circle with some tables and on my record player we played his favourite music, *Zorba the Greek*. We were all clapping as the music played. Peter had tears running down his face. We were all a bit pissed and emotional.

Parkhurst was brilliant. It had had a lot of trouble previously in other wings, so they tried to keep everyone quiet by giving us extra concessions. It was a little longer before I had my own catering arrangements and special kitchen facilities, but I'm getting ahead of myself.

I had to learn to work the system. The most effective way to do that was to mentally stay out of it. I never got involved in the prison culture as such, other than to fight to make things better for everyone. Apart from that, my life was outside. I had my family, my letters. My mind was beyond the walls, was free, not locked up. I'd learned how important that was when I was in chokey in Wandsworth; the guards had played their tricks on me, tried to convince me they were my friends and induce me to pay them to smuggle in cigarettes and drink just so they could shop me. They were perverse in their cruelty too. I was victimised because I didn't want to have a trade with them. The only outside line I had was letters from Maureen or my mother and when I was in chokey block they'd come around with your mail every day and open the cell door. I'd get up to go get the mail and they'd sneer: 'Not for you!' and shut the fucking door. They tried it again and again but after the first time I don't get out the chair, do I? They say, 'Mail' and I say, 'Put it on the side.' I was not going to stand for that game. Of course, that gets you branded for being 'difficult'. I swore when I was in Wandsworth that 'difficult' was going to be my middle name and I never ever bought into the system in all my years in prison.

I met extraordinary characters throughout these years and I can only tell you how I got on with them: you can feel how you want about them. I know my mind. I found the easiest way to survive in prison was to deal with every person as I found them on the day. I never truly concerned myself about what other people were jammed up for. It wasn't up to me to judge Peter Kroger or anyone else. He was a Communist, a convert, and we argued about it, but he did what he believed in. It was the Cold War and Peter was very much part of it as one of the key members of the Portland Spy Ring, the lot that nicked secrets from the Royal Navy. His wife, Lona, was also an agent and banged up in Holloway Prison. He talked a lot about her, for she was unwell and he was worried. He wrote to her all the time, as often as the Press were always writing about them. I understood that separation.

Peter had a soft American accent and was happy to talk as he was simply 'waiting'. His motto was *zorba* – [in Greek] *live each day*. He said he'd always been convinced a deal would be done after their arrest [7 January 1961]; Moscow, he said, always brought their *sleepers* home. We'd play cards and we'd talk and, as I said, it was an education. He gave me a copy of *The Spy Who Came in from the Cold* [John Le Carré, 1963] and said that was more like reality than Bond: 'I'm no James Bond.' He might have been, he was a cool enough fella. He and his wife had been recruited in America but he was in Parkhurst with me for his role alongside Konon Molody, who I knew from the newspapers as Gordon Lonsdale, the boss of the spy ring which stole naval secrets [from the British Admiralty Underwater Weapons Establishment at Portland in Hampshire, England; the team captured great amounts of classified material, including details of Britain's first nuclear submarine, HMS *Dreadnought*. In Moscow it was seen as one of the grandest coups of the Cold War].

As I was told it, Lonsdale's main catch was a sad little Englishman called Harry Houghton. In 1950, he was a Royal

Naval clerk at the British Embassy in Warsaw and after two decades as a sailor, liked the diplomatic good life, especially the gallons of cheap drink. One of Houghton's barroom friends told him: 'If you don't make a pile here, you're a mug.' Houghton went into the coffee business, getting it supplied through diplomatic couriers, and moving his cheap supply at a good profit. Then, a tantalising new female client appeared, long, dark hair and a body to commit crimes for, who had the cash for big shipments. Harry did. I can understand it was with some sadness two years later he left all that behind and returned to the UK. He went to work at the Portland Underwater Weapons Research Establishment, lost a wife to divorce but became engaged to Ethel 'Bunty' Gee, a filing clerk and secretary at the Portland base. Like the life Houghton had created, she was built for comfort, not speed.

They seemed to spend every weekend decorating their bungalow. Harry Houghton was surrounded by new rolls of floral wallpaper when, in 1955, he answered the telephone to a heavily accented man. He had a message. Three days later Houghton met the go-between at the Dulwich Art Gallery in South London. It was made clear to him the Polish secret police knew of his affair and the black market business and offered silence and cash in return for secrets. Houghton spun Bunty Gee a tale about the black market problem and said he was being blackmailed by a CIA agent known to him from Warsaw: the Americans believed the British were withholding nuclear secrets. He would go to jail unless he gave them details of the research at Portland. With a man in her life for the first time, Bunty was in. Houghton got a Minox camera the size of a cigarette lighter – there was a bigger, sharper version he kept for documents he could take home. The tradecraft for clandestine meetings and handovers was mundane. It was done by a code of pinpricks on life-insurance brochures sent to him by Royal Mail. The material, about nuclear submarine development and anti-submarine weapons, was invaluable to the East. In turn, they kept Houghton happy with money, as well as 'protection' from his black market past. He bought more than his fair round in pubs, drove a new car, and the Sanderson wallpaper was top of the line. And he worked at a top-secret nuclear establishment at the height of the Cold War: for nearly four years Houghton provided Gordon Lonsdale and the East with crackerjack material.

Peter Kroger moved the information to Moscow from Ruislip, from *Ruislip in Middlesex*. He and 'Helen' Kroger had a bungalow, and a high-speed transmitter, used to communicate with Moscow, was next to the kitchen. Peter's front was as a book dealer, so he was always sending parcels abroad: full stops on the pages of many books contained microdots giving secrets including details from the Holy Loch nuclear submarine base in Scotland.

This grand theft might have gone on and on but Peter Kroger said the Americans got intelligence that buggered it all up for them. MI5 and Special Branch rounded them all up. Then, it was a trial and all that stuff about dead letter boxes and bits of film in tins of talcum powder. It seemed and still seems fantastic, but they were risking their lives for it. Peter's friends, his fellow travellers Julius and Ethel Rosenberg, were also American citizens and they were given the electric chair. [The Rosenbergs were executed on 19 June 1953, in Sing Sing prison, Ossining, New York, after being convicted of spying for Moscow.]

But he always believed his Russian mates wouldn't forget him. He kept pointing out that Gordon Lonsdale had been 'swapped' [in 1962 for the British 'businessman' Greville Wynne], but rumours in the papers about the Krogers getting exchanged were bringing a lot of heat on my old pal Harold Wilson. The Prime Minister was getting flak 'for agreeing to release dangerous Soviet agents like Peter and Helen Kroger in exchange for Gerald Brooke, a mere propagandist'. Peter said Brooke was a British spy but I don't know: presumably he had some clout or Wilson wouldn't have made the deal which saw Peter wish us all a swift goodbye that October in 1969. We saw him filmed getting on to his plane to Poland on the television news. When Peter finally got to Moscow he sent me a postcard wishing 'mud in my eye' and 'Cheers!' When he was there he met George Blake – another spy but one who caused me a lot more aggravation than Peter.

Blake had gone over the wall from Wormwood Scrubs in October 1966, only nine months before I got weighed away with Charlie, Frankie Fraser and Roy Hall – we were each in a different secured police transit van – to Durham as many miles as possible from our South London manor. The thinking was 'out of sight, out of mind'. It was also to bang us up in 'E Wing', which was the all-new state-of-the-art prison within a prison, an impregnable Alcatraz in the north of England.

The Beaujolais-slurping Roy Jenkins was the Home Secretary and terrified of losing his job after George Blake, who the papers called the greatest traitor of the Cold War, had done a runner. The opposition Tories, with 'Grocer' Ted Heath doing much of the shouting, were on about national security, and being a frightened politician Jenkins set up 'an urgent inquiry' asking Lord Mountbatten to sort it out. That didn't get rid of his problems, so Jenkins had his Labour lot pumping money into Durham, and Parkhurst and Leicester jails, setting up security cameras and the usual barbed wire about the place, but I have to say I've seen better-protected allotments. The gullibility of the bastards – they thought they were running Colditz, with surveillance towers and the like – but the only people crawling about the place were reporters from Fleet Street. Durham was a 'celebrity' hang-out. I was part of the new attraction.

Happily, kept well away from me and the others in E Wing was Ian Brady, the Moors Murderer, who was locked away in an isolation area along with other sex offenders, the nonces. As in the outside world, there are limits, arguably even more defined, in prison about social contact. There were plenty of *faces* on the E Wing. And we were all living in an unpleasant environment following the breakout of George Blake. Roy Jenkins had ordered the construction of our secured unit, which was on four floors and linked by those rattling iron staircases. It was as if The Incredible Hulk was on the way anytime someone climbed up them. The screws – it was mutual hatred, them and us – locked themselves up more than we they did us. They had little steel enclosed cells on each of the unit's landings. For all the mod-con security there was still slopping out. Buckets were splashed down an open drain every morning. It stunk, almost as much as the food, which was prepared in the main prison kitchen and went cold before it got to us. I was receiving the benefit of Blake's escape artistry – if the powers that be had only known how he really did it. There would have been a bigger stink than the shit buckets.

Blake had been locked up for forty-two years, the most

severe sentence ever handed out, and for good reason as his spying for the Soviet Union against Britain in the early Cold War years cost many lives. He was a double agent, an MI6 officer working for the KGB. Officially, his escape story is that on 22 October 1966, after serving five years, he scaled the wall of the Scrubs on a ladder made from knitting needles. He was helped over the wall and hidden by Irishman Sean Bourke who was jailed for seven in 1961 for sending a bomb in a biscuit tin to a policeman. A couple of save-the-world merchants, anti-nuclear blokes, Michael Randle and Pat Pottle, had been in the Scrubs with Blake. They were out and got him away to the East German border and he was on the bus, as it were, to Moscow [Blake was in Moscow in 2018 and preparing to celebrate his ninety-sixth birthday in November].

Well, yes, Blake did go over the wall with the help of Bourke, but the escape and its successful aftermath was due to an elegant Indian woman who had strong Communist sympathies. She helped him get out with a child's toy, a two-way walkie-talkie bought from Hamleys in Regent Street. Inside prison, I heard the whole story but can only now tell it as those involved are not around to be worried by any interested plods. First, you must meet Lilamani Kapoor, who was born [on 26 July 1927] for the pages of *The Arabian Nights*. She was a most glamorous, unique woman and she provided money and herself helped Blake escape.

[In the late 1940s Lilamani Kapoor scandalised her native Ceylon by leaving her husband, the biscuit heir Nicky Seneviratne, for the Italian film director Giulio Petroni; in 1951, they married and moved to Italy, where with her husband's show-business connections she became a star. She had studied

Bharata natyam, the classical religious dance of southern India. She often danced with Ram Gopal, the 'Nijinsky of India'. She was a fixture in Rome's *dolce vita*. Her friends included Marc Chagall, Jean-Paul Sartre, and Jean Cocteau, who painted her. She also appeared as a maharani in *Roman Holiday* (1953) and was courted by Marlon Brando, although in Rome was much friendlier with Steve McQueen. Her marriage suffered, and while working for the Indian Embassy she accepted the offer of going for a drive with Shiv Kapoor, a wealthy ship-owner 'from a princely family in Assam'. They married in 1958 and set up home in London and friends included Stephen Spender and Princess Margaret's set. The Queen considered buying their country home, Buckhurst Park, near Ascot, as a wedding gift for her sister. It was bought by King Hussein of Jordan. The Kapoors had a home built for them in Virginia Water, Surrey, made only from stone and wood. In the 1960s they rented it to Diana Dors and her then husband, Denis Hamilton, and it became infamous for two-way mirrors and sex parties.]

Lilamani Kapoor was as rich as can be and had the Midas touch. Her old man was a bit of a rogue, the arms dealer in that TV show *The Night Manger* was modelled on him. They had money but she was a bit in love with love, as such people can be. There was a lot of anti-fascist sentiment about in Rome when she was there and that's when, I was told, she began to see the glory of Communism. She was, of course, a touch naive about it all. She thought Blake getting forty-two years was inhuman. She offered to help in the Saturday-night getaway.

Blake's escape was all a bit of a farce from the start. Bourke smuggled the walkie-talkie Lilamani supplied into the jail so Blake could talk to him outside the prison wall. On the night, while most of the other blokes and guards were at the early-evening film show, Blake went out of a window at the end of a corridor, slid down a porch and ran to the wall. He climbed up and over and fell down on the outside, breaking his wrist. That's where Lilamani came in. She arranged a relative as the driver of the getaway car, but in the rush racing away it was involved by chance in an accident. It ended with Blake being shoved into a wheelchair and whisked away by Lilamani to another car and onto a safe house she'd arranged. The siren were blaring all over London on the hunt for Blake and her, the lady in a sari wheeling him along in Shepherd's Bush. Scotland Yard and the Government were going ballistic and there was a manhunt on. Security and police were off to airfields, seaports, the Russian Embassy residences in Kensington Park Gardens, the cross-channel ferry train at Victoria Station and the London docks, especially Eastern Bloc ships. Lilamani helped some of the searchers. She wore a nurse's uniform – she made it herself – and told a car patrol that she'd seen the getaway car drive towards the North Circular, as though it was heading to the A1 and Scotland.

Harold Wilson was at Chequers and they told him with some certainty that the Russians had done it. Special Branch were tipped that Blake was hiding in a harp case belonging to a member of the Czechoslovakian State Orchestra who'd just performed on London's South Bank. The Czech airline flight was stopped and searched, musicians, harps, cellos and the rest, but no Blake. He was having cups of tea and brandy at the first of the houses set up by his sympathiser Lilamani. As the house-to-house investigations went on, Blake stayed with Lilamani and her family in Croydon.

George Blake was in the kitchen one day when a Special Branch officer, on a routine call, knocked at the front door. It was opened by her toddler son, Mangal. The rather weary and bad-tempered copper went through his routine and asked the boy with a laugh: 'Is there anybody hiding in the house?'

'Only Mum's friend under the kitchen table,' he was told.

The cop was an arse, for out of the mouths of babes... He was also dismissive, rude to the boy, never stepped into the place and walked off. Blake got out from under the table and put some hot water in his tea.

He did the rounds for a couple of more weeks before he left the country for good. The political fury was incredible but if they'd only known the half of it. Lilamani [after struggling with Parkinson's disease, she died on 27 December 2007, aged eighty] set Blake up for a few days in St John's Wood at the home of the Rev. John Papworth whose wife Marcelle was having regular sessions with a head-banger. She told her therapist that this man whose face was always on television and in the newspapers was staying with her; she saw him all the time. The head doctor said for her treatment to work she always had to be totally honest. When she insisted, he declared she was hallucinating and should forget all about it.

It was stories like the Blake escape that encouraged me to fight the system, for it showed that, with friends, it can be done. The right friends. When I hear that people get depressed and hurt themselves I can't understand it. I've never been in that situation where I got overtaken by the crap I was stuck with. I never give up, I'm always fighting. I never even thought about getting depressed, it was not an option; in lock-up I'd be even more positive in my attitude.

Blake was befriended from afar and done a good turn he didn't deserve, but it got him out. I was suffering under the regime imposed because of his unexpected departure. I was also a *Double Cat A* inmate. I was a public enemy, officially a very dangerous man indeed. After Blake hopped it, Jenkins had the Home Office bring in *Cat A* as the styling for prisoners who'd been done for serious crimes. So, I was reckoned to be double trouble. Of course, what was spooking them was if I escaped, if any of us Torture Trial boys made it over the wall. That wouldn't look good. So, I was under the cosh and they were a rough lot the screws and they had no time for us London blokes: Charlie and me and Roy Hall and the like were treated like dirt by them.

It made us a tough team. I was furious about the way it had all gone for us. Now, I was stuck in E Wing, in a goldfish bowl, encircled by endless, claustrophobic corridors and always being peered at through spy holes; the more I dwelled on it the angrier I got. I thought Charlie had been rubbish when he was quizzed in court – that fucking judge had asked him if he wanted to sit down while giving evidence and he did, he subjected himself – but inside we were *the Richardsons* and there was every reason to use our reputation. As a unit of men within the unit we had a chance of taking on the bastards who had been ordered to keep us down, do all they could to break our spirit. Inside prison, everything becomes larger, more important, for you have all the time in the world to stew over things.

As a first-time prisoner I should have enjoyed better treatment, some privileges, a half an hour extra here and there out of my damp cell. Spies, probably responsible for a lot of people's deaths, used to be let out. I would ask: 'Why can't I go out on recreation?' Ah, they were 'star' prisoners, first-timers on long terms. Well, so was I. Ah, but I was different; it wasn't the same for me. The screws didn't mind the traitors getting a nice deal because they were 'yes sir, no sir', Oxford accents and all that. I was entitled to be let out on recreation like them. We used to get out but we didn't get the same association periods. In the night-time you had the television. I went and complained and they went on saying it didn't apply to me. I went on about it, I was a fucking terrier in there, and they had one of the kick-it-down-the-road inquiries which still ruled that I was different from every other bugger in there. Talking of which, one of the 'star' first-time prisoners who did get a bit of VIP treatment was the notorious spy John Vassall. At first, he wasn't keen on me watching him play bridge.

I knew Vassall and another bridge player, Frank Bossard, a Naval spy who was in for twenty-one years for also playing footsie with Moscow.'

Vassall's plight fascinated me. He was so much my opposite in upbringing and lifestyle but here we both were under the day-to-day law of prison warders who were mostly as thick as pig shit. He played it cool but I was a paid-up member of the angry brigade and very much in credit. Vassall might have been from another planet to most of us; he highlighted to me how powerful the class culture was in Britain. He'd got eighteen years at the Old Bailey for 'selling his country for lust and greed' but inside was still treated with some courtesy. Vassall was convicted after a trial held partly in secret. He got away with his dubious story that because he was a poofter he had been compromised by the KGB into spying. He operated in a world where, if you spoke and behaved in a certain way, your actions were unlikely to be questioned. He was an assistant private secretary to a junior minister at the Admiralty, was vastly overspending, much of it along Savile Row, buying from the most exclusive stores to present himself as a gentleman. I ask you, this character happily sending classified material to Moscow, was living in a luxury Dolphin Square flat and better dressed than the Duke of Windsor himself. But no one noticed. Why would they? He was a gent.

[John Vassall was a clerical grade Civil Servant, earning £750 a year. When arrested on 12 September 1962, Special Branch officers searching his apartment found thirty-six suits (almost all bespoke), three unwrapped cashmere overcoats, twenty-nine pairs of custom, hand-lasted shoes, custom-designed silk shirts, bespoke silk pyjamas and underwear. For his collection of Burberry mackintoshes he had a specially designed clothes stand. He also had two drawers of beachwear, used on Caribbean holidays. On arrest it appeared that he had some sort of private income – no one at the Admiralty had noticed, other than that John Vassall 'always looked smart'. This explained why some of his trial was held 'in camera' – it wasn't the spy stuff the Establishment wanted hidden – it was Vassall's fashion secrets, for this spotlighted how fragile British intelligence was and that had to be hidden from the Americans. When Section DI of SIS listed an inventory of Vassall's Dolphin Square flat it comprised a Praktina document-copying camera, a Minox and exposed 35mm cassettes recording 176 classified Admiralty and NATO documents. These were hidden in the secret drawer of a fake antique bureau. The contents of his wardrobe were clearly more embarrassing. As were the endorsements given about him by his superiors, who enthusiastically praised his piety and impeccable character. They did not say that he was known around the office as 'Vera, the Admiralty Queen'. The Establishment attitude to Vassall was gathered concisely in the words of Prime Minister Harold Macmillan, when his spy chief, Roger Hollis of MI5, announced the traitor's arrest: 'When my gamekeeper shoots a fox, he doesn't go and hang it up outside the Master of Foxhounds' drawing room, he buries it out of sight.']

Vassall and Frank Bossard, who liked a laugh and home-made hooch, if we got some yeast from the kitchens, showed me how patience worked playing bridge and in negotiations, but I was still too young and too angry to understand that. I wanted action – now. I decided it was the correct moment, that February in 1968, that we had a mutiny at Durham.

CHAPTER TWELVE

NINE TALES

The Durham Prison governor, 'Flash' Gordon Chambers was a disciplinarian. While the toffs like Vassall and Bossard could stroll around Durham prison yard, we were allowed out for about an hour and only three of us at a time. Along with Charlie and Roy Hall I'd been suffering the high security of Durham for about seven months when the new governor, 'Chambers of Horrors', arrived. We'd been making progress on getting privileges by acting as one. I encouraged ganging up because I knew that if we stuck together, we would get what we wanted. You've got to know the fucking wankers you're dealing with to make special units worth living in. The trick was to complain about this, about that, but not with aggravation, just make the point.

But 'Flash' arrived and laid down his law. It was strict stuff. When you have tough nuts around you in jail it works to have some of them onside, but the new governor alienated everyone and that included a string of high-profile, controversial prisoners as well as new boys like Charlie and me. These were men who the public were terrified of. And 'Flash' was just as terrified of them causing trouble or escaping. It was all about incarceration of the largest number of Cat A cons in the country.

Of course, inside almost all of them were my friends. When I got into Durham the armed robber John McVicar, he'd got twenty-three years for robbery and assault, let me know that I was getting verbals from some blokes who didn't like the look of me. I did what I have always done and confronted the trouble meaning to deal with it and then move on. I told the blokes to complain to me, not whinge on to others. I said it quite forcibly but that wasn't what changed their attitude. It is the look you give people, the look that tells them you will follow through with your threats, follow through no matter what and how much you may get hurt, to your last breath: that's what melts their legs. After I made my point I never had a whisper again.

Our unit had been dumped on enough; all the promised changes about exercise facilities and times didn't happen, we were treated like schoolkids about what we could and couldn't wear. And there weren't any kids in Durham jail. Dennis Stafford was in for killing Angus Sibbet [on 4 January 1967, at South Hetton up in the north-east of England]. It made big news shouting that gangland had arrived in Tyneside and inspired the Ted Lewis book, *Jack's Return Home*, which became the Michael Caine film, *Get Carter*. It intrigued me because supposedly Sibbet was taken care off for skimming cash from a fruit-machine operation – so called 'The One-Armed-Bandit-Murder'. Stafford [with his named changed to Dennis Scott, he continued to maintain his innocence in 2019] was a new boy like me and had a huge profile. Of course, so did Harry Roberts and John Duddy and John Witney. That trio had sparked petitions for the return of the death penalty and for British policemen to be armed following the 'The Massacre of Braybrook Street' [12 August,1966]. Harry and the other two were parked in a car in Braybrook Street out near Shepherd's Bush but close to Wormwood Scrubs prison. There had been all the noise about George Blake and others going over the wall and maybe that's why they were approached by three plainclothes cops. Or it might just have been that there was no tax disc displayed on the estate van.

All these questions had been asked over and over again long before I met Harry and the others in prison. The cops [CID detectives Sergeant Christopher Head, thirty, Temporary Detective Constable David Wombwell, twenty-five, driver PC Geoffrey Roger Fox, forty-one] are thought to have used the missing tax disc to go and have a word with Witney who was in the driver's seat. Their talk went back and forward about paperwork and Head asked Wombwell to take a note of the details. He didn't get much chance to do that. Harry Roberts, perched on the front passenger seat, pulled out a Luger and shot Wombwell stone dead, through the left eye. Sergeant Head ran towards his undercover squad car but Harry fired off a shot, missed, but hit him in the head with the second shot. By now, John Duddy was out of the back seat and holding a .38 Webley [an Army Service revolver] and he went over to the police car and put three bullets through the window and into PC Fox. You can see why these men were notorious. [After a long manhunt the three were arrested and convicted of murder and jailed for life. Duddy died in prison in 1981.

John Witney was released from jail in 1991 and died in 1999; Roberts, one of the longest-serving UK prisoners ever, was released after forty-eight years in 2014 and there were protests that he should never have been freed].

So, no schoolboys so far.

Although Tony Dunford looked like one. He was only seventeen years old when he stabbed a guy to death, and in jail in Lincoln Prison in1964, with the help of another couple of guys, he murdered another prisoner. When I met him in Durham he was serving two life sentences.

Johnny Hilton was also a lifer. He'd killed a guy during an armed robbery in our manor, in South London, in 1962. He had a lifetime's commitment to armed robbery, he was up for anything. [A month after his release on licence in 1978, he shot a diamond jeweller in the back during a robbery and, accidentally, shot his accomplice, who bled to death.] He had a run-in of kinds with the Moors Murderer Ian Brady, for his cell was beneath Brady's. Johnny thought he'd give Brady some stick and in the night banged up on his ceiling with a broom handle.

Never mess with a lunatic.

Brady retaliated by banging though the night back at Johnny. He was relentless. Brady was a fucking vampire; I swear in Durham you could feels his evil vibes. But even that was overwhelmed by my anger, and that of most of E Wing, over the rule of 'Flash' Gordon Chambers. One of our big hates – and most of E Wing was made up of Londoners – was how difficult it was for our families to visit us. It's a fucking long trek up and back down from London to Durham. Maureen was managing it once a month travelling with Jean Lagrange.

I wasn't happy but 'Mata Hari' Jean Lagrange was staying at our house in Chislehurst, Kent, claiming to have nowhere else to go. I never had time for her and I was worried she'd bring trouble for Maureen and our girls. And she did because Special Branch were watching her and we had the house turned over a couple of times. That made me even more disgruntled.

In E Wing we'd got the hump when one of the Wing's footballs vanished. The screws said they knew nothing about it but our resentment got really busy and we wanted to act. It kicked off and we barricaded ourselves in the AG [Assistant Governor] office. John McVicar was involved, but he knows Johnny Hilton was our point man on the mutiny.

I was watching my old pal Roger Moore as *The Saint* on Saturday night ITV along with the rest of the lads. We were pretending to be entertained while Johnny Hilton watched for the evening guard looking after our landing. When he saw him leave his armoured office Johnny rushed him, slammed him against the wall, gave him some fucking verbals and had his keys off him. We went on the rampage and burst into the office and locked ourselves in just in time, for the screws were like attack dogs after us, barking at our ankles. They were snarling too outside the locked doors. But I could hear more of them on the way, the sound of their boots echoing around the prison wing as others were putting on riot gear and oiling their batons. The office was crammed in with chairs and desks and filing cabinets and we used those for our barricade. There was a chapel next to the office with a big altar, heavy solid oak, so we smashed that all about and used it to strengthen the barricade. It sounds as if this is taking for ever but it was going at full speed.

My heart was thumping and with all the shouting and

chanting going on it was like we'd scored the winning Cup Final goal. Then some screw was on a megaphone telling us not to be naughty...

As soon as we were in the office, Dennis Stafford, who knew the phone numbers at the *Daily Mirror*, was straight on the phone to them and we had a result there. He told them we weren't out to hurt anyone but just get humane conditions on E Wing. They stuck us all over their front page and with that publicity the screws couldn't take liberties or keep our mutiny under wraps. Everyone knew about it. We just had to keep our nerve. The mugs at the prison left the phone line on, so I called Maureen, and the other lads got in touch with their families and friends. We went through all the prisoners' files and I found mine and they didn't like me. It was all 'notoriety' and 'escape potential' and 'violence' and Charlie's file read the same way. As the others went through their files we were shouting 'Snap!' as they were much the same.

Still, Charlie and I, *the Richardsons*, had ten out of ten on the chart for being the most dangerous men inside Durham Prison.

To make that context clear: the most dangerous two inside the secure unit, E Wing, constructed on the orders of the Home Secretary, to cage the most dangerous men in Britain.

We had truly pissed the Establishment off.

That rating still makes me have goose pimples when I remember the Moors madman Ian Brady's paperwork: in it he called us 'the animals'. I suppose we were during the mutiny, which went on for nearly two days. People needed to go to the toilet, so we used the chapel and it was a mess; when I saw the chaplain later he looked disgusted with all of us but it was needs must. I was quite a young man. Corporal punishment wasn't on [it was abolished in 1948] but flogging was allowed for attacks on the screws until 1962 when the 'the cat', cat o' nine tails, was outlawed. As the news went out about our mutiny there were calls for the return of 'the cat'.

By then the phone had been cut off in the AG's office and the atmosphere was getting cranky. John McVicar said we'd made our point, but Charlie didn't want to give up. So there was a little bit of conflict there with him. Charlie never trusted McVicar. He'd have been better off not trusting a lot of people. Inside the barricaded office we were pretty united, ready to wait it out, at least until our supply of water ran out. Outside the politicians wanted an end to it. 'Sunny Jim' Callaghan was the Home Secretary by then and he sent up an envoy to negotiate. A deal was done that our complaints would be looked at. Charlie, of course, wanted to carry on the mutiny, but with the assurance that no one would be badly treated we voted to end the protest, which was good sense as our water supplies would have dried up soon enough.

I think the screws could have killed us as we wandered out of the AG's office when the barricade came down. Observers had been shipped in, local magistrates mainly, to see fair play, to see we didn't get beaten to bits by the screws who were very much up for just that. I could feel the anger as we walked out in little bunches, two, three, maximum four at a time. In the eyes of the screws just two of us talking together made us guilty of conspiracy. I felt we had done something positive but inside, when you live *in* the goldfish bowl world, everything is magnified.

I was in lock-down for forty-two days and that meant I was allowed out of my cell for two thirty-minute periods. I was also unlocked to go and get my food from a communal 'hot' plate, but that was manipulated by the screws to take ever so long. I'd take the plate back to my cell where I'd be locked back in again. The food, bad as it had started out, was by now a shrivelled, dried-up offering; I ate it for there was nothing else. I had built myself up in the previous months working out with weights and I didn't want to lose that strength and power. Maureen was as good as gold and came up on a visit, again with Jean Lagrange, soon after our rough and tumble with the prison. The newspapers were all over her and she made all the good points about our caged and 'inhumane' conditions. Some of the papers had gone on about us 'dangerous men' being pampered, but she said that was nonsense. But that never stopped the hang-'em-in-the-village-square crowd for wanting us in solitary full-time on bread and water. Maureen was there for me and I'll always be grateful for that.

Jean Lagrange hung around for a while for Charlie but their relationship faded and so did she from our lives.

The screws were present every twenty-four hours of my life. They would bait you with stories of their weekends, their big dinners and their sex lives. I could cope with all that, but after our protest nothing happened; all the promises of improved recreational time and food came to nothing.

So, with our grand belief that we were terribly important, nineteen of us on E Wing went on hunger strike for ten days. I found there are some inevitable results from taking part in a hunger strike: you are starving, you lose nourishment, weight, your health, clear thinking and there is a definite weakness at the knees. The most aggravating of all is that in Durham Prison no one cared. In my mind I was like some romantic novelist's idea of a hero doing the right thing for not just myself but my prison community. All I did was refused to pick up my food when they opened the cell door. The guards shrugged and locked me back up. After a few days I was weak and quite ill and if I hadn't given in after ten days I don't know what would have happened. I went down about 20 pounds in weight and that's a lot to drop on a big fella like me. Two of the blokes couldn't go on and we stopped. McVicar had stopped. Charlie wanted to go on, fucking yin yang those two, in that Charlie was self-destructive – he had an addictive personality. He never accepted anything in moderation and that was his denouement.

I learned early in that first spell in Durham – oh, I went back there – that it is pointless to hurt yourself in prison. The system is there to do that for you, to break you down in spirit, make you give up. I never did that even after our appeals against the Torture Trial convictions were rejected at the Court of Appeal in London, that spring of 1968. You hang on to hope rather than letting hope hang you. My big one was that I'd be out of Durham soon after the bit of nonsense and the hunger strike. As soon as you've been a bit of trouble, have caused grief for any section of Her Majesty's Prison Service, they want you gone. I always used to be number one on their list. I was always trouble. I was waiting to be *shanghaied* out. Being shanghaied is the prison service's VIP limousine service, a bit like going to the Oscars. It's just you're trussed up so it feels you're wearing a straitjacket not a dinner jacket. Still, it's certainly special treatment.

It's always an early start, not much after 5 a.m. I was a Cat AA prisoner, so the rules – and these are the days before health and safety – are that as soon as your cell door clicks open the screws come in mob handed, at least half a dozen of them, and are ready for trouble, fists up as it were. They want to catch you half asleep and get you handcuffed and out of there without too much of a struggle or fuss. Struggle? I was delighted to be leaving the hellhole of Durham Prison. Arsehole of a place. And the first of my many experiences of being shanghaied was wonderful for it was, of course, from Durham Prison. There should be a ballad about the place.

The drill is you are handcuffed and then handcuffed again to a prison warder. There is no time to collect your belongings or any of the debts, cigarettes, cash, owed to you from around the prison. I wasn't worried about that. I knew people wouldn't tuck me up. But as a shanghai virgin I was amazed at how elaborate my move from one prison to another was. I was cuffed to one screw, another one was part of my escort and a third was the driver of the van I was forcibly guided into. To combat any outside attempt to free me during my mystery trip – I wasn't going to show weakness and ask where I was going – there were decoy vans leaving Durham Prison at the same time as me. There were two motorcycle escorts, a police car in front of my van and one behind. The keys to my handcuffs and to the doors of the van I was in were in one of the other vehicles and for obvious reasons I had no idea which. I never had the opportunity to try and find out. The Home Office created the 'dispersal system' which distributed *dangerous inmates* through the seven high-security prisons considered able to hold and cope with us, and moved you on from one to the other when there was trouble. We were never anywhere long enough to be cleverly dealt with, to be 'rehabilitated'.

I was always a Cat AA prisoner, the highest security, and the money they must have spent moving me around the system: I had two screws with me everywhere I went. When I saw that movie *Silence of the Lambs*, I thought of my years of being transported around the penal system rather like Hannibal Lecter, trussed up like a Christmas turkey. I proved I could bite too when I got myself organised in Leicester Prison; it was nearer to home but still one of the 'magnificent seven' security prisons and with the highest wall of any jail in the country. I planned to get over it, and a plan soon took shape; you've got to have a situation where you can escape. At the same time the other important essential is to make day-to-day life as comfortable as can be. I took control and I had power. I was able to organise and, as we did with the mutiny, get things done if I had to. OK, I lost 450 days of remission for being a rebel (no one has ever lost that much) but I also earned myself and the others better conditions. I still wanted to get out and here in Leicester was Joey Martin who'd not made it out with McVicar in his escape from Durham [in October, 1968] and been shanghaied out to Leicester. My brother Charlie had wanted to go out with McVicar and Joey and Wally 'Angel Face' Probyn, but they thought he might blow it for them and shut him out of it. He was livid to lose the chance to get out of Durham but McVicar just made it and was lucky to stay out for a couple of years.

Leicester, like Durham, had our unit secured within the prison so if you made it out of high security you still had a way to go. Joey Martin, who was a London lad, from Tottenham, was in for an armed raid a week before Christmas 1965, on the United Dairies Depot Dairy in Wood Green in London. Joey had only been free for six months, after six years inside for shooting a girlfriend, when he got done again.

NO HANDCUFFS

He and a couple of others [Francis O'Connell and Bernard Beatty] wore stocking masks and had a shotgun, a revolver and iron bars. They meant business and it was tragic: the gateman Andrew Philo was shot in the head and killed when the alarm went off and he tried to stop them getting away. They'd stolen 3,060 milk tokens and £886 and half a crown [two shillings and sixpence].

Joey was in for life when I caught up with him again in Leicester. He was making table-tennis tables for local youth clubs, a nice little job in the woodwork room organised by a volunteer chaplain called Simon Beesley. A couple of my South London pals were there too, Tommy Wisbey and Bobby Welch: they'd already got the system working and that first night in Leicester I had strawberries and cream for tea. And that was after the jellied eels. I finished up with a nice cup of coffee. Our little security unit was a holiday camp compared to Durham: there was an exercise area with weights for training, a snooker table and, of course, a television room where we followed the football and the cricket. The visits weren't so controlled, so you could get personal bits smuggled in and good bits of steak for a nice fry-up tea. If I got new trousers brought in I had my own personal tailor, a trained 'cutter' called Arthur Hosein. He was alright was Arthur, although he missed his much younger brother Nizamodeen who was locked up somewhere else on the circuit. They were Muslims from Trinidad, who hatched some crazy scheme to kidnap Rupert Murdoch's wife Anna [in what turned out to be, in December 1969, the first kidnap and ransom crime in Britain] but got it all wrong. The Hosein brothers kidnapped Mrs Muriel McKay, the wife of Alick McKay, one of Murdoch's top business boys running *The Sun* and the *News of the World*.

It was to be only their first mistake. When it started to go haywire they murdered Mrs McKay. The body was never found and there were all kinds of stories including the most believed, that they'd fed her to their herd of pigs.

I asked Arthur about all that but he stayed silent. It was an extraordinary story and I followed every move of it. It's still one of those mysteries you think about, like Lord Lucan, for there's never been a clean answer to what really went on. [Arthur, thirty-four, and Nizamodeen, twenty-two, bought Rooks Farm, near Stocking Pelham in Hertfordshire, on a mortgage in 1967 and moved into the seventeenth-century farm set in eleven acres in May 1968. Arthur liked himself and was known locally as 'King Hosein'. Keeping pigs and chickens and making trousers, Arthur was a tailor by trade, could not make the fortune he felt he was entitled to. The apparent answer to their problems arrived when they saw newspaper owner Rupert Murdoch being interviewed by David Frost on television. Here was a very rich man who would pay a small fraction of his fortune for the return of his wife, if she happened to be kidnapped and held to ransom. The brothers followed Murdoch's Rolls-Royce to Wimbledon, and planned the kidnap. On 29 December 1969, they broke into the house and abducted the woman they found there. Unfortunately for them, Rupert Murdoch was in Australia on holiday. They had kidnapped Muriel Freda McKay, fifty-five, the wife of the deputy chairman of Murdoch's UK empire, who was using the company car while his boss was away. Alick McKay returned home about 7.45 p.m. and found the telephone ripped from the wall and the contents of his wife's handbag scattered on the stairs. He called the police from a neighbour's house at 8 p.m. At 1 a.m. the next morning the McKays received a call demanding £1 million from a man calling himself 'M3'. Over the next few weeks eighteen telephone calls and three letters were received from 'M3', demanding money and threatening to kill Mrs McKay. There were also letters from Muriel McKay. After an attempt to deliver the ransom failed instructions were received from 'M3'. They said £500,000 was to be placed in two suitcases and taken to a telephone box in Church Street, Edmonton, at 4 p.m., the next day, Friday, 6 February.

A policeman and policewoman, disguised as Mr McKay and his daughter Diane, took the suitcase to the call box. They were told to go to another call box in Bethnal Green Road. From there the trail led, by Tube, to Epping. Next they were told to take a taxi to Bishop's Stortford where they were to leave the suitcases by a mini-van on a garage forecourt. The taxi arrived and the two officers set out. Just up the road they got the driver to stop. When he did so, another policeman leaped into the back of the taxi and curled up on the floor. They arrived at the garage in Bishop's Stortford and drove past. They dropped the extra policeman up the road and returned and dropped off the cases by the mini-van before returning to Epping. It was about 8 p.m.

The third policeman kept watch on the suitcases, and the traffic on the main road. He noticed a blue Volvo with only a driver which passed four times between 8 and 10.30 p.m., usually slowing as it passed. He took note of its registration number, XGO 994G. The car was the same one as used in the previous attempt to deliver the ransom. At 8 a.m. the next morning the police raided Rooks Farm. They found an exercise book whose torn-out pages matched those received in the letters from Mrs McKay. Arthur's fingerprints matched those found on the ransom demands. Police searched Rooks Farm for several weeks but could find no trace of Mrs McKay or of what had happened to her. The brothers' trial began on 14 September 1970 at the Old Bailey and ended on 6 October with guilty verdicts and life sentences for the murder despite no body being found. It was and is generally believed Mrs McKay had been drugged, shot, butchered and fed to the Hoseins' herd of Wessex Saddleback pigs.]

To this day, no one knows what happened to Muriel McKay, except Arthur and his brother. They served about twenty years before they got out and faded away But Arthur did get some extra punishment in Leicester from a character I knew who was chucked in with us from the main prison: Harry – Hate 'Em All Harry I called him. He did not like or have time for anyone, which is why he was in with us. Harry Johnson was his name and he was a big bloke and a right-on racist, so not one to mess with. In the snooker room the deal was you put your name down and you played the winner of the previous game. Arthur who was good with a cue was waiting for his next opponent. Up stepped Hate 'Em All Harry who was a bit of an ace at snooker and expected to give Arthur a good hiding. Oh, it didn't go that way and Arthur was clearing all the balls and was on to the colours and looked the winner. Now, Harry hates everyone and here is this man who is not a white man beating him at snooker. Harry paused for a moment and then smacked Arthur a bloody great bang on the head with his snooker cue. A real crack on the head. He walloped him and Arthur had a huge shiner. I was amazed and questioned Harry:

'What's that for, Harry?'

'He was laughing at me.'

'Like fuck he was.'

'His eyes were laughing at me.'

I was laughing then. I thought that was brilliant.

Prison life had its moments but Joey Martin's plan to escape was more tempting.

CHAPTER THIRTEEN

THE MAGNIFICENT SIX

I was going to be first over the top of the highest prison wall in the country and it was all down to a neat piece of lateral thinking by Joey Martin. And because all we lads in the escape-proof top security wing of Leicester Prison liked our shirts and pants nice and clean and neatly pressed.

I knew we were taking big chances. We'd have to be rough on the screws, might have to really hurt them, if we were to get away. I just hoped threat and surprise would give us the luck of the moment.

Arthur Hosein had been marched off somewhere else and Hate 'Em All Harry was back in the main prison, so there were just seven of us left in what I called our little submarine, for we were cramped together and that was often too close for comfort; Joey Martin, being a lifer, was keen to get out, and when he brought his escape plan to me I saw it was a good scheme, it could work. The premise was that the escape plan involved making life easier for the screws, which was something they'd grab at. Joey was a star carpenter and as I explained spent his days in the woodwork room making table tennis tables. Our unit comprised two ranks of cells, the TV room to the side of a recreation area with our snooker table, the kitchen area and the woodwork room and another set of cells on the other side of the oblong set-up.

The guards' office was glass-fronted so they could monitor us 24/7 and next to that was a cell used as a laundry room. We went in and out of their offices all the time to get fresh shirts or pants and that annoyed them: they had to stop what they were doing – or sleeping – and unlock and lock doors to allow us to get through to the great bundles of clothes which were all neatly stacked in sizes. We used to look over all the stuff in the office and they didn't like us going through their place. There was another free cell that was never used as it led on to the exercise yard. There was an electronically controlled door from there into a corridor to another remote controlled door, an exit to the exercise yard. Joey Martin's plan which he worked on with me was straightforward: persuade the security to create a new laundry room in that 'exit' cell and out, up with a ladder and over? Ladder? That was easy, he was going to make one. It was clever. The security agreed to moving the laundry to the cell where we already stashed our weigh-lifting gear and to Joey making a clothes cabinet. The cell was 13 feet 6 inches deep and Joey made the cabinet fit along one wall and above it were shelves turned into pigeon holes for the different clothes. Slotted together all the bits magically became a 26-foot ladder.

The yard was surrounded by a 26-foot high mesh fence, hung together with steel posts placed at regular points. The posts branched into a V at the top of the fence and as another deterrent barbed wired was coiled through the Vs. Around the mesh fence was another yard and beyond that the prison wall proper, which on our side matched the 26 feet but had a drop of more than 40 feet down to freedom. What we didn't have was something to get us from the fence to the outside wall. We made planks of sturdy plywood, but we had to have the exact distance between our unit compound and the outside wall.

I hit on the plan to get the screws to tell us: there was always one standing about the outside wall while we were on exercise inside the wire mesh fenced area. We'd call him over and ask for a light for a cigarette and count his steps. It helped but we couldn't risk the plan on guesses. We hit on a plan where we looked like we were having a lark with the boys who collected the litter in the yards. They pushed their barrows in the outer yard and we tied a cigarette to a string of cotton and chucked it out as far as we could. When the litterbugs went to pick it up we yanked it back and all had a laugh. The screws joined in the fun; they liked everyone having a laugh for it meant no trouble. We played it for time and a few days later got a screw 'for a laugh' to place the cigarette out right by the outer wall. We were patient and when the cleaner came along to pick it up we snatched back the cotton line and, with all of us laughing, had an exact measurement of 19 feet 2 inches. We calculated the width of the base of the wall and the top and worked that in, too. Joey Martin had plenty of plywood but I had to get bent screws to post letters smuggled outside for me – it was the same screws that brought in my brandy – so that I could get the nuts and bolts that we needed for the escape brought in during visits: they were going to keep the ladder and runners to the outside wall together for us. It was all stashed in Joey's laundry room cabinet, which the screws never bothered with. They searched our cells as routine but, of course, there was nothing to find. They relied too much on their closed-circuit cameras and electronic locking devices. Then, this guy Brownie, he made himself busy – he wanted to be in it and all that – made a rope out of sheets which he plaited together. We collected our own sheets and simply took more than we needed. First time around Brownie didn't do an ace job and the 'rope' split and broke. We learned and used more sheets. This was to get us halfway down the outer wall for I didn't think we'd have a problem dropping down 20 feet, especially if it got us on our toes.

I'm making this sound as if it happened in days but it took weeks of planning and organising. We needed everyone in on the plan and Joey Martin didn't want Tommy Wisbey on the escape, so I got that straightened out. Tommy Wisbey was in it. I explained to Joey that it couldn't be any other way. Going with us was Brownie, Ron Brown who'd done quite a term of his thirteen-year stretch, Bobby Welch and George Elliot. Now, it's who is going over first and all that. We worked out I was going over first. Joey Martin would follow me and then Brownie, Tommy Wisbey, Bobby Welch and George Elliot.

We were in a high-security unit for one reason – we could be trouble. I wanted to really show that off before we made our prison break. I started getting a bit wide-eyed and noisy, slamming about and cursing. I wanted the screws to be intimidated by me as I moved about the prison. I wanted them to think twice about ever taking me on.

The exercise routine was that – routine. We were escorted in and out by two guards: you always had to have a white-collar man, a Principal Officer (PO), and an ordinary screw, two of them to bring you in. We were out in the yard exercising and using weights and all that; when the time was over and we came in and we bring the weights in, just inside the door. The PO, who is normally the one in the office, had to come in with us. He was getting on and was a bit doddery. I didn't really want him, and he was scheduled to be on duty the Saturday we'd set for the escape as Leicester City were playing at home and the town and streets would be busy, better for us to get away and get lost in.

Still, if it had to be.

Luckily, as event unfolded, it didn't.

On the day, the old PO had for whatever reason got our physical training instructor, a young bloke who was also a white-collar man, to bring us in from the yard and that's when our escape kicked off.

As he came in, I got hold of him with my arm around his neck and thumped him hard on the floor. I was sitting on top of him and had the middle of the dumbbell over his nose. There was a bit of vicious verbal. He wasn't a problem.

Then, the other five of them are struggling with this other fucking screw. This Brownie, who was supposed to pop that geezer, didn't, and Tommy Wisbey jumped in and with the help of the others got him quietened down nicely. We got their arms tied tight around their backs and shut them up with tape across their mouths and stuck them in the corner all wrapped up.

Now we'd see if the ladder design worked. The two pieces went together perfectly, locked on and in place. It was a beauty as in that corridor between the doors we saw it for the first time. We ran it out to the fence and I went straight up the ladder to the top with two foam gym mats on my shoulder. I stuck these thick mats over the barbed wire so I could balance and sit in the

V of the concrete posts. The security cameras were on us and I could see them swivelling about, up to me and down to the guys supporting the ladder. But if we were quick... Joey Martin was up top on the fence with me and Brownie was feeding up the runner to take us over to the wall and out of the place. Then the other one was coming up, which went through the top wire and to the outside wall; Brownie, the geezer on the bottom, when he still had about six or seven feet to go, fucking tipped it up. If I say I'm going to do something, I'm doing it. Know what I mean? Brownie bottled it all up and the runner hit the wall on the other side and fell towards the ground.

I was trying to pull the runner back into position and the skin was being torn from my shoulder. Joey was helping me and we nearly got it coming back when a screw in the yard between us and that prison wall jumped up and got the end of it. He was swinging on it. Once they got the end of it we had no chance. That was it. It was quite a brilliant little plan and it would have worked if we had had the proper people, if Brownie had made sure it went right up to the top. It was a fantastic escape. They say it is in the Police Museum, the ladder and all the pieces that comprised it are in the Police Museum at Scotland Yard. I don't know if that's true, they wouldn't want to boast about it would they?

I do know that if Tommy Wisbey had been on the bottom of the ladder it would have worked. Freedom was so close I could taste it, but it was over. In a moment the yard was covered in screws, from up there they looked like an army of ants except ants don't carry batons. I'd have had a tear-up with them but there wasn't much point. The governor appeared and it was over.

Well, all the crew from the submarine were on lock-up: our

cells had a bed, a table and a chair. The bedclothes were handed out each evening at 8 p.m. and collected at wake-up, so there was no daytime bedding. The library books we could get were not so much previously read and loved but previously ripped about, the final chapters of mysteries torn out for a laugh. At the next reader. By law, we got our one-hour a day of exercise but if the screws could make that a walk around the wing take place in the rain they did.

One lucky break on that escape was that I didn't have to deal with the older Principal Officer. He died from a heart attack two weeks after our attempt and if I had roughed him up and he'd died on the day, the result would have been much worse than it already was. We all lost six months remission, the maximum following an internal investigation and hearing. It was all kept as quiet as possible – our story was not good PR for HM Prisons.

And I knew it. I was on bread and water for fifteen days and banned from contact with anyone for fifty-six days. On top of that I got forty-two days of non-associated labour, working on my own. No contact with anyone. They thought I was the Mr Mastermind of the whole escape. Maureen and some of the other blokes' wives staged a protest at the prison to highlight the conditions. Simon Beasley, who'd got Joey Martin into the woodwork shop, said he was so upset about our day-to-day living conditions he resigned. Afterwards, we had the Roman Catholic guy come in. I said to him: 'Don't it prick your conscience, Simon Beasley resigned?' He said: 'No. It's not this world you have got to worry about.'

Lord Longford was doing prison visits [he began them in 1936 when he was an Oxford city councillor] and I met him for the first time. He was a completely genuine man but his kindness wasn't of the effective sort. They said he was misguided to champion the case of Myra Hindley [Ian Brady's partner in the Moors Murders], but he did it in good faith and never gave up no matter what abuse was thrown at him; everyone is redeemable, and so was she. The tenets of his religion. I liked him, but at these meetings in Leicester I never thought he could help me in my prison life. I was still an angry young man. Angry enough to lose twelve weeks more remission on my sentence: I used hardback books from the library and placed them right in the doorjambs so that if you really slammed the door shut you'd buckle the hinges of the cell door. I wasn't going to take what they handed out, for the conditions were all wrong: they were exactly as Maureen had complained they were – inhumane. And as long as that went on I was going to have a turbulent time. Especially when it involved my family and their visits. I was furious when they set up partitions in the visiting room: the new arrangement stopped you being able to hold hands with your wife or girlfriend and clearly you couldn't have your children sitting on your lap. The submarine men and I planned to have a real go in the visiting room when we'd ended our summary punishment. I was all set to be the first to do it.

Maureen was all booked in for a visit just before Christmas, right on the cusp, 23 December. It was a long trip for her, especially in a cold winter, but no one told her I wouldn't be there. I was shanghaied out to Parkhurst on the Isle of Wight before she arrived. It was the usual, handcuffed, officers around me all the time, special vans and outriders who changed when we drove through the different police jurisdictions on our way to the island. I wouldn't say it was paradise, but compared to what I'd dealt with so far it might as well have been. You could tell how open it was from the story of the Soviet spy Peter Kroger's farewell party. That couldn't have happened anywhere else. Parkhurst was brilliant in that way. Everyone had their own cells. Parkhurst was very quiet, and very lenient: that was for us, the special unit prisoners like me, a Cat AA. If there were problems in the other wings, and they had their trouble, their riots, we were separated and allowed to get on with it. They had a riot, but we had what we liked.

We used to have the tables laid out in the section. We all sat down together and food would come up; we did our own cooking. I once did a Christmas dinner for sixteen with a huge turkey and I always had an after-dinner brandy. In one prison we had so much food – legs of lamb, joints of beef, chickens – that we couldn't get it all in the prison fridge. I had to apply to the governor for permission to buy another fridge and it was granted. They liked me happy. In Parkhurst, when I first arrived, there was a special security wing. You'd never think they would let us live like that but Parkhurst was brilliant. It had had a lot of trouble previously in other wings, so they tried to keep everyone quiet and gave us extra concessions to persuade us to be good boys. Harry Roberts used to run the greenhouse. Cucumbers and tomatoes, and all that. We used to get bloody thousands of them and we sent them over to the prison hospital because there were too many for us. Quite a talented boy, Harry. Nice fella.

CHAPTER FOURTEEN

TERMINATED!

B y now I was learning how to live life in prison. I was lucky for I always had 'resources' – access to cash. How you get resources in prison is by only getting a small wage. Some people, they go in and they work on the machines, piece work and get extra money, because they are knocking out so many shirts or whatever they are producing. So when they've got a lump of cash in their canteen because they are not spending it, they come to someone like me and say they have seventy quid in the canteen, money in prison is worth a little bit more, say a hundred quid. 'Where do you want the money sent?' They would give me an address, and it was usually to their families, and I'd arrange for the cash to be delivered. They were happy to be helping out the family and I was delighted to get my extras. I'd give them a big list of Jersey Royal potatoes, steaks, chickens, a list of food. The food was coming from outside. You would put an order in with an outside supermarket with your canteen money and that supermarket delivers the order.

Sometimes the screws would actually go out shopping for you. They were in charge of the canteen side, so that was their job. If they can't get it delivered, they go and get it for you. To keep us quiet. Keep everyone happy. They want no more trouble.

There was a lot of trouble going on in prisons then. All sorts of things like that going on. I didn't really suffer because I had good friends who would send in tinned food and fresh bread. You were allowed, I think, £15 a month to take out your private cash into your canteen. They did allow you a little bit. If you want to live well, you need more than that. The same with the phone cards. The same sort of thing. You'd have phone cards off people, and buy the same way. Send your money to their address outside, for there is always a bit of money floating around. Money would go out to the right people and the good stuff would come in. That's how I would do it. There was always a way to get what you wanted. If you had resources, if made a difference.

People were selling drugs in there, selling heroin and all that. A lot of trades were going on. For many it was still trade with tobacco. A half ounce of tobacco was, I tell you, worth its weight in.... I sound old fashioned but I was happy to be living well in prison. I wanted a pair of trainers and one of the younger lads got his mum to size them up for me and send them in, and I'd have the cash and a bit extra delivered to her or give him the price in phone cards.

A handful of the Train Robbers were in Parkhurst including Roy James who was a goldsmith by trade. He made jewellery inside and was allowed to have gold sent in for his work: he told me what gold and amount to get sent in, and the size and specifications, and he created a gold ring for Maureen. I always thought the sentences handed out to Roy and the rest of the lads was a travesty, far too harsh. A lot of people agreed with me and not just people who'd had run-ins with the law. As well as Roy James, I had Gordon Goody, Jimmy Hussey and Charlie Wilson, who I got on well with, alongside me in Parkhurst. We were to take French lessons together but in a different venue. I got booze inside without much trouble, there's a bent screw or more in most prisons who can fix that, but there was always the home-made brews. Some were good, some just undrinkable, and I never really binged on it but I'd drink it if we were having a party. In the secure units I was in, the yeast for the hooch was brought in from outside the prison walls; in regular prison the yeast would be from the kitchens. Normally, it was fermented apples or oranges all mixed in with sugar and water. Most of the time I was happier with a cup of tea with my daily newspaper.

I got *The Daily Telegraph* every day – we were allowed papers if we paid out of our own funds – and Reg Kray, who was in Parkhurst with me, got *The Times*. The idea was we'd read our papers and then swap 'em. Ronnie Kray had been in Parkhurst with Reg when I arrived but had been taken off to the hospital wing. After our spell in Durham, I was never locked up with my brother Charlie anywhere. They thought we were far too dangerous together. But 'Colonel' Ron and Reg? They were a double act for a long time in prison. I got on OK with Reg, there was no aggro. Inside, it was all of us against the Establishment. In prison, you're fighting the system.

Outside we were supposed competitors, but it was a different situation. In prison, the Twins wouldn't do anything to me, interfere with me in any way. They were like two lost sheep in prison, lost sheep who had no idea how to get on with it inside. The Krays vanished in prison, didn't know what they were about. They got by on reputation. Reg and Ronnie were all right for a quick cup of tea but they had no conversation. Ronnie got certified and went off to Broadmoor and Reg was left to amuse himself with the young lags. Outside they were never up to properly taking us on, inside it was all a bit sad. The Train Robbers, however, got nicked for doing a bit of work and they accepted it and got on with it.

When I was at the end of my sentence I worked in the compound stores at Parkhurst where goods used to come in and we'd deliver it to different departments. It was an easy, cushy job. We used to play bridge. We didn't have a problem. Reg and Ronnie used to come out on exercise and they'd come straight round to the store, which was on the exercise yard. It would be 'You alright?...' I'd talk to them for a little while. They would have a cup of tea and all that. There wasn't any proper conversation. I used to read the newspapers cover to cover, follow the politics and the news and sport. I'd read mine and then switch with Reg, and his newspaper was always still stuck together. I had to unstick it. He hadn't even read it.

Reggie just immersed himself in prison culture and didn't look beyond four walls. That was it for him. He and Ronnie were like two dummies. They didn't make use of their time and it was like they gave up on life. They were nice, polite people in there. They were not bullies and I never heard of them losing a day's remission in there. But that tells you something about their attitude. They were beaten men. During my first stretch I lost 450 days remission for the Durham Mutiny and the escape attempt at Leicester. It was a prison-system record. But inside it was live and let live with Reg. He was never a bother to me. I wouldn't say we were close, bosom buddies; we got handcuffed together and that was close enough.

I was sitting one Saturday afternoon in the recreation room at Parkhurst Prison and the BBC News came on previewing a story in a Sunday newspaper. According to Norman Lucas, the crime reporter on the *Sunday Mirror*, thousands and thousands of pounds in taxpayers' money was being spent on keeping the Krays and the Richardsons apart in prison. Just at that moment, Reggie Kray leaned over and asked me: 'You want another cup of tea, Eddie?' That lifestyle ended abruptly for both of us. As I said, Parkhurst was as close to paradise as I'd found in the prison system so I wasn't happy to be shanghaied out. Reggie was moved with me and we shared a prison wagon. We were double-cuffed: handcuffed together and then each handcuffed to a screw on the other side. Whenever you move, to the toilet or wherever, it was a piece of dance choreography. For this trip with a Richardson and a Kray, we had ten prison officers with us and they were all happy, in a holiday mood. They get overnight allowances and overtime on long distance prison-to-prison moves so it's a jolly for them. I wasn't so cheerful as I suspected we were going to Leicester where I'd had a lot of trouble and lost remission.

The Richardson name wasn't too good there either: my brother Charlie had been there while I was doing my Parkhurst time and he'd chucked a bucket of piss and shit over a very senior prison official. The tourists on the ferry didn't know any of that as they tried to see who was in this prison van going back to the mainland with them. There was remarkable curiosity, for the ferry was being patrolled by armed policemen, and when we docked all the other vehicles and passengers were held back as our transport wagon rolled off. When I was certain we were going to Leicester I said it again to Reg and he went all tough guy, found his old arrogance.

He'd gone down for the murder of Jack 'The Hat' McVitie [on 29 October 1967, at a party in Stoke Newington, London] when Ron had urged him to kill McVitie. The brothers, Chris and Tony Lambrianou, were there and charged with disposing of the body. Ron Kray had bunged McVitie £500 in advance, with another monkey to follow when the job was done, to kill their friend and business partner Leslie Payne. who they believed was about to turn on them and go to the police. McVitie messed up and still kept the money.

He was lured to the party but Ron and Reg got there first and Reg, at Ron's urging, was to 'do' Jack by shooting him as he walked in the door. The gun jammed and Reg stabbed McVitie many times and to death. Jack 'The Hat' was a low-level thief with a big mouth. It was a terrible liberty to kill him and totally unnecessary. The Twins took another liberty by having Frank Mitchell killed after springing him from prison. Ron Kray had got on with Mitchell when they were in Wandsworth Prison together as young men, in the mid-1950s. When Mitchell was up for attempted murder, Ron hired a lawyer for him, but Mitchell was convicted and ended up in Dartmoor Prison. Ron decided he and Reg should get Mitchell out and they did and bunged him in a flat [in Barking Road, East Ham].

It was big news and there was all the usual carnival of MPs jumping up and down, Royal Marines and police in manhunts over the Moors, and helicopters whirling above them, and all the time Mitchell tucked up with some bird he's falling in love with over in the East End. Mitchell was a big man with a short fuse, so when he started being a nuisance for Ron and Reggie they decided to get rid of him, kill him. On Christmas Eve, 1966, Mitchell was led like a lamb to the slaughter, taken into a van where several blokes with revolvers pumped a dozen bullets into him; his body was never found but Freddie Foreman, who said he was one of the gunmen, also said he dumped Mitchell's body, weighted down and wrapped in chicken wire, into the English Channel. I told Reg that killing Mitchell was a liberty. He said it was his biggest mistake and he had never wanted Mitchell killed. But Ron had insisted.

Ron? He used to have tots of very powerful medication to keep him calm. One of the guys tried half a dose once and it knocked him for six. Who knows how their brains worked? Reg blamed the other brothers, Chris and Tony Lambrianou, for being part of his and Ron's downfall. He said they'd made statements. He wanted to 'do' them in Leicester where they were being held. The last place I wanted to hang about was Leicester, so by joining Reg in a bit of real trouble I knew I'd be a prime candidate for being instantly shanghaied. It would be worth losing more remission. The Lambrianou brothers, who I'd never met, would be collateral damage. All this was going through my head as we did indeed arrive at the hellhole of Leicester Prison.

Charlie, who'd been there, had been shanghaied out that day. The sights that did greet me were not good. I walked along beside the visiting room and the partitions separating prisoners from their loved ones were still up. No one had smashed them to pieces as we'd planned, had the nerve to have a go at them, make a protest, make the point. I was furious for I thought we'd all agreed to work together to change the rules.

When we got there, the Lambrianous had been moved. When I said that this was the only unit with a partition, Freddie

Foreman, who was doing ten years as an accessory to the killing of McVitie, said, 'If you get a good screw, he lets your kids come round.' That sent me off: 'I'm not waiting for a screw to do me a fucking favour. This system's all wrong.'

I got evangelical and told the others in the submarine that Leicester was the only place that had such cruel visiting rules. Parkhurst was Cat AA and didn't have that sort of arrangement. It was an unhappy start to a fucking terrible bit of jail time for me. I really didn't like it there and the plan of using the Lambrianou brothers fizzled; they were moved out, which in retrospect was a good thing as I caught up with them later and we got on fine. It also saved Reg Kray from having to do anything, show some muscle, but the Kray name forced him into another bit of bother. Harry Roberts's partner in the Shepherd's Bush police killings, John Duddy, was in the submarine and enjoyed making comments about Ron Kray being a poof. Now, nothing travels as fast as gossip in a prison, so Reg was soon made aware of the poof comments. And as he knew about them he had to do something, show his loyalty to his brother. He got Duddy in the TV room and, being fitter and younger, was all over Duddy. I was keeping an eye out for the screws but realised Reg was truly going to hurt Duddy and in turn do himself a bad turn. I pulled Reg off and he turned, snarling. 'That's enough,' I said and he was going to have a go when he realised it was me and slowed down.

I was a totally different proposition and Reg didn't fancy it. I was the only one there who could have done that without having a fucking row with him. I was alright like that. Still, he'd made his point to the submarine that he wouldn't be taking any unpleasant remarks about Ron. And done so without any bother from the screws.

TERMINATED!

I was the one who was about to get that. And it was all about standing up for your rights no matter what you've done or been fitted up for. Especially the right to have time with your family. I've known some amazing women in my time. My mum and my grandmother, who had a shop in Camberwell, were great ladies. Mum never stopped loving us unconditionally, although she knew what we were. She knew a lot of the stuff they said about me was grossly exaggerated. Mothers are the one constant. In prison, men lose wives and girlfriends, but their mums stick by them. But my wife Maureen was a wonderful wife and mother. I was a womaniser – it came on a plate to me – but Maureen always stood by me. She kept the family together while I was away, and our girls are a credit to her. She also campaigned on my behalf when I was inside. I kept a lot of the business away from my family. But the family never, ever went without. Which is part of why I was so adamant that on their visits I should have an enjoyable time with them.

It was never easy. Maureen complained about the lack of privacy, of the inability to be normally together. Inside the visiting room there was always an atmosphere of anxiety. Her view was that a long prison stretch destroys a marriage and it's true, for neither of you have any idea of the future; you can't discuss it, you can only talk about the day to day, what's been going on in prison, what's happened at home. Melanie was eight years old when I went to prison but Donna was only a toddler, a two-year-old. She thought she was coming to see me in hospital when she visited.

On this Leicester visit, she was six years old then, she and Maureen were across the partition from me. We were busy talking and Donna slipped around and sat on my knee. There were about a dozen screws in the room, three sitting down and watching from a table, and the others dotted around the walls of the room. One of them marched over: 'This visit is over, TERMINATED!' Donna was on my lap and looked up at me, bewildered. Maureen kept saying to Donna to come back over to her side of the partition. She had no idea what was going on, she was just a child. I looked at her and I lost it, completely kicked off.

I busted up the partition and with all my strength pulled it up and threw it into the air. The dirty dozen or so screws were on top of me bashing at me with their batons. My odds were not good but I kept on fighting. I was so angry and I struggled and struggled but they got me flat out, a bunch of them hanging on to my arms and legs. I knew I'd had enough, but one of them began beating me, punching me up my bollocks, and that fired up my energy again and I caught a couple of them before they had me back spreadeagled again. Maureen and Donna were watching all this when two policewomen rushed in. One picked up Donna and the other bent Maureen's arm behind her back and frogmarched her out of the room like some terrorist.

Some 'family visit' that was. I lost six months more of remission and spent fifty-six days back in solitary, but I was quite content with chokey, I wanted to be alone. I refused any scheduled visits by anyone under the Leicester Prison rules, although I saw Lord Longford on his prison tour. I preferred it in chokey, I didn't want to come up, I didn't want to be with those wankers who wouldn't protest to get the visiting rules changed. I stayed down the chokey block. I wouldn't move back to the special unit in Leicester. I was there for about twelve months all together. You can get used to anything after a while. I was there on my own. I was quite happy to come out and Reggie Kray would say: 'Eddie, come back', and I'd say: 'I don't want to fucking come back up there with that load of wankers.' Reg was worried about my wellbeing. It was a funny thing that, us and the Krays. I always used to get a Christmas card from Reggie and I would send one to him, wherever we were at the time.

Maureen was on the warpath, to our MP, to the National Council of Civil Liberties and forcibly to the Home Office about how I and the other blokes were being treated like animals. She also protested about being roughed about by the plainclothes policewoman. What those running the prisons feared most was trouble and I was marked down as that. Every time there was a hint of bother I was the first one out, for they considered me someone with influence. I had six lay-downs [locked away in a cell on your own] three times at Durham, twice at Bristol and once at Liverpool. I don't think anyone else had that many. They move you out for six weeks or so and you never knew whether you're going back to the same nick or a different one.

It was miserable in Leicester, and even in chokey I had constant trouble with the screws. They can sense you're pissed off and do as much as they can to wind you up.

I wanted to keep a busy mind and Maureen sent me in one of those grand ship models that you have to put together; they are fiddly and so detailed, with the rigging and gun flaps where the tiny toy cannons would pop out. Harry Roberts was good with jobs like that, clever with his hands, so he helped me. Truly, he did the artistic stuff and it was me who just gave him a hand. Before we completed it, ready to launch, I was shanghaied again. It was a short stop in Chelmsford but I was now used to seeing familiar faces like the Train Robber leader Bruce Reynolds and, this time and very briefly, Charlie Kray: were all high-security prisoners going round and round the prison system like a carousel. Charlie Kray had got a raw deal, ten years on thin evidence of helping the Twins dispose of Jack 'The Hat' McVitie's body. He denied any such thing to the end of his life. The people running the prison weren't the usual Gestapo types, so I got plenty of keep fit time and I'd do running laps of the exercise yard with Bruce Reynolds. I felt so much better getting some weight on – the screws shopped for us, so we cooked good meals for ourselves – and for a secure unit we had more quality of life.

I was on the football team and we played against the screws. It wasn't a great shift in attitude in Cheltenham but enough to make being there more humane: you were being punished but you were still a person. Doing it the other way only breeds renegades, and that's trouble, within the system. After you are moved in this dramatic early-morning pantomime, shanghaied, with great fanfare, they send on your stuff and when I got mine the galleon was with it. Somebody had put their hand through it.

Luckily, Harry Roberts's mum used to visit with Maureen and between them they arranged to get the galleon back to Harry. As good as gold, he mended it and completed his job on it. I have it and it still looks a grand ship and I admire it every day. It was a good omen, for finally I was moving from a high-security prison, no longer a public enemy. The bad news was it was to Hull, which is a long haul, whichever way you look at it, from South London. I had to feel it was the system finding yet another way to make the life of my family more difficult than it had to be, the usual *merde*.

CHAPTER FIFTEEN

THE FRENCH CONNECTION

There were enough friends for a Londoners' football team when I got to Hull, which was my first time in an open prison. It was like walking down a crowded pavement after the space of the high-security units. There were prisoners everywhere I turned and lots of familiar faces.

We were partisan, the Scots guys kept together and had their football team and as did the lads from Manchester and Liverpool. We London boys were like glue, stuck solid, and lost at some of the football matches. Roy Hall was on the same wing with me then and he was the Birdman of Hull. He bred budgies in his cell and kept them in cages in there, for the cells were huge compared to what I'd seen. Underneath the cages he stored our betting 'money'. It was a tobacco stash for that was the currency of prison. We had betting ring going, taking wagers on the racing on television or the score of a prison football match. We'd cover any bet. We ran it like a proper betting operation with betting slips and the rest. The screws knew and some of them even had a bet with us. People who didn't smoke managed to save canteen money quickly and I'd have it off them with the usual rules, sending cash from outside on to their families. Smokers rarely had resources and had to suffer the prison food but probably they couldn't taste it properly anyhow. I never went without

Being off the stricture of the special security-unit life I found myself wanting to learn more about life. We had loads of visitors who wanted to help us who came in for Monday-evening talks, from Quakers to the MP John Prescott, which is a big stretch. We had one fella who knew all about witchcraft and wanted to give us his facts of the supernatural, but I explained the facts of life to him instead. I was interested in learning. I certainly had the time. But not for bollocks from warlocks.

Among the usual suspects in Hull was the Train Robber Charlie Wilson. We both wanted to speak and understand French and we decided to learn it together. We got textbooks out the library and all the dictionaries we thought we needed. He used to come round my cell and I'd go round his. After a little while we said we would only speak French to each other. It went well and I felt we were really progressing. This went on for about six months or more and we were terrific at understanding each other. Then, they started a French class in the prison and we signed on but, of course, not as beginners. We thought we were good if not fluent French speakers by then. We didn't learn phonetics, it was out of a textbook. The French teacher got up at the first session and I couldn't understand a word being spoken. I tried to explain to her, in French, how hard Charlie and I had worked to learn her language. What we'd done, of course, was learned our own form of pidgin French – French only we could understand. We looked at each other and shrugged. *C'est la vie.*

The French classes did establish one thing – my poor hearing. The teacher was dictating all the time in English and I had to write it down in French; my work sort of made sense but a few of the words were wrong. The French teacher explained to me I was tone deaf. She guessed it and she was the first one. When I didn't hear something I wouldn't keep saying: 'What?' I just used to leave it, and not worry. I used to make out I heard when I never did. Now, I've got two hearing aids. I don't want to miss a thing. I've always had a problem. I never heard the words pronounced properly because I cannot hear consonant sounds; I can hear the vowel sounds. The hearing aids emphasise the consonant sounds for me so I can hear now, but for years I never could.

Luckily, there was a good sound system and we didn't need subtitles to watch *The French Connection*, that great movie with Gene Hackman in his pork pie hat chasing about New York for the French drug smugglers. We had a film club in Hull and we all chipped in a few pence each week to get a movie in that we'd voted to see. John Daly, who I'd known since I was a kid – he was nicked with me for stealing that torch – was the boss of a film company, Hemdale, which he set up with actor David Hemmings. John kept in touch with me all his life [John Daly died from cancer, aged seventy-one, November, 2008] and wrote to me all the time I was in prison. He sent me scripts to look at and comment on including *Rambo: First Blood*, which kicked off that set of Sylvester Stallone's action movies; I certainly saw the potential in that and told him so. He produced *The French Connection* and sent in a copy to Hull.

John was a good friend. He was the son of a docker and a south London boy and my neighbour and he produced or distributed more than a hundred films including some real big successes like *The Terminator* with Arnold Schwarzenegger. He was also a great boxing fan and along with Don King, the American fixit fella, was the official co-promoter of the Muhammad Ali v George Foreman fight in Zaire, the 'Rumble in the Jungle'. One of John's great gifts from *The Greatest* was a photograph of Ali standing over Foreman sprawled at his feet, signed by Ali and inscribed: 'John, you told me I could do it. Kindness to others is the rent we pay for our room on earth.' I received a photograph of Ali signed by him: 'To Eddie, All the Best.' That was arranged by my pal Billy Williams, known as Bill the Bomb, who was an East End boxer working out in America after a bit of bother back home. My friend and partner in the Soho Rangers football team, Leslie McCarthy, fixed it up for Bill the Bomb in the States through Chris and Angelo Dundee who looked after Ali. Bill won a dozen heavyweight fights and gave exhibitions with Ali and it gave me a real thrill looking out at that world of boxing. It also shoved me on and made me keep working on my fitness. I lost my Cat AA category in Hull and applied through the system to be moved to a prison closer to home for Maureen and the girls to visit. That was agreed but it was a fuck-up. As a regular prisoner you have the privilege of being told which prison you are moved to and given time to pack up your belongings.

You also have the time to whip round the prison and collect anything you've lent out and any money owing you. But no, a handful of screws arrived in my cell and told me I was to be shanghaied. I went off on one and told them I was no longer a Cat A and they could kindly please fuck off. It was 5 a.m. and they're six-handed to move me to another prison. I said: 'I'm not getting shanghaied any more. I'm not going to get told where I'm going and that is that.'

This happened because of a little AG [Assistant Governor] on our wing. The little bastard was on my back all the time I was in prison. It was because of him I'd got moved back from Parkhurst to Leicester. I used to be the first person to get shanghaied out of prisons. They used to get rid of all the people that caused grief for them. I always used to be number one on their list. I got what they call 'lay downs'. I was in Durham three times, Bristol twice, Liverpool once on lease. In Liverpool, I was in the chokey block down and I got a message shoved under the door by one of the cleaners. The prison population knew I was there and said 'Hello'. I was supposed to be allowed the humanity of exercise but the screws were horrors. Exercise? Two of them let you out and watched you. The first time I was let out it was into this little chokey block. I must have looked bewildered, wondering when we'd move on from this tiny corridor to the exercise yard. I looked at the screw who said to me: 'You going on exercise then? This is it.' It wasn't much bigger than a cell, and this was the exercise in the chokey block there. Unbelievable. Not all good news, obviously, but if I have been in some bad prisons; I've also been in some of the best restaurants in the world. I've seen both sides. I've had good cars, and a lovely house. Things like that.

When they tried to shanghai me from Hull I stood for my rights and refused to go. The screws weren't expecting that and went off for a 'conference', which gave me two days to gather my gear including a collection of cuddly toys, teddy bears and bits I had had made for the girls. They returned and then one of the other assistant governors came to see me and explained properly what was happening. I was going to Parkhurst. He was plain speaking, saying Parkhurst had a new governor, George Thomson, and he would be helpful towards me. I took that with a pinch of salt.

I could have been a regular holidaymaker, the lack of fuss they made taking me back to Parkhurst. I rather missed the escort and the outriders but it made for a quieter trip. As it was, in Parkhurst. Governor Thomson was one of those 'new brooms' and he wandered around the prison happy to talk to anyone. I'd lost fifteen months remission and I wanted it back, I wanted to be out. I needed to pick my moment. I got a job in the compound stores through a couple of friends of mine who were already in there. I kept my eye on the governor and the time to approach him. He was a rugby player, a proper man's man. I got on with him straight away. He knew what had happened to me at the other prison and he was sympathetic. There was a new law about reclaiming remission and I asked him about it and that led to me filling in loads of forms. He phoned the Prison Board and I got forty-two days back, which I was disappointed with: I was hoping for my 450 days. The governor was straight with me when I told him I was upset with the result: I'd been there a month and got forty-two days back off my sentence, keep my nose clean and he'd see what he could do next time around. I had six months to wait for the next time, when I got 300 days back. It was a godsend.

I was very lucky that I happened to have the right governor at that time, who knew and understood the situation that I had been in, and who was on my side. I applied for parole and was refused but, again, the governor helped out and sorted me to be placed in Pentonville on a loose licence: they had a hostel there, which was inside the prison proper; you were allowed out each day but had to have a job to go to. But in the summer off 1976 I was off the island, out of Parkhurst, back in London and more or less a free man. I just had to follow the rules.

John Daly arranged through one of his other friends for me to be a driver for a demolition and rubbish clearance company and I was on a wage of twenty-five pounds a week. The pay went directly to the hostel and when I was free properly, the cash for my board and lodgings would be taken from my earnings and I could keep what was left. Terry Mills, who was the boss of the company, looked after me in that I didn't have to actually do any driving or work and he'd head off any prison people checking on me. That way I could keep myself busy catching up with family and my life. I was back at the hostel by 8 p.m. every night, followed all their rules, and after a month I was able to spend weekends at home.

After six months I was back at doing what I'd always done best – grafting hard to make a living. I'd been inside for a decade plus a few months and my good friends had treated me to a lunch and a grand for every year of my term: a gift of £10,000. It was enough to bankroll my next venture into the world of artistic photographs. It was the world before mobile phones and the internet and all the freehold glories on offer on computer screens. In those days pornographic magazines and films were the prime titillation for indulging in solo sexual satisfaction. I suppose you could say I went into the porn business. It was profitable for me.

When I got out of prison I partnered up with a friend who already had interests in two London pornography shops. We opened a third in Hogarth Place not far off the Earls Court Road in West London. It was a good business from the off, so much so that after six months we needed a manager to run the operation and I recruited my future brother-in-law Paul. My sister Elaine had gone out with him for eighteen months before telling him who her brothers were, but when she told him it didn't bother him one bit. Paul was a shrewd man and you had to be in that business, had to judge people, know all the peccadilloes and what sells to each individual group.

Our shop had sections: big tits, bondage, whips, high thigh leather boots, thongs, crotchless knickers; female domination; male domination; rubber fetishes (the rubber section was always popular), chicks with dicks and a variety of gay interest magazines. There was a huge gay community around Earls Court so that trade was always busy. We got the material from California or Amsterdam but ruled out importing anything involving children or animals. The punters would go straight for the one they wanted. There was no looking at one or another. They all had their own particular area of interest. Some of the specialisations were way out of my comfort range, but there was a fella in Paddington, one of many, who dealt almost exclusively in material devoted to coprophilia [pleasure in faeces and defecation].

Paul and I took a business trip to America with him and met with porno producers in Los Angeles – the home of one of them was at the top of Mulholland Drive near a trio of houses that then were owned by Marlon Brando, Jack Nicholson and Warren Beatty – Las Vegas and San Francisco, where the most astonishing choice of gay magazines were available. We ordered up bundles and when we were back in London I had them printed off in their thousands. I traded with other porn shops, a bundle of their bounce mags – that's the big tits ones – for a bundle of our provocative gay ones. Sex sells and we were rolling it in.

I knew that for a business to prosper you have to keep improving, changing tactics, giving the customer more of what they want. I introduced 'What The Butler Saw' type booths into the store but they were much more sophisticated than the seaside town versions, a little more racy. For 50 pence a time, and we had plenty of change on the premises, customers could watch a minute or so of a movie and had to keep pumping in the 50-pence coins as the action developed. We offered gay movies or straight ones and they were equally popular.

I reckoned that to take more control and make more profit we should make the films ourselves. There were plenty of people willing to get into action for the cameras and the only difficulty was making enough movies to offer new material as much as possible. As with the magazines, we would exchange, sell on and buy back material, for as our business grew so did our contacts around the porno movie industry. Much of the really popular material came in from our regular suppliers in the Netherlands, and the Amsterdam producers had a syndicate of lorry drivers who would smuggle the films over the Channel. I paid up on delivery. It was good money for everyone involved. Paul was an ace at it. I had explained everything to him and that he was going to work in the porn shop – with a good wage. It was like a fucking duck to water with him. He really fell into it. But after about twelve months, out of the blue, the shop got raided and he was sent off to Middlesex Sessions charged with selling pornography. There was a lot of this going on and

Paul got hit. We were just selling normal magazines, films and material that was not offensive to those that liked it. I went to the court case with a girlfriend and expected to be going for a drink with her and Paul after the case.

As it turned out, she and I found an empty lawyer's office and spent too much time enjoying ourselves and missed the case. When I walked towards the court it was to see Paul in handcuffs and being led away to the cells. He'd got a month.

It was silly and the judge even apologised for having to send him to prison. He said he had to do this because of instructions from, of all people, the Torture Case judge, Mr Justice Lawton. Paul served eighteen days in Pentonville and during his time there I sent him a telegram. In those days if you sent a telegram to someone the screw had to take the telegram round and loudly read it out. 'You've just been offered three quarters of a million pounds for your share in Bradshaws. Let me know what you want to do.' I did it to piss off the screws but a young lad who was sharing a cell with Paul said to him: 'I knew you were a millionaire.' It was just a little bit of fun. When Paul got home we went down to visit my brother Charlie at Parkhurst. Paul and I arrived and we're telling Charlie that Paul's just done his time, his *eighteen*. Charlie's saying he has just done eighteen and people are listening. Reggie Kray was there and hearing this and nodding: 'He's done *eighteen*. People are saying 'Oh he's done eighteen,' shaking hands with him and asking about it: 'Where did you do that?

'Pentonville.'

'I didn't know you could do that sort of bird at Pentonville.'

Eighteen. Eighteen days... it was best to keep quiet and leave.

We were going into the more formal entertainment business,

mainstream movies, a nightclub, gala boxing evenings, unlicensed fights including a boxer who knocked out the 'The Guv'nor', Lenny McLean, and it was all going along very nicely indeed. Then, my brother Charlie escaped from prison and I was lumbered with looking after him. I couldn't blame him – he'd done fourteen years and been turned down for parole seven times. It complicated my life, as did an unfortunate incident at my nightclub where a young man was stabbed to death.

CHAPTER SIXTEEN

TEN COMMANDMENTS

My life in film was short-lived. On reflection, I believe that John Daly, who'd been a friend for so many years, before and after becoming a highly successful producer, was simply being kind when he said he'd support my efforts in moving from blue films to mainstream movies. I don't think he believed I'd try my luck, but I've never said I would do something and welched on it. I follow through, study the detail.

Which is what the lady in charge of the London Dungeon, where we'd arranged our first day of filming our documentary about torture through the ages, did. She'd checked out our film company address and found it was above a porn shop in Paddington. When we arrived at the Dungeon with a full film crew, cameraman, sound people, lighting, continuity, the whole works, she looked me in the eye.

'You're going to make a porn film. You can't come in.'

No one had shouted Action! and I was already disenchanted with the film business. Yet, I wouldn't give up and with the help of my pal Leslie McCarthy, who bankrolled much of the budget, we decided to make a short documentary about London's Soho, the Soho you never see or hear about: we went behind the scenes and filmed the floor shows at the clubs and turned out a thirty-five-minute film called *Chameleon Soho*, which played along quite nicely. John Daly did distribute for us but it went out with one of his adventure films, *The Passage* with Anthony Quinn, a movie that for once wasn't a great success for him. No money was showing and Leslie McCarthy pressed him for payment, which I thought was wrong. I didn't feel happy about any of it, although I made a profit from the film.

Still, and I've said this many times and can only emphasise it: I made more money throughout my life in straight business than anything bent. I went back to where it all began – the scrap metal business. I discovered a business for sale in Greenwich for £27,000 and I was able to get a help with start-up money, from my friend Stan Woods, who I'd worked with before in the metal game. It was a straightforward arrangement with Stan who held the deeds to the premises and I paid back the money by banker's order.

I went full throttle for all I could do. At the time they were building the Thames Barrier and I had contracts with them for scrap, in time thirty-six skips on both sides of the river. Some of the scrap was too huge for the skips and I had to move it on lorries. Other consignments, up to nearly 100 tons, had to go by barge down the river to be unloaded. I was the sole contractor in scrap metal, a serious business. It was the sort of construction job where workers started the job by cycling to work and by the end of it were driving off shift in Mercedes saloons. I was running a proper business. I was legitimate. It was nearly three years of graft and by then I had paid off the bank, squared Stan Woods and had the deeds sitting with a healthy account in my own bank. It was going great and I finished up buying a warehouse on the river at New Caledonian Wharf in Rotherhithe, before you get to Deptford, where the river comes out. It was an opportunity impossible to turn down.

It all happened by me being a bit of a sportsman after I got out of prison. I'd always kept fit and enjoyed playing sports. After being inside I got hooked on skiing and take every chance I have to take a holiday on the slopes. I was also a regular squash player and that's where I first met Patrick O'Nione, always known for obvious reasons as Paddy Onions. He was the one who took fifty quid off me and then told me it was my deposit on an Austrian ski trip. I was reluctant to go but I took to it like a duck to water – I owe Paddy for first getting me on skis.

He was a Jack-the-Lad and had spent time inside for smuggling watches and bits and pieces but by the time I met him he was the ultimate salesman – he could move anything. He made his living making deals that usually involved big shipments of slightly damaged goods. He was always great fun to be around, so when he approached me about the warehouse deal I was happy to see him. He kept his stock in a small rented warehouse, but the neighbouring property to it was on the market for a very reasonable £270,000. It looked out on the river and had potential and the owners had offered it to their manager, David Patterson, but he needed investment help to get it. I set up a company covering all the legal bases I needed and became a director with Patterson and Paddy Onions. I just needed the cash and I knew my mate Terry Mills, who had been so good to me with the van driving 'job' when I got out, had it. He joined us. He sent his bankers, who valued it at nearly 150 grand more than the asking price, and fronted the money: the shares were equally split between the four of us. The annual repayments were heavy, about 60 grand a time, but before the deal was even signed off we had rented out some of the building with assured income of £75,000 a year. The money we were collecting from the rent from all these people was covering everything. We had a good deal. Never cost a penny. David Patterson knew the ropes and we bunged him a good annual salary, 10 grand and a car, to continue managing the warehouse. It was a smart business move in every way, but events, those bastard things, brought me back in the middle of happenings I had no control or responsibility for. Still, I was connected by fate to it all and that included the death of three men and a massive gold robbery, which was one of those other jobs the newspapers called 'the crime of the century'. It certainly involved loads of money.

Big Peter Hennessy, who I'd had the straightener with that terrible night at Mr Smith's when the guns came out against us – he was never arrested for we didn't grass him – was with a pile of his mates at a charity boxing show. It was one of those black-tie evenings when a big crowd from South London get dressed up for a night out and to raise a few pints and some money.

It was being run by Beryl Gibbons, who had the Thomas A' Becket pub on the Old Kent Road where I'd trained as a boxer, and there was quite a crowd including Paddy Onions and some of his friends. Hennessy was pissed up and had words with Paddy who gave him some back. He had a go at him at the table. Hennessy continued being a nuisance when he decided to stage an extra collection for an invalid wife of a friend. A row broke out and Peter Hennessy ended up getting stabbed and killed. I wasn't there, so I don't know what went on, but he was stabbed half a dozen times in the back. Then, Hennessy's brother and all his mates decided that Paddy Onions had done the villainy. Hennessy's brothers hired two people at the time, two fucking lunatics that were gun running, to take out Paddy. They had already tried once, tried to shoot him through the window of his house and missed him. I told him I'd look into it but he said: 'Nah, I've got it sorted out now...' Then, he gets fucking shot and killed. I'd sworn to sort it out for him but Paddy insisted it was not necessary, he could take care of himself. By then he'd sold his share in the warehouse to one of Terry Mills's directors and invested that cash in a wine bar near Tower Bridge. He kept to a schedule. About seven weeks after Hennessy's death [on Tuesday, 30 November 1982] he was shot in the back of the head walking out to Tower Bridge Road from his wine bar.

A copper who saw the attack chased after this gunman but lost him, but the coppers tracked this piece of crap, called James Davey, down to his home in Coventry. He was being prepared to be brought back to London from the cells up there when he supposedly lunged at a policeman and died when he was 'restrained in a headlock'. It was an almighty mess and a tragedy for Paddy Onions. All I could do was help with a charity event to raise funds for his widow. The police, of course, were inquiring into everything to do with Paddy Onions's life during their investigation and that brought them quickly around to the business at New Caledonian Wharf in Rotherhithe. My fellow directors were panicking; they didn't want any of this police attention. They were all shitting themselves, weren't they? They really wanted to unload it.

Well, they wanted to unload *me*.

And to do that they put the property up for sale. By this time it was worth £1 million. We had permission to make the top two floors residential, which boosted the value no end. Nevertheless, outvoted by my fellow directors, I agreed to sell and they got an offer from Selective Estates from Jersey for £750,000. They wanted to take it. I didn't but I wasn't complaining, I was still getting a lump of money out of it. They sold it short, for they just wanted to get rid of me to be honest. They were frightened men and naive – they were selling the property to a man laundering the proceeds of the Brink's-Mat bullion raid. I'd just been on a skiing holiday with him. He was a nice fella but I had no idea – and neither had he – that we were doing a business deal together. [The Brink's-Mat robbery was on 26 November 1983, at the company's warehouse, Unit 7 of the Heathrow International Trading Estate, near Heathrow Airport. Six men believed they were going to grab £3.2 million in cash but got more than £78 million (at 2019 value) in cash, diamonds and gold bullion – almost all the three tonnes of gold has never been recovered and four of the robbers never convicted.]

Johnny Parry was a master money launderer – even the people who people who finally put him away admired his skill and said in court that he was 'quite brilliant' – and was good on skis too. We'd been on a trip to the Trois Vallées in France and stayed at Méribel, which was a lovely village. Back in England he saw my name on our headed notepaper, which was among the paperwork for the sale of the warehouse. When he knew it was really me, he came round and was lovely: 'Ed, come here...' and all that. What a coincidence? John was 'investing' the Brink's-Mat loot in London Docklands, which was at the height of its development. Even with our million-pound property we were just one small deal among many. He arrived at our meeting in his red Bentley – that was his style. When I knew it was him we tried to do a deal under the table which would have suited him and us, but because the contracts had already been exchanged, it was too late. He bought it with the gold money. I went out with him and we went on the champagne, the Dom Pérignon. Later, we did do a quiet deal for another Docklands property the company owned, another Rotherhithe river property.

The 'company', this is my fellow directors, wanted shot of that too following the murder of Paddy Onions. It was a weird string of coincidences, for one of the Brink's-Mat robbers, a man called Brian Perry, was shot dead in daytime outside that Rotherhithe warehouse [November 2001] as he got out of his car. The newspapers went on about the curse of that job and it was unlucky for a lot of them. Charlie Wilson, who I'd learned a unique take on the French language with at Hull, and who was suspected of being one of the robbers, was involved in investing some of the money from the raid but found himself in trouble when £3 million of Brink's-Mat cash went missing in a drug deal. [In April 1990, a young British gunman knocked on the front door of Wilson's hacienda north of Marbella and shot him and his pet husky dog before riding off down the hill on a yellow bicycle.]

NO HANDCUFFS

Only two of the actual robbers, Mickey McAvoy and Brian Robinson, were jailed for the job and I knew both of them. They each got twenty-five years at the Old Bailey.

The consequences of that raid were still going on more than thirty years later. John Palmer, who was said to have set the whole job up, was shot dead a couple of years ago. [In October 2015, John 'Goldfinger' Palmer, sixty-four, was the eighth person linked to the raid to be murdered. He'd been tried and acquitted over melting down gold bars stolen in the heist, but the ricochets from the robbery found him shot in the chest six times in the garden of his expansive home in rural Essex.]

So, John Parry is lucky for I know he's still around. [In the immediate years after Brink's-Mat the big-spending Parry bought Crockham House in Kent, spent £60,000 on curtains, gold-plated all the taps and a free man in 2019, was reportedly still living in the £2 million, nine-bedroom home with his wife Irene.] He was on the run for a time and came to see me wearing a beard when he was ducking the coppers. He spent time on the trot in Spain but was extradited back to the Old Bailey [in 1992] when he got sent down for ten years.

He got a big lump of a sentence but if nothing had been said he wouldn't have got that sort of time. The solicitor who was arrested with him told them everything and he got top dollar. That was it.

———

For all his antics, Charlie was my brother and I regularly visited him, and by 1980 he was in Spring Hill Open Prison in a rural spot between Aylesbury and Bicester in Buckinghamshire. He'd done fourteen years and for the past few had been a good prisoner apart for being nabbed for puff [cannabis], but he smoked dope all the time inside. He was doing Open University degrees and was only a few credits away from one in sociology. Charlie knew he'd get out sometime soon but he was never a patient man. I was working full out with my business interests. The Earls Court porn shop was ticking along nicely and I'd also got back into boxing – I think out of everything it is one of my greatest interests – and with the ever-ready Leslie McCarthy I'd put on gala boxing evenings. It was all a little magical. We'd get a venue like the Cat's Whiskers in Streatham and stage three or four fights and the moment they were over the boxing ring would disappear, dismantled in no time, and dining tables would appear and a smashing dinner would be served. It was always a great night. We'd have raffles and dancing.

I also promoted unlicensed fights, not the eighteenth-century bare-knuckle stuff, but with gloved boxers who weren't regulated. Our main man was Harry Starbuck who was a nightclub bouncer and Mr Popular. I made sure he never lost a fight by carefully selecting his opponents. Harry worked the doors at lots of clubs and people liked him. They didn't want to see him get knocked down. He got a grand a fight and his opponents picked up 600 quid for doing the right thing and falling down at the right moment. One of Harry's opponents was a regular who had to dye his hair so the fans didn't catch on. A lot of the fight fans knew Harry wasn't doing it for real but they wanted to believe.

Harry's boxing life ended in a fight I wasn't involved in putting together: someone matched him with Roy 'Pretty Boy' Shaw who I'd spent time and trained with in Hull prison. I knew how lively Roy was and feared for Harry. I was right. Roy popped Harry down twice and gave him a true going over.

There's been a lot of applause over Lenny McLean being 'The Guv'nor' of unlicensed fighters but my money was and is on Cliff Fields, who worked for me in another little business I developed. He was my doorman at J. Arthurs nightclub in Rushey Green, Catford, and he knocked out Lenny a couple of times. Cliff didn't have the discipline to be a professional boxer as he could never stick to a fitness regime but on the door at J. Arthurs he was the job. My brother-in-law Paul and I had looked at the club, which had been cloned off one in Chelsea but hadn't taken off south of the river. We thought we could make a go of it as it was in a good location across a couple of floors of a building on Catford Broadway. I wanted first class all the way – and I got it. I used to put shows on there upstairs, a variety of acts from comedians to singers. Joe Longthorne who was funny and did impressions and could sing was always a big hit. Lots of different acts and a free buffet, nice turkey, sliced ham, a nice plate of food and nothing costs a penny for it was all covered by the entrance money. Downstairs we had a nice white grand piano and Joe Longthorne used to sing with our piano man downstairs as well, so we used to get a double event with him. My resident on the piano was Ian Gomes who plays the piano in The Ritz in Piccadilly. Every time I go over to The Ritz I go in there and see Ian Gomes and he says I'm the best guv'nor he ever had. Good as gold is Ian. Sometimes [in 2019] I go over there for drinks, and get them to play up the tunes for us. In the Palm Court, where they do the teas. Five sittings for afternoon tea they have. They are booked up about three months in advance. At J Arthurs performers like

TEN COMMANDMENTS

Georgie Fame and Lonnie Donegan entertained for us, and it was a good going business. We had a disco set-up and that brought in the youngsters. Thursdays were a quiet night and Roy Hall managed it for me those evenings. I couldn't do it all and I know now I was overstepping myself trying to juggle so much.

I'd get home at three in the morning, have a couple of hours' sleep and then I'm up again. I'd open the scrapyard premises Saturday morning. We were manic with the Thames Barrier jobs. I was fucking burning the candle at both ends, rarely getting more than five hours' kip:

> My candle burns at both ends
> It will not last the night;
> But ah, my foes, and oh, my friends –
> It gives a lovely light.

Which is why I was happy to let Roy Hall handle Thursdays when we didn't even charge the kids to get in. Roy had got out of prison in 1972 and had been troubled with heart attacks. It wouldn't have mattered much if I'd been there the night it all went tits up. There were a group of youngsters in and some of them began arguing, two brothers and another fella in the upstairs room. One of the blokes [David Sommerville] got himself a knife from our kitchen and stabbed one of the brothers [Martin Klimcke, twenty-two] and killed him. All the people there said they hadn't seen anything, so the coppers got very upset at that and the family of the dead boy were screaming for justice. The knifeman was convicted of manslaughter and got five years. Of course, the Richardson name was brought into it and it was only a matter of time before the licence was taken off me and I had to sell up, but that took for ever, for any deal brought objections from the police that the interested buyer was working under the table for me. It eventually got done.

Charlie's patience ran out in May 1980. Now, everything you've heard or read about Charlie from Charlie is concocted stories.

Now he wants to escape, he wants to come out and I sorted it. It didn't work the first time. Paul went to collect Charlie from an area close to Spring Hill Prison and waited and waited and waited. After three hours he thought better of it. Charlie, meanwhile, was having a farewell party back at the prison and couldn't be arsed to be on time. When he got to the arranged spot Paul was driving away. He had to hop it back to prison. Of course, when he phoned the following day he blamed Paul for not hanging about. The next day he stayed on schedule and escaped and I was looking out for him and bankrolling him. I got him to our dad's place and then a flat I arranged for him. Charlie, being Charlie, wanted to go to Paris, and I sourced a good passport under some Irish name for him and off he went running a merry dance around the Continent until he landed in Spain.

Wherever he was on his toes, Charlie campaigned for his release from prison and got his picture on the front of most of the Fleet Street papers. The MPs were leaping about that 'Britain's Most Wanted Man' could be chatting to the papers but the coppers couldn't find and arrest him. He wrote a letter to *The Times*, which grabbed a lot of positive attention, but then their clever-clogs columnist Bernard Levin took space for two consecutive days to have a go spouting all the Torture Trial claims and decrying Charlie's education efforts in prison. I was furious and they published my letter pointing to the flaws in Levin's arguments.

What had some sideline benefits for me but was overall a big mistake was Charlie co-operating with a writer called Robert Parker on a book [*Rough Justice*, Fontana Original, 1981]; Charlie worked with him on it and asked me to co-operate too. It wasn't on Charlie's side at all. But what Parker did highlight was the 'confused evidence' at the Torture Trial that had me convicted.

Following this questioning of the evidence over the beating of Bennie Coulston, the National Council for Civil Liberties and the *Sunday Times* asked for the Home Office to look at my conviction. The Sunday paper made a good case for it, but however it went I was never going to get back the years I served. Or the aggravation I'd suffered. And, indeed, was suffering with Charlie on my doorstep. He'd returned to England and had moved into a flat on our manor near our dad. He'd got involved with some girl and they were shacked up quite nicely.

The coppers didn't seem bothered if they knew. He was about South London quite openly and happily drinking in the pubs – and sending his friends around to J. Arthurs. It was my pound notes after pound notes for Charlie. I had the cash. I also bought what I thought might be useful in spiriting Charlie away. My best mate Harry Rawlins – he postponed his wedding to his lovely girl Della until I got out of jail and could be his best man – was the only one I knew who had any clue about being out at sea. He and Paul went with me after I bought this boat [*The Oceana*, a five-berth, 32-foot fibreglass Norwegian motor boat] for fifteen grand off my friend Kenny Bloom, who was the master of the long-firm business. Ever heard that story about the two happiest people in the world? Someone who just bought a boat, and someone who just sold one. It's so true. The boat was in Southampton and I checked the fuel tank before we left the marina but 11 miles out to sea we found out the reading was wrong, there'd been a blowback. Harry Rawlins who knows a bit says the engine has gone. Then the other one went. It had a ship-to-shore radio on it, too, and we got on it and put out a Mayday.

We get the coastguard: 'Where are you? What do you hear?'

Harry was saying: 'There's a buoy about 10-foot high and it's blinking every half minute or so and...' then telling them where we were.

There are these different buoys and they've all got a different signals. It took a couple of hours before a big RAF launch comes and I said: 'Are you going to tow us in mate?' He said: 'No. The lifeboat is on its way to you.' He continued: 'We'll stay with you, but the life boat is on its way to you. Don't worry, you'll be alright.' It was in the main shipping lane! We're in this light boat bobbing about and every sort of ship and tanker is battling around us. We got towed in by the lifeboat. They all do it for nothing, them lifeboat guys. One guy came to us and said: 'I come from Camberwell. I live in Denmark Hill.'

I think they suspected I might be Charlie, for when we got into Chichester harbour there were teams of coppers and sniffer dogs waiting for us. We ended up in the nick all night, me, Paul and Harry Rawlins. Harry was going barmy: 'You fucking fitted us up.' We didn't know what was happening. They kept coming round to the cell door and peering in at us. They said they'd found a substance on the boat and had to analyse it, but it was nothing, some sailing oil or something, and an excuse to keep us locked up. Eventually we got away about five o'clock in the morning and got the train the Waterloo. I didn't relish my life as a sailor. Which was good instincts working for I wasn't much cop at it.

When I got the boat going again I hired a proper captain and we were heading towards a berth in Dover and I said: 'Are we going in then?

He said: 'Not at the moment – you have to wait for the green light.'

Then, just as I wanted to push full steam ahead, a giant ferry sailed out in front of me – it would have been a disaster if I'd been left at it, lots of aggravation.

Every time I went out on the boat there was a drama. I went with Eddie Rivers and Peter Cundell, two friends of mine, to move the boat from Dover to Ramsgate, and as we came over the top at Dover, you could see the sea. I could see it was rough.

I said: 'The sea's rough.'

Cundell said: 'Where did fucking Nelson come from?'

When we got out of the harbour the boat was going crazy in the wind and I said to Cundell: 'Where's Nelson from?'

We did get to Ramsgate eventually, although the wind gave us so much trouble and we didn't really know how to control the boat, to steer it properly. It was hitting other boats as we came in, one guy threw a rubber boat device down to stop the damage, and finally we get parked up. What did we do after that? We went and had fish and chips. That's what I like from the sea, a nice piece of fish. I sold the boat for a wash-its-face price and with not too many regrets because it only truly cost me for the berthing and fuel. I never ever used it for Charlie anyway.

NO HANDCUFFS

Eventually he got nicked. At a place and time which cost me dearly and was totally unnecessary, which was completely out of order, a true liberty. Much of what I had coming to the business was going out to keep Charlie going. Britain's Most Wanted Man, for fuck's sake. He arranged to have photographs taken of himself dressed as Santa Claus upstairs at my shop. Father Christmas among all the porno magazines. The arrogance was too much – and it upset the coppers too. They'd been leaving him alone but then he did some newspaper interview, with the *Daily Star* for God's sake, and said he was living it up in London and that brought the house down on him.

And, as always, on me.

CHAPTER SEVENTEEN

NOT SO HAPPY RETURNS

It was Charlie's forty-seventh birthday on 18 January 1981, but there wasn't much to celebrate. He got nicked outside the shop in Earls Court. He'd all but advertised where he was and the police couldn't ignore him any longer. He'd been on my phone all day and wandering about like a free man, which was an almighty piss-take. Charlie wasn't daft, he knew what he was doing: the cops raided the shop and arrested him and with that location were able to be all over me too. Charlie's story of it all is some romantic fantasy of wrong man, wrong time, wrong place. Nonsense. In everything he said or did he paints himself as my champion, but it was me who did all the heavy lifting.

He left me in the lurch time and time again. This time, with all the police activity I had to close down what was a thriving business. He was an absolute menace but, still, he was my brother and even then, and I don't know why, I remained loyal to him. I visited him in prison, joined in campaigns for his freedom including helping with a petition to Mrs Thatcher, and generally supported his case. I did so financially too – a lot of my money went up in smoke with Charlie chain-smoking cannabis. There was a lot of noise about the length of his sentence and demonstrations by his family. Mrs Thatcher wasn't that bothered, having the Falklands War to win. Charlie got out on a weekend pass in October 1983, and I picked him up – I said I was a bit flash with motors – in a lime green Rolls-Royce Silver Shadow. I don't think the screws at an open prison near Woking had seen one of them before.

It, of course, wasn't simple. Charlie stayed away an extra day through the Monday and was punished with two weeks' remission being lost. He got more time out in the real fresh air when our mum was poorly in June 1984, and then he was out proper in August that year. Charlie was free to look after himself, but that didn't mean he would stop helping himself to what was around. Right away he wanted 'a testimonial', which was something you did for retiring West Ham players not your relatives. Charlie was on and on at me about it because of what I did for Frankie Fraser when he came out after Charlie. Frankie had got another five on top while he was inside, so when he came home I had £50 tickets printed and hosted a benefit for him in the West End. Some people bought £500 worth of tickets each and it finally added up to £18,500. That was a lot of money in the late 1980s. I made it up myself and gave him twenty fucking grand. When I came home I never got a pint of beer. I don't expect it because he hadn't got the brains to be able to do it. He wouldn't have had a clue. I'd done my bit for Frankie over the years. When Charlie came home it was a different thing. You couldn't go and do that. So I laid on a dinner for about ten of us and everyone put a grand in.

Charlie had changed, and I don't mean in that he was older

or tougher or nastier or more selfish. He'd *changed*. In that he was a different person. He'd never been easy but as kids and as teenagers and even in those busy years as young men we'd always had a good connection. I couldn't say exactly what it was but it seemed he even looked at me differently. I'm not being silly, I couldn't tell what he was thinking; there was no hint, for he presented a blank pair of eyes to me. Was it the dope or the system or a bit of both that truly fucked him up? I didn't know. What I did know was the scrap business and what had been a truly successful business in Greenwich was all that was keeping me in the style that I had become very used to.

What with the Earls Court shop shut down and J. Arthurs not bringing in anything, it was starting to be a struggle. After a lot of paperwork shuffling I got J. Arthurs off my hands. I'd much rather have held onto the nightclub but with all the police trouble there was no chance of that. The burden I felt was that I had always been the perfect provider for my family and for the people who worked for me.

It was a difficult year, 1988, as my dad died – he'd got to seventy-nine and was living with Lizzie, the woman he'd left for – and my relationship with Maureen was not good. She'd been right about the way a long prison term can destroy a marriage. It wasn't either of us that made it difficult, but the circumstances that made it increasingly impossible to stay together. As I've said before, Maureen was a wonderful wife and mother. She always stood by me, although she got a divorce to get the house. She kept the family together while I was away, and our girls are a credit to her. She also campaigned on my behalf when I was inside. I had so much respect for Maureen and I think that was reciprocal. She sold the house for £500,000, which was a lot of money in 1990. She deserved it, and was welcome to it. She never wanted me to suffer. We had been out of touch for years when she died in 2008. When it was clear she was on the way, she made our daughters swear not to tell me that she was dying as I would be sad. I only found out some years later.

The legacy she left me with our daughters Melanie and Donna, both lovely grown women now, and the grandchildren are a wonderful reminder of how good she was. All Donna ever wanted from the age of six was to be a ballet dancer and her discipline was extraordinary. She concentrated on ballet from the moment she woke and that's the way you become exceptional. You don't succeed like she did without enormous hard work. She worked and trained every day; very few of them get into the Royal Ballet Company, but she did. It took a bit of a manoeuvring, because she was wanted elsewhere, she was popular.

She was with the Royal Ballet for about two years with private lessons and everything that could help. I might not have been a good husband, if you like, but I was a good provider. The family always had money. Maureen was happy with all the money she got in. Donna was working hard at school, she got plenty of O levels, and two places came up for the Scottish Ballet. All the ballet schools put down for these two places and my daughter got one of them. We carted her off up to Glasgow, got her all the gear and settled her in the accommodation. Before she went, one of the top directors from the Royal Ballet suggested she should go there, but she'd committed to the Scottish Ballet. Donna didn't really like it in Scotland miles away from the family. I used to go up there quite a lot but she was on her own most of the time.

Later, she wrote to the director who'd been interested: 'I don't know if you remember me, but if there is any opportunity of ever getting into the Royal Ballet, if ever there is a place, could you possibly keep me in mind for auditions?' Then, he wrote back to say: 'I do remember you...' One place was available at the Royal Ballet but Donna had to try out; she did loads of trials, lots of eliminating contests, if you like, when they get rid of them. It came down to one girl – her mother was a ballet mistress – and Donna, my daughter, got it. (Just to get an audition for the Royal Ballet is an honour.) So now she's got the place. But we had to get her released from the contract with the Scottish Ballet. Once they found out, they didn't have the needle with us, they had the needle with the Royal Ballet, but they were sensible and she took her place. She went all over the place – South Korea, Russia, China, all around the world. An American artist came round the Royal Ballet and did a series of paintings and one of them was of my daughter. I often went to see her dance and I always booked seats in the Royal Circle, pushed the boat out, the proud father. I'd take guests and after the performance I'd take them all to dinner and drinks at the Savoy's River Room.

We went to the invitation-only Royal Ballet Christmas party, which was attended by Princess Margaret, and we were only feet away from Prince Charles with Princess Diana. One time my mother was in the box above the Royal Box with the Queen Mother.

Melanie, my other daughter, has a first-class honours degree in pharmacology and runs a hospital pharmacy. My two girls are a source of great pride to me. They've both turned out well, as has my granddaughter, but they never wanted for anything, even when I was inside. They got private tutors, the lot. Of course, that was what was hurting most in 1988 – trying to keep up my living standards. I had quite a successful company in Greenwich but it wasn't gonna last long; it was being taken over. A lot of the companies in Greenwich were moving out, being offered more money. I was losing customers, left, right and centre, and I had people working for me like my brother's son, and people like that. That's what really got me involved in the drugs. I knew my legitimate business companies weren't going to last for ever, so I thought I'd get a lump of money and sort them out. But it didn't quite happen.

I wasn't on hard times but difficult times, and that's when I was made an offer I couldn't refuse. It was, to me, a business proposition that would, after all the ups and downs, bring in the cash which wouldn't just balance the books but balance out my life. In a daft way I got into trouble, made a big error, because people knew I was straight in business, I was reliable. People were always coming to me with business for I had a reputation of efficiency, of getting things done without making a noise. I was always being offered 'opportunities', but this one was irresistible: a partnership with a top Colombian cartel. This was not the world of *Narcos* that I was getting into, but simply an association with the South Americans, the Cali Cartel, in which I'd use my contacts to move on their consignments. I didn't need to invest anything other than my time: any money paid would be *to me* after shipments of drugs sent on credit had arrived.

The projected profit for me looked like £4 million, which in 1988, at any time, is a lot of money. The politics of the South American cartels didn't bother me for I knew nothing of it. [The Cali Cartel, led by brothers Gilberto and Miguel

Rodríguez Orejuela, was named from its base in southern Colombia in Cali in the department of Valle del Cauca. When Eddie Richardson began his association with the cartel in the late 1980s, the Rodríguez Orejuela brothers had gone into deadly competition with Pablo Escobar whose Medellín cartel they had deserted. The Cali cartel soon controlled 90 per cent of the world's cocaine market – and the same percentage in the European customer base they had exclusively developed. The cartel created their US$60 billion empire from the success of their original marijuana trafficking and the US Drug Enforcement Agency called them 'the biggest, most powerful crime syndicate we have ever known'.]

The Cali Cartel wanted me to find buyers for their drugs, having been told I was able to securely provide what they wanted; they got to me through a friend who was engaged to a girl from Colombia. As I remember I put them in touch with people in Liverpool and that's how it all came about. I was more active when they returned to London and I wasn't too nervous about the deal but I was careful, for I was doing business with people I didn't know.

I've always wanted people, friends, around who I knew would have my back. Still, they seemed legitimate when I first met the two men I would have direct contact with. The cartel's main man in Britain went by the name of António Teixeira, but he could have been Tex Ritter for all it mattered. He lived with his family in Blackheath in London. To me, he was a little bit too chatty for his and my good. But the other Colombian, a chemist who processed the cocaine, vouched for him, said that 'Tony' was reliable.

I was under a lot of pressure, juggling all the businesses, and this made me a touch vulnerable for I had no idea how cut-throat this lot were. The Colombians had mountains of cocaine they were desperate to unload throughout Europe, and Britain was a starting point, a bridgehead. It was an edgy, deadly business. But under the arrangements I wasn't even going to see a line of cocaine never mind tons of the stuff.

My Colombian connection and what it involved for me was set out at meetings carefully held in parks or noisy restaurants: I was to organise the collection and distribution of the cartel's cocaine shipments and my money would be paid when the drugs were sold. I went to work with Donald Tredwin who dealt in cars but boasted the big expertise of having excellent contacts among baggage handlers and customs workers at airports and docks. We bunged the Gatwick Airport baggage handlers many grands to take our cases with the drugs off the planes and 'lose' them before they got to customs. Our first deal of 24 kilos of cocaine slipped through without a whisper of trouble and I got close to 100 grand out of it. As I saw it I was very much an agent. What I didn't know or see was that the coppers, the drug squad detectives, were already on top of them, they had already been fucking stamped on before they ever got it over here to England. I wasn't being paranoid. I was used to being watched – I was a Richardson – but this was heavier. I dodged a couple of tails, cars following me through Docklands and other parts of London. A couple of times police 'copters suddenly appeared above my car and trailed me.

The shipments were ambitious: one involved 153 kilos of cocaine valued at about £40 million, but that lot was itself disguised within a two-ton, £6 million consignment of cannabis and all wrapped up in a container of balsa wood like a Russian enigma. It was en route to Southampton where Don Tredwin's handlers would secure and store it until it was safe to be collected and distributed. The plan was for the shipment tagged as ceramics or whatever to arrive at a legitimate venue and then be stolen. If you were cheeky you could even go for the insurance.

I had a container coming over to England with four tons of puff, which would have been good if I'd got it through. With such deals, the manifests, the paperwork, has to match exactly the information the import agents have; there must be no suspicion from them or customs agents. But they already knew more than me. The drug detectives and customs job 'Operation Revolution' had started in 1987 and the South American Teixeira had been on an 'obso' order – they're 'observing' you – for a long time. With our cocaine shipments the details of that very essential paperwork had to be sent to Colombia with details of how the drugs would be wrapped, addressed and to where and whom. The customs boys had all that information, having got warrants to secretly turnover Teixeira's house where they found the shipment details – and my name linking me to the cartel. The fact that he was bunging money back home in half-a-million-pound bundles a time was also unhelpful advertising. They simply followed the money.

Happily unaware of all this, I thought my next big moneymaker was on the high seas heading for Southampton when in fact customs had redirected the ship, the *Silver Happiness,* and what they said was then the largest shipment of cocaine coming into the UK, to Portsmouth.

My thoughts were all about buying Christmas presents and all the food and trimmings for the 1988 celebrations. I was caught on the hop when I was pulled by the cops not long before Christmas Day. I got nicked with £17,000 cash on me. It was the Christmas party for the scrapyard workers the next day and I wanted the money to pay out for that and the rest; I'd chased up the cash which was owed to me from the first cocaine shipment and I'd got it from a go-between at a quiet meet at a cab stand in Elephant and Castle. I thought I'd get lost in that spaghetti of roundabout and streets but I reckon the coppers were on to me from the start, watching my every move. I had the cash in a plastic bag and was driving towards Greenwich when the drug squad pulled me over. They turned over the car, which was like a fruit and veg shop I had bought so much stuff for Christmas. Of course, they had the money and they had me up to Eltham Police Station. I got out about five o'clock in the morning, less the £17,000. I'd told them that scrap was a cash business and that I often had two or three times that money with me.

It took ages to get the money back and I was on an 'obso' order all that time. I got the money back about 4.30 p.m. on a Friday and much too late to put the money in the bank. I was messing about with Joan Harris at the time and she lived down the same street as me, at number 38, so I got the money, ten grand of it, stashed away under her stairs. The rest of it went the way of scrapyard kitty and Christmas. They'd marked the money thinking I was paying out for the drugs but they got that arse about tit. They wanted a connection with me and the South American, but I didn't have to give the cartel anything. I didn't owe them anything, so he never got any money, and their little plot failed if only in that way. I got nicked the same night, the day after they'd picked up the South American they knew as Antonio Teixeira. They'd nicked his wife and children, too, and that heaved the pressure on him and he blabbed and pleaded guilty.

They were tooled up when they came to get me. They really put on a show with an armed raid on our family house in Chislehurst in Kent. Donna was at ballet school in Scotland but Maureen and Melanie were upstairs when the squads of cops arrived, some of them armed. There were a couple of dozen of them and more and they came in through the front door by smashing it to pieces. Screams of 'Police!' and what they'd seen on television. I'd have opened the door if they'd knocked.

It was 4 a.m. or something like that and I'd leaped downstairs and I was standing by the door in my underwear with guns pointed through the windows at me. House lights were flicking on all along our street. They had a metal bar jammed across the door and the frame was hanging around it in jagged bits of wood and splinters. Then they were all over the house and I kept shouting that Maureen and Melanie were there. I thought they'd be shot by some panicking copper. It's happened. I was handcuffed around my back and nicked proper and they marched me off leaving my girls and a great bloody mess behind them. They also turned over Joan Harris's house and took the money, the ten grand, which I never saw again.

There was a lot I didn't see for a long time.

CHAPTER EIGHTEEN

MY BROTHER'S KEEPER

The *Silver Happiness* was in dock when I arrived at Southampton police station where I was charged with importing drugs said to be worth a nice round headline figure of £80 million. They rattled along about the amounts of cocaine involved being bigger than this, larger than that. I was portrayed as some Mr Big of the drugs' business when I was in fact acting as a salesman. The Drug Enforcement people and the police didn't harass me to talk for they knew I'd say nothing.

I'd given the South American that advice and, after he realised his wife and kids weren't going to be weighed off and hurt, he tried to go back on his statements, but the damage was done and I was back in that criminal cavalcade, the justice system Monopoly game, dealt a go-straight-to-jail card. They whacked me into Brixton prison while they prepared the case against me and I was transported to Winchester Crown Court for the pre-trial hearings. They used a little van – it was like being in a sealed box on wheels – to ferry me back and forth cuffed up and with my outriders, the chorus of sirens, and feeling anxious for I knew who I was would be a problem. They didn't want the embarrassment of a 'not guilty' verdict on a Richardson, especially with all the front-page headlines. This court commuting went on for about eighteen months before I was moved to Winchester jail for the trial proper. Winchester prison was an unruly place with protests and moaning I wasn't involved in. The only way it intruded on me was the noise stopped me getting a good night's kip. I hadn't time to be involved in prison life as I was constantly preparing for my court case.

I was a Category AA prisoner once again and all visitors were vetted, only allowed in by application. I couldn't see people who might have legally helped my case but they let in Charlie and Frankie Fraser, which is another of life's mysteries. Yet, there was little chance of nobbling a jury outside of London. I had my romantic triangle to be concerned about with the ten grand being found at Joan Harris's place and me being nicked at home with Maureen who was in Winchester for the court case. I was nervous about what would be said in court about where that cash was discovered. I don't think at that stage I had any clue at the enormity of what was facing me. I'd been hauled in for drug importing for indulging in dodgy business. What with being me, a Richardson, and the new way of the world kicking down hard on drugs and white collar crime – the world had moved on from the days of the Torture Trial. If not the methods.

They brought me to court with a bloody great fanfare, as if I was going to a Royal Wedding. In court pointed concerns were raised about the safety of the jury. The implications were left hanging in the air. I was fearful of the evidence the South

American might give from the witness box, but it wasn't a problem because he pleaded guilty. Now I believed I might stand a chance at my trial. I should have known better. The odds were stacked against me. As the long slow days and days of the trial went on "I wanted a robust approach by my lawyers. II had no drug-related convictions, I had very few knocks against me, but none of that was brought out. I had a lot to shoulder when I defended myself in the witness box. I think I did a good job but for two days the questioning was relentless. My defence lawyers sat still and let me get on with it.

Which is what the jury did after sitting in court listening to some fantastic flights of imagination for forty-seven days. They didn't come back quickly when they went off to consider their verdict. I thought it was a good sign, but that was false hope, the sort that snarls you up, and I was found guilty of a plot involving which – the next day's newspapers headlined – 'Britain's Biggest Ever Cocaine Haul'.

I went down for smuggling two tonnes of cannabis and more than 300lb [153 kilos] of cocaine into Britain on the *Silver Happiness*.

I got off on some nonsense about bringing cannabis through Gatwick in 1987, which I wasn't involved in, but I also got convicted of importing cocaine through Gatwick that Christmas of 1988 and of money laundering. As I said, the world had moved on: you could rob a bank with a gun and be in less trouble than I was for what they called 'financial wrongdoing'.

I had a long wait to be sentenced. The courts, the customs were after any profits I had made from the drug deals and I was fighting to hold on to what I had and what I'd built up through straight money. The wanted the lot, the house and everything that was somehow linked to my name. It was consuming, and in a way that was lucky for I hadn't time to think about how much time I was going to get. They valued the scrap-metal business at more than £100,000 but only got £7,000 out of the safe there. That business, and I had a decade of straight accounts, was worth nothing without me working it, just the lease on the place. So, they went after the family house in Chislehurst where the kids had grown up and we'd had for nearly thirty years. Maureen had begun to get a divorce after I was nicked and waiting for the trial. It was nothing heavy between us just that the time had come to officially separate. She had a smart solicitor who suggested it as a way for Maureen to get our home and have somewhere to live and I knew, in time, my daughters would get the benefit of it. The bloody customs fought tooth and nail over it, but Maureen got it in her name simply because she was entitled to it. For many reasons.

While I was on remand I had my brother Charlie's son, Charlie Boy, run the yard. He'd worked for me for years so taking over was natural. He was a good lad and the weekend before I got nicked I had given him a grand in bonus. That was a lot of money. I was looking after him. He was working for me but he was like a bit of putty in his dad's hands. Maureen was also working the metal yard while I was on remand for that eighteen months. It was smart to keep the business going as I reckoned if the customs thought they were getting this magical £100,000 Maureen had more chance with the house.

I had a helper, Chicken George, who wasn't the full ten bob but was a reliable worker and could do the heavy lifting and deal with the call-in traders. I'm in prison and I let Charlie use my offices but I said to give £100 a week to my wife. He gave her fuck all. He spent our money on phones and all the rest. He walked off with some paintings I had at the office and even took my paperwork including my depositions from the fixed-up Torture Trial. Charlie couldn't leave anything alone. He wanted it all. Charlie Boy sold off, all but cleared out, all the metal in the yard but left the 10 per cent VAT outstanding. But then we got broken into and it happened every time Maureen bought in more stock. It was neatly done and happened three times. It seemed when they looked around that the thieves were hopping over a back wall and clearing out the metal. It, of course, was my brother Charlie. My brother robbed my premises repeatedly. Robbed it. I still can't fathom it. The local greengrocer tipped off Maureen that Charlie was turning up with his keys and moving out the metal and tarting it up to look like some thieving had gone on. The morning she was told this, she got a VAT bill for £5,000 – 10 per cent of the value of the stock. Charlie had cleared the yard out and had made off with £50,000. Had all the fucking money. Fortunately, Maureen had money to pay for the £5,000 VAT bill. Charlie tried to fuck up my business.

I don't know now why I was ever surprised.

No one had ever mattered to him except himself.

I had worked, along with a lot of people who were on his side, to get him an early release from prison and to keep him in puff and good wine and food. When he got in to visit me when I was in Brixton on remand for the drugs I asked him to contact someone who might be helpful in my defence. I wasn't asking for anything dodgy, but he leaped up and staring at me screamed out that he wasn't going go back to prison '*for you*'. They say to me there's a touch of Cain and Abel about our relationship but I don't know about that.

NO HANDCUFFS

Maureen visited me in prison and told me all about Charlie's doings in the office and the robberies. I could only mutter something about changing the locks. Charlie was now a stranger to me. I said he'd changed, but had he? Maybe he was always a bastard and I hadn't wanted to believe just what he was. He asked me to pay for his daughter Susan's wedding and I willingly did so – and danced at her wedding reception. It was family and that's what you did. I never knew it, but Charlie was jealous of me. I've had good friends all my life. People trust me and ask my advice. Charlie didn't hang onto friends. He was too self-interested, he just took people to promise-land, like the Train Robbers and their 'investment cash'. He struggled when he came home from prison but I always helped him. Even my mum told me to steer clear of him. She loved him but knew what he was like. I swore never to deal with him again. I had a lot of time to think about Charlie's behaviour, his betrayal. As I waited to be sentenced I was kept locked up on my own. My longtime friend John Daly wrote to the court on my behalf and made an argument for leniency. Lord Longford, who'd rather 'adopted' me, asked to be at the sentencing hearing and 'plead for mercy'.

It was kind but I didn't believe it would help and I was right. They sent Don Tredwin away for fifteen years and gave the South American Teixeira twenty years. For me, Mr Richardson, they threw away the key. It was 1990 and I was fifty-four years old and originally sentenced to thirty-five years. I was made a scapegoat again and whacked up for thirty-five years: twenty-five for the drugs and ten for the money laundering. I got ten knocked off but it remained a quarter of a century in jail.

It's a shock when you hear these sort of numbers announced

aloud, but in time it sinks in and, as I always have, I applied myself to dealing with it. It might be hard time but you don't have to do it the hard way. I was older and wiser and prison life in for me the second time around – in Full Sutton Prison near York, where I was double cuffed off to after my drug sentence – was more mellow although I was a Cat AA prisoner again, the highest security, and I had two screws with me everywhere I went. They were scared of me. My resources brought benefits: I had my own television, access to the exercise yard – I could never workout in the cell, too claustrophobic – and a few of us took turns to cook for ourselves. We played lots of bridge.

Charlie Kray got nicked when he was seventy years old for conspiracy to supply cocaine. [Ron and Reggie Kray's elder brother Charlie was jailed for twelve years at Woolwich Crown Court on 27 June,1997, for, according to the police and prosecution, 'masterminding' a £39 million cocaine plot. He died in prison of natural causes on 4 April 2000, aged seventy-three.]

He never supplied anything. They got it up for him. He got done for the mere fact that he said he *could* supply cocaine to two policemen. Juries aren't stupid. The coppers offered Charlie fifty grand for a kilo and he knows that the price is forty grand or so, so he knows he can get someone to supply them at those prices. So he says he can and gets done. What an idiot. That's what happened with him. He had people like Frankie Fraser as witnesses for him saying that he wouldn't do something like that. Frankie Fraser testifies: 'Charlie Kray wouldn't do that.' I ask you. It was so ridiculous. He should have said he was fitted up instead of having Fraser and other people up there in court as 'character' witnesses. I said: 'Charlie look, tell the fucking truth and everything.' He was saying yes he was going to do that. I explained everything to him. Yes to everything.

'Yes I'm gonna to do that, Ed.'

Then I saw one of our friends, Joe Pyle, and he said: 'Everything you say to Charlie is right but he won't do fuck all.'

He was right. He had done nothing. He went along with the same fucking story, and Frankie Fraser's spiel and it was ridiculous. He finished up getting twelve years. The Old Bill were after him. He was alright inside, Charlie. Brian Keenan, the number-one man in the IRA, was a neat card player, too. Brian was my bridge partner in Full Sutton Prison. He got eighteen years [in 1980, for conspiring to causes explosions], and as an IRA commander whenever there was any trouble he'd get involved. We'd be playing bridge and someone would come rushing in and Brian would have to leave the table and go and help sort out some crisis in Ireland. When he got out he played an important part in the peace process and arranging a ceasefire. If John Major as Prime Minister had paid more attention to Brian, the Manchester IRA bombing, Canary Wharf and some other nasty things wouldn't have happened. I enjoyed spending time with Brian for he was determined man [Brian Keenan died 21 May 2008] and really worked at getting a solution in Northern Ireland. I partnered him at bridge and at badminton and I wasn't surprised at how important he became.

Of course, there are those who are born important. Or think they are. We had one in Full Sutton – a female prison warder. Yes, times had changed and having women as these particular kind of screws, so to speak, was as surprising as the amount of drugs going around. There were 'clean' blokes coming into the prison system and being turned into drug addicts inside. Soft and hard drugs were available if you had the resources. I was happy with the brandy in my Coca-Cola bottle brought in by a well-rewarded gentleman screw. He was a different class to some of the women screws. They could be right bitches. This one at Full Sutton put a lot of passion into frisking female visitors and prided herself on being unpleasant to anyone she came into contact with. She was on a power trip as much as any of the screws and eventually two Geordie kids had had enough. Those Geordies know exactly where they come from. They are all pretty game. This screwess is giving the women a lot of aggravation. The women are coming in and she's patting them down and going through their hair and things like that. So, the Geordie boys, they want to do her. They came around to me and I agreed we'd have a whip round of cash so they'd have a few bob when they came out of chokey, for they knew their plan would get them bunged up. They poured a bucket of shit and piss over the screwess, shitted her up properly. When I talked to the boys they said: 'We'd do it for nothing.' They despised that bitch and when the real word got around about her she was moved on.

It wasn't all one way. There was a Geordie female prison guard and there's a big black man in there giving this screwess aggravation. The Geordie boys wanted to put one on him so they asked me: 'Do you have any objection if we give him a going over.' I didn't object and they went ahead. That's the opposite side of it. They were doing that to protect this Geordie girl and it seemed a plan to me for she was getting a lot of stick. The black prisoner wasn't doing anyone any favours: he'd splashed boiling cooking oil over a male screw burning the hell out of one side of his face. That stopped us getting the use of cooking oil, so he fucked up any chance of a fish supper, no oil for battered fish and chips. The cells at Full Sutton were full of Geordies and I got invited to a party and there was plenty of home-made hooch. This is a high-security prison and we were going at the booze and singing having a good time there and everyone in the nick could hear it. Even the screws were laughing. It *was* a laugh and I got on well with these Geordie lads. I was always consulted about the antics in prison and I suppose that's because by then I was the elder statesman, not that rioting young man from the Durham days.

My approach by then was live and let live unless, of course, I reckoned someone was taking a liberty, and in my case was usually the prison governor or his staff. I was content in myself and that's what allows you to survive intact. And there are all the friends, the eccentrics and the wild men, and I met all of them. In some prisons just about everyone was, a headline name. And they're not at all like their publicity.

Charlie Bronson is 'known as 'Britain's most violent prisoner' and he's been inside [in 2108] for forty-three years. He's always kidnapping screws or having a turn but it's all part of keeping himself busy and having a laugh. Every time he gets remission he goes off on one and has it blanked off. I went to the celebration of his third wedding [in November 2017] when he married a girl off *Coronation Street* [Paula Williamson] up in Yorkshire. They got married inside Wakefield Prison and we had the drinks and sit-down at the York House Hotel. I was happy to be there, for I always got on OK with him inside. We would exercise together and he was fit. He had his own workout regime in his cell and that was his method of dealing with prison. I did as much thinking as exercising as it's inside your head you have to keep things straight.

I walked round with Charlie and he was quite funny, a bit of a comedian. He was alright Charlie. He told me when he was in Broadmoor they'd come round and cut the grass and he got the grass clippings and dried them out in his cell. Then he put the dried lawn grass in little plastic bags and he said the other prisoners couldn't get enough of it. They were smoking it – getting 'high' – and coming back for more of it. Psychological – it's all in your head and I was determined to use mine. I knew if I could be as close to a 'model' prisoner as my temperament would allow, I'd get out much faster. I learned to play rather than disrupt the system and I also started reading more and wrote some poetry. I also became a Muslim for they had a better menu.

I didn't have to participate in Friday prayers as going along to the meetings qualified me for the special diet. I was something of an evangelical trendsetter as friends in prison also 'converted' to get the better food. Our Church of England enthusiast, the prison chaplain, was not pleased at losing supposed members of his flock and told me: 'You've sold your soul for a bowl of curry.' I saw it more as leasing it out. I wanted to do more things for myself as well as making life inside as pleasant as possible. I found the other prisoners knew when to let me alone. It's all in the way you look at people that tells them to stay clear. It was in Full Sutton, which was a maximum security prison, that I went back to the future. As I said, growing up and as a school kid and a littler later I was only interested in woodwork and technical drawing, which had got me the job at Durrants in Great Dover Street in Southwark.

I went back to the art and craft in prison and took a variety of other classes – anything I thought would improve my mind and chances of getting out of jail sooner rather than later. I never imagined art, painting, would take me out of myself the way it did. It made a new man of me. I could spend hours at a time working on a painting, and in prison time is the demon you must control. It didn't happen right away – it took time for me to find my place, find what I wanted to do and could do well. I've never wanted to do anything that I couldn't have a chance of getting done properly. On my first sentence I was quite a young man and still quite active, which is why I lost all my remission by getting involved in all the aggravation and the tear-ups. I was older, I'd reached fifty-four, the second time inside.

At first, I wasn't sure what to do except I knew I wasn't going to waste my time in there. If I went to the library, I got a book out that would educate me. I read about psychology and anything that would improve my mind. I went on full-time education but the classes were boring on about life outside that I knew wasn't going to happen. I was a regular in the gym and I met Peter Cameron working out. I got lucky with Peter, who was in Full Sutton for a long stretch for cannabis smuggling but was an artist, and he suggested I take the art class. I went a couple of days a week and I finished up full time. I was painting out of my head, from memory, and I was struggling with it. The woman who was in charge of the class was mainly into pottery, so not a great help with this, she wasn't really the best person for me. Then another art teacher came in once a week and he said what I wanted to do was almost impossible.

Peter worked at his painting in prison and he was helpful and encouraging to me [Peter Cameron in 2019 was a successful artist based in Liverpool] and later explained to the outside world what it meant: 'Prison is a dark world, where so many things are denied you. You cling to anything that will take you away from the drab, mundane existence.' Which was correct, and with him and the weekly lessons from our art teacher I began to learn. You can be a natural but you must have the technique.

My first painting was of J. Arthurs Club in Catford and I did that from memory but it was tough; it was difficult to get it right and being me I wanted it to be perfect – and be perfect quickly. I soon learned patience is a gift to a painter. In art class I was told to copy pictures, to learn by painting from photographs or other art. I copied a Degas portrait and that worked out well. Constable and the countryside were subjects and I learned about perspective, the art in the art, if you like. It was so easy after I had been told what to do. In the end I started to get quite good at it. I got better and better as I did more and more of it, became quite a good artist.

My prison visitor, Lord Longford became a friend of mine. He was a guest at the wedding of my brother Charlie's daughter Susan and for all that was said about him and for all those who attacked him, he had a tremendous heart, a good heart, which possibly wasn't always in the right place. His pleas for the parole of Myra Hindley [with Ian Brady responsible for the 1966 Moors Murders; she died in November 2001] made him hated by some people but he was dedicated and loyal to his belief in religion. He was a great prison reformer and co-founded an organisation to help prisoners survive in prison and do well after release [the New Bridge Foundation in 1956] and that led to the launch of a newspaper, *Inside Time* [first published 1990] for all those in nick in Britain. The paper published one of my poems. And I painted Frank Longford's picture. I persuaded him to give me a photograph to work from and because he had some life in his face, the lines, the experience, I was able to produce a good likeness. He thought so, too, and liked it and I gave him the picture, which he donated to a prisoners' charity.

If you had a skill in prison you were in demand. Blokes used to ask me to draw stuff for them but I liked to do my own thing. They lined up but I shied away from that and even when I was offered big cash for a painting I turned it down. I was learning to do proper painting. I had to trade for materials and one young fella was getting out and he had quite a lot of canvases and paints that I bought off him. I finished up with two 5 by 4 foot canvases; I wouldn't have gone as big as that normally, but I took the chance of having all his stuff as he was going out.

On one of them I did a painting of a horse auction with an old pony in the middle being sold off with the details of all the different faces around peering at the auction ring and it came out quite well. The bloke going out said to me: 'I'll give you a grand for that Ed.'

I thought about it; I was sending home all my paintings and I had a pile of them. I said: 'I don't really want to sell that.' I blanked him. Afterwards, going back to my cell I thought I must be mad. The man was offering to pay. I regretted it afterwards. When I did get home I sold it for £3,000. I had done the right thing. At the time, three grand was good money for what I was knocking out all the time. It was a big painting. Some of the work that followed was prize-winning and that came about through a man who knew a lot about being incarcerated.

The philosopher and writer Arthur Koestler was punished for his beliefs and when he was free he set up up a charity to endow art and writing in prison. [Arthur Koestler, the Hungarian-British author of *Darkness at Noon*, was jailed in three in separate countries: General Franco's Spain, a WW2 French concentration camp, and as a suspected alien London's Pentonville Prison, but was sentenced to death in Spain. From a spy hole he saw others shot by firing squad. In the 1950s, Koestler was a leading campaigner for the abolition of capital punishment. When that was almost achieved, he turned his attention to jails. As an intellectual, he had survived by playing mind games; he set himself a 'timetable' – an hour for mental French, an hour for maths. But he knew the barren years most prisoners endure. 'The main problem is apathy, depression and gradual dehumanisation. The spark dies.' He approached the UK Home Office, and was allowed to set up the Arthur Koestler Award (in The Koestler Trust) to give prizes for art to prisoners, detainees and 'patients' in special hospitals like Broadmoor. He committed suicide in 1984, leaving £10,000 to his trust: 'I wish a little cheap immortality.']

I won my first award for painting in 1994 and it really chuffed me for it meant the painting I was doing was worthwhile – unlike my French language efforts with Charlie Wilson. It was the satisfaction of a job well done. Koestler helped me and Peter Cameron and many other people. The Koestler Award was my first pat on the back and I went on to win one every year – I've got twelve of them.

CHAPTER NINETEEN

POSTCARDS FROM THE EDGE

I didn't get rich on my prizes but they won me art supplies and I was already better off for I'd quit smoking, so no more big tobacco spend-ups. I had the system wrapped around me but, although I was a pussycat compared to my first jailhouse runarounds, I remained a Cat AA prisoner. I'd put in my Full Sutton Christmas orders – a couple of turkeys, shiploads of little sausages, gravy, cranberry sauce, hats and crackers and a huge trifle we'd fix with our own sherry – when in the early hours I heard the clanging of doors, the jangling of chains and the march of the steps of ghosts of Christmases past.

The day before our big Christmas dinner I was shanghaied off from Yorkshire to Cambridgeshire, to Whitemoor Prison, another of those so-called 'secure' nicks. It was the same as usual: I was hustled out in handcuffs, in the van, sirens, outriders, and off to the south-east with the escorts changing county by county. I'd learned to lean back and enjoy the journey even if I didn't know the destination, and Whitemoor Prison was no paradise. It was a dispersal prison divided into two blocks, one for the nonce cases, and the other half for normal prisoners like myself. The nonces, the sex offenders, worked in the kitchen and cooked all our food. AIDS was still the hot topic and there had been banging on by daft MPs and the like that the nonces had to be supplied condoms in prison so they could have 'safe' sex. The nonces were kept well away from us otherwise there would have been riots, real trouble. Our food was wheeled over on trolleys to a central hot plate and our lot served it up. One lunchtime a lad spooned out a ladle of custard and screamed: 'There's a fucking Durex floating in this...'

There was. And it had been used.

If you've never been inside and you think about it – food is really important. It's like being on a long-haul airline flight when they served up shit food and you take it because it's something to do, something to take up the time until you reach your destination.

In prison meals are a weapon against monotony.

The condom in the custard was an outrage. Everyone went fucking mental and on strike. There was a banging of trays and shouts and all manner of bollocks threatened. I'd rarely eaten from the hotplate and I never did again. I had the money, the resources, to do that, but even the lads who were mostly skint tried to exist on a diet of canned stuff, mostly baked beans. They smoked, so they really had to have the prison food. This went on for some time and I didn't eat anything at all from the kitchen other than maybe a bit of bread. You had to hope they hadn't had a wank in that.

I cooked for myself with our food boats: there might be four of you together, and each one does a meal from the few quid you each put in every month. It goes around like that. You get three meals and then you get to do one yourself. You do a curry, chicken or tiger prawns, your speciality. That was for people who had got resources. I didn't really suffer because I had good friends who would send in supplies. People without resources suffered for they never had control, while those who did had the influence. Someone like myself, I've always had, if you like, a reasonable life in there, friends I would ring up and ask for anything I wanted. If you have resources, it makes a difference. People sell heroin and all that in prison, a lot of trades go on. I stuck to my painting which was going well, and I kept winning Koestler prizes, and the Koestler Trust turned my paintings into postcards and greeting cards which were sold to benefit it.

I was also concentrating on appealing against my sentence and that landed me in the horror that is Belmarsh Prison during my hearing. I got many visit from friends, with Belmarsh being in South London, but the place was an advertisement for all the corruption and disgusting unpleasantness of the prison system.

There were bent screws around and you could get high just by taking a deep breath. Inmates weren't just trading in the drugs brought in by the screws; they were dealing in the specific quality of the heroin and cocaine, like settling a good year for wine. Puff was available on every corridor.

My appeals didn't go well but one good result was that I was shipped off to Parkhurst and of course there would always be people there that I knew. When I went, there were gardens where you could grow your own vegetables and get yourself a little plot and it was fantastic. I had tennis lessons: instead of padded cells we had a padded tennis court where I played and there was a football pitch and good kitchens. I got on a food boat immediately with some old friends, including Bill the Bomb and a lad called Dick Reid who was in for murder. He had big hands and if it was his turn on a Friday he always used to do skate and chips: a bit of oil, get that hot, do the business. That was his meal; I was the one who would try various different meals. Dick Reid was also the admired gardener at Parkhurst. He got gardening societies from outside coming to visit him for talks and information about plants and planting and what time of year/in sun/in shade. He was never stuck for an answer. He could recite the names of plants in English and Latin. He was a wizard at growing rare plants – his long fingers were certainly green – and he'd trade them for food with the prison guards. We'd also bung them the cash to go shopping for us and they found great cuts of meat and fresh fish to go with our fresh veg.

The governor knew how good Dick was with anything to do with gardening and when a beehive formed on one of the paths, which was a dangerous place for beehive to be, they asked him to move it. Dick said he would move it but only at night because he wanted the bees inside the hive before he moved it. They thought he was up to some midnight escape plan but he insisted he couldn't move it in daylight. He told me that if the bees were not inside the hive they would just fly around where it used to be until they died. He didn't want to lose too many bees and he didn't want the bees to suffer, to get lost, to not be able to find their home – their hive. At night, most of them are in, and at best they'd only lose a few. Dick moved it at 10 p.m. at night. He was a gentle soul and very different from Victor Castigador. As I said, I never asked what people were in for but Victor's story arrived in Parkhurst before he did.

Victor was an illegal immigrant from the Philippines and he was real loyal to me. He was a little villain and was jailed for trying to rob a gaming machine arcade in the West End and killing a couple of guards by locking them in and fucking setting the place alight. [Victor Castigador was given a 'whole-life' sentence in 1990 for murdering two guards at a Soho amusement arcade where he worked. He tied up the guards and the female cashier, doused them in white spirit and locked them in a wire cage in the basement before tossing in lighted matches. He was labelled 'The Human Torch' and 'The Killer from Manila' and responsible for 'The Human Torch Murders'.]

Victor was a right solid little lump. He was as good as gold with me and we'd play chess and he was quite a good player. A geezer came into Parkhurst who was a champion chess player, or said he was. He was bragging about it and we thought he was suspect, a 'mole' brought in to get some inside track on what was going on in the prison. Victor challenged him to a game and a betting ring started. Almost everyone backed the other geezer. I was the only one betting on Victor. They had three games, and Victor won two out of three. I get up and then all of a sudden Victor jumps right up onto my shoulders. It was a big thing because everyone thought this other guy was going to win and in victory Victor, quite a strong little bloke, jumped up, straight up on my fucking shoulders. Right up on my shoulders. We paraded around didn't we? The two of us giving it to them! Victor, as I said, was very loyal to me. I had an argument with someone out of the window one night and Victor heard it and he turned up with a knife, a big fucking blade: 'Let's go down and get the geezers.' I calmed him down but he was there for me. When he killed another prisoner I thought he wasn't worried about doing that for he was inside for his life anyway.

[Victor Castigador was sixty-one when he bludgeoned to death Sidonio Teixeira in the prison workshop at Long Lartin, near Evesham, Worcestershire, in June 2016, using a rock from a prison fish tank he had hidden in a sock. His victim was imprisoned for killing his three-year-old daughter and attempting to murder his nine-year-old son. Castigador told his prison guards: 'He pissed me off, he deserved what he had. He won't need an ambulance, he's dead.' Castigador himself died on 21 March 2017, following a stroke at Woodhill Prison, Milton Keynes, Buckinghamshire, where he was being held in a 'highest security' Close Supervision Centre (CSC).]

The more I was inside the more I could see how broken the prison system was and is. It forces people to see life a different way and that can harm rather than rehabilitate them; the suicide rate is high and I know people say: 'Good riddance.' But if it's just a young bloke or girl who's messed up a little, made a mistake, and they're thrown into the system, it's tragic. It's always tragic when someone dies broken inside.

I was back in Whitemoor when I got an official artistic job from the *New Law Journal*, a legal magazine, who wanted me to draw a cover illustration for their story on prison suicides. Lord Woolf had led an inquiry into the mess of British prisons and his findings – 'The Woolf Report' – had been kicked into the long grass by the Government. My drawing was of a young prisoner placing a noose around his neck and stepping up a ladder comprising the letters from W-O-O-L-F to hang himself. The two Os were drawn as handcuffs and I could do them from memory. I was pleased that Lord Woolf asked how much I wanted for the original of the cover artwork. I told him he could have it in return for a few years off my sentence. He told me he couldn't help with that but would make a donation to a prisoners' charity. We had a deal. He sent a note to say he'd framed my drawing; it was an endorsement that I was doing well with my painting and, like that magazine commission which paid me a couple of hundred quid, only made me more keen.

In Parkhurst I had art class twice a week with a maximum of eight in the group at one time so we got individual attention. He was a good teacher not just in the art of painting but in the mechanics of it – how to mix the paints, how to find just that right movement of the brush for the shade you wanted – and when he wasn't around I was still able to use the art room. I also painted in my cell and I think by being able to concentrate there I achieved the best I could.

That interest, obsession maybe, with my painting kept me away from the fights and the drug deals going on all around me. There were always bust-ups and knives being smuggled in and scores being settled and during my time inside Michael Howard was the Tory Home Secretary – he's the one that Ann Widdecombe said had 'something of the night about him'. He liked to play to the balcony and brought in measures to certify that 'prison works'. Well, of course, it bloody doesn't. No society has found a version of the system that does one job or another, neither too soft or too harsh.

Howard personally pissed me off by closing down art classes and there was none of that when I moved to Long Lartin in the Vale of Evesham. The *Daily Mail* readers loved it that he was being tough on crime and criminals. But they never saw the full picture. Howard brought in mandatory drug testing and that was applauded, but it wasn't thought through. In most prisons the inmates were doped out on cannabis and dreaming of flowers in their hair and what makes the world sing. Marijuana stays in the system for days, for a couple of weeks, so that would be stopped with the drug tests. Users didn't get caught if they indulged in heroin, however, which flows throw the system in forty-eight hours. Arguably, Michael Howard turned Britain's prison population into junkies. He certainly made my life inside more miserable. I was now a Cat A and that meant on way towards release from prison; a long way to go but on the right track as I'd had to lose the Cat AA to get into Long Lartin. I signed for classes and courses, anything to win points with those who would have a say on whether I got parole or not.

Reggie Kray was in Long Lartin with me. But, really, he was a stray in the system. Ron was the leader and with him gone, Reg couldn't function properly and he was more lost than ever. My mind was outside prison but Reg knew he wasn't going home. We went for a walk and I was talking about preparing to get out. Reggie said: 'I'm not talking to the probation people.'

'Well if you don't, you won't get out because they're the ones who decide,' I said. Lifers also get a psychologist appointed to them but Reg wouldn't talk to them either.

I added: 'You don't have to do anything clever for them, just act normal.'

But he wouldn't have it. He and Ron always thought they were bigger than they were. But as I said, they were lost in prison and their reputation over all these years was built on pub talk and prison gossip, myth.

I was far more positive and all for standing up for my rights and taking action; I launched a fight against the ban on art. I argued, told the truth, that it was therapeutic and therefore part of the intended rehabilitation. They went on about how the turpentine I used to work with could start a fire, but there were plenty of alternatives and finally I was allowed acrylic paint and some luck. The P. O. on my particular wing asked me to paint two murals for the wing's recreation areas and I agreed – if the paint was supplied. I got enough to happily paint my way through to freedom. The murals I did in a couple of days: upstairs a tranquil scene with a bloke fishing, and a lively Caribbean picture in the downstairs recreation room. [Eddie Richardson's murals, which measure 10 foot by 6 foot, were still in place in Long Lartin in 2018.]

Prison life worked OK for me at Long Lartin. There were faces I knew, like Mick McAvoy [still serving out his Brink's-Mat sentence], who I played tennis with, and Ronnie O'Sullivan whose son is such a genius at snooker. I did a lot of cooking with Ronnie including a Sunday-morning fry-up. Ronnie Senior was done for murder [in 1992] and got an eighteen-year 'life' sentence but that should never have happened: it was a bar fight and it got out of hand and a knife was used. It should have been manslaughter. [O'Sullivan, who operated sex shops in Soho, killed Bruce Bryan, a driver for Charlie Kray, in a club on the Kings Road, Chelsea, London. He was released in 2010.] It was good to see his son visit him and being so loyal. Pleasant as the company was, I wasn't going to sit about. I needed to be a Cat B, and I got there and was shipped on nearer to London to a dump, to Swaleside in Kent, on the Isle of Sheppey.

I simply kept myself out of the mess that place was, with its fights and bent screws supplying drugs, and the conditions which were miserable. I kept on painting in my cell and pursing my release and survived that two years. I kept doing every course I could from computer class to the evangelical Christian Alpha course and applied for parole four times. God and the Home Secretary Jack Straw weren't listening and I was turned down every time.

On my fifth application for parole I was approved for release but wasn't told the date. By 7 June 2001, after a General Election, there was a new Home Secretary, David Blunkett, and he didn't stand in my way. At 11.30 a.m., after thirteen years spent of my second jail term, I was given a couple of hours to pack up and go. I had no warning whatsoever. I didn't tell anyone I was getting out, coming home. I thought I'd surprise my mum and the family.

I quickly did the rounds giving away all my gear, my clothes and plates and cups and the little knick knacks that you use to try and make a cell your own room, but especially the game boards like backgammon, and reference books and my dictionary and encyclopaedia: the ones you leave behind need it more than you. That's a lesson I learned, that kindness is never wasted.

I'd alerted my close friend Joan Harris and she collected me from the Isle of Sheppey and drove me back to South London, which after thirteen years hadn't changed as much as me. I'd grown up.

My brother hadn't changed. Or so I was told.

I never spoke to him again in any meaningful way.

CHAPTER TWENTY

TOMORROW

My mother was the constant in my family life and when I got out the second time she'd moved to Kent, to a quiet life in Beckenham, and was living with her sister, my Auntie Doll. They'd got my room ready before I even stepped out of my cell. And organised the welcome-home party.

And I hadn't even told them I was out.

Somehow, the word had gone round that I'd been released. When I got home, after a nice afternoon with Joan, all the family and friends other than Charlie and his sons had been waiting for hours. It was me who got the surprise. It's hard to walk straight back into the regular world like that even if it is your family, but I felt their warmth – and protected.

I't takes time and adjustments to fit back into society. Other people got leave, rehabilitated; I didn't, I was straight out on the street. I wanted to be out, but I was going around in circles for a while. I found it easier with my friends who had never deserted me when I was in prison – I never wanted for anything – and who certainly helped me get back on my feet.

My friends had a whip round for me, and before I even got around to selling my paintings – thanks to Peter Cameron's idea – putting on my first exhibition, I had a few thousand quid in the bank. I was encouraged by how well my paintings [selling for several thousand pounds each in 2019] went down with people.

Sadly, my mum, aged eighty-nine, died a few months before that exhibit in 2003. I had time with her, which was good as she was poorly with diabetes towards the end. She'd coped with everything over the years – our dad, Charlie and me – but was most hurt and devastated by the early death of my brother Alan. She could see my sister Elaine, she could visit me and Charlie in prison, but Alan was gone for ever. She had grandchildren and great-grandchildren, but for all these years she could not display in person her love for Alan and that constantly upset her.

Yet, as I said, she coped, she fought on through the power of her relentless personality. Much of that was her attitude in that, to her, taking care of each day was important. There was little point in looking over your shoulder at what might have been – better to get things done today and look towards tomorrow. I believe so much in that and see no point in getting all moody over regrets. I use every day I have to enjoy my life with no handcuffs. When you've lost so much freedom, there is an added joy to having it back. It happened the second time because I was tempted and those people who lecture me about that never had such temptation: because I am thought of as a reliable and trusted man I was getting such offers all the time. If my critics had been made the same offers wouldn't they have been tempted, too? I think they would. What I do accept is offers to organise lunch for my mates: they come from all over and we sit down – sometimes a dozen or more of us – and we have a good time. I'm still devoted to boxing and get invites to events like one [around Easter, 2018] as a guest on Sugar Ray Leonard's table for an exhibition evening.

It was at another black-tie evening out, a snooker event with Ronnie O'Sullivan and Jimmy White and names like that playing, that I last confronted my brother Charlie. He was sitting at another table and I went over and gave him a slagging in front of these people. I did give him a right slagging but afterwards, to be honest, I fucking regretted I hadn't given a whack. Then I saw him at a funeral and I ignored him when I should have taken the opportunity to have gone over and done something. He was diabolical. He destroyed my family. He was absolutely, unbelievably jealous of me. He never got over how well I was doing on my own. I was thriving and he had fuck all and he couldn't take that. I went inside and he was thieving from me, his own flesh and blood. Even in his own death, Charlie made it difficult for me.

I'm at the age where old friends have gone and, despite the many lunches I arrange with my mates, we seem more and more to see each other at funerals. Harry Rawlins, who had been with me most of my life died. Mum left us and my Auntie Doll died at the start of 2018, and that was a great sadness for she'd always been there for me.

The aftermath of Charlie's death was a pantomime. The funeral was at New Camberwell Crematorium on 8 October 2012. I felt obliged to go along but I stood outside and did not attend the ceremony. I said I would wait outside and that's what I did. People kept coming up and asking me to go in but I stayed put. Charlie's wife Veronica wanted to do the reception and went on to my sister Elaine saying she'd arrange it. She did. Elaine and her daughter Emma went over to Sainsbury's and got a lump of sandwiches for the mourners. That Veronica also put a white floral tribute on one of the ten Jaguars in the funeral cortege spelling out '240DC' and helping headlines for a reminder of all the stuff about the black box at the Torture Trial.

I didn't want anything to do with it. A load of people from all over came to see me at the funeral. We had a separate drink at another pub and we had a good afternoon there for a few hours. After Charlie died I wrote: 'He will be missed by his six children. I can't say he was a good father, but he was a father. He leaves a big family behind him. I'm sure they will be upset and losing a dad is difficult. It came as a surprise to some, but not to me. He had been ill for years and has suffered with breathing problems, emphysema, for a long time due to smoking.'

The usual people like Frankie Fraser were there and the usual music, Frank Sinatra singing 'My Way'. I've heard that song too often recently. They played it again a couple of years later in December 2014 when we sent off Frankie Fraser at Honor Oak Crematorium in Camberwell. It was busy and many people couldn't get into the church if they'd wanted. They crowded around the open doors to hear the services. Frank's family had all the trimmings, the floral displays and the cars and the tributes and I suppose you have to, for that's what's expected.

[Many gangland funerals say it with flowers. When Shirley Pitts, the 'Queen of the Shoplifters', was buried in a South London cemetery in 1992, one 6 foot long display read 'Gone Shopping'.

There was also a floral Harrods bag in tribute to one of Shirley's favoured venues. She was buried in a £5,000 Zandra Rhodes dress (no receipt), while a trumpeter played the 'Heaven, I'm in heaven' line from a favoured song, 'Cheek to Cheek'. Ronnie Kray's funeral in 1995 was a grand affair. The procession from St Matthew's in Bethnal Green to Chingford cemetery was led by six black-plumed horses followed by twenty-five limousines. He was also sung away by Sinatra offering 'My Way' and given a reading of W.E. Henley's poem 'Invictus', with its lines 'I am the master of my fate, I am the captain of my soul.' Reg Kray was allowed out of jail for what was an *event*, handcuffed to a prison officer. Famous faces lined up to kiss Reg Kray on both cheeks, a custom developed since *The Godfather* film trilogy. 'Colonel' Ron's other farewell song was Whitney Houston's 'I Will Always Love You'. When Reg Kray followed his twin along the same route on 11 October 2000, things in the East End were not what they used to be. When the Krays' mother Violet had died in 1982 around 60,000 people lined the funeral route and a similar number turned out for Ron Kray. His brother only attracted 2,500. Still, they got 'My Way' (original rights belong to the singer-songwriter and increasingly wealthy Paul Anka) once again. But some of the criminal fraternity who had worked with the Krays, including Tony Lambrianou and Freddie Foreman, snubbed as pallbearers, boycotted the funeral. Roberta Kray, who married Reg Kray three years earlier in Wayland Prison, Norfolk, strongly indicated it was not to be a day for honouring men from her husband's past.]

When you go to these funerals there's always someone at the drink afterwards who says:' You know who'd have really enjoyed today?' And, of course, it's whoever you have turned up to say goodbye to. There's a lot to be said for the argument that funerals are for those left behind not for the person in the coffin.

I was back at the New Camberwell Cemetery in February, 2017, for the funeral of Train Robber Tommy Wisbey [aged 86] who'd died at the beginning of that year following a load of strokes. The only one of the train men left is Bobby Welch [aged 89 in 2019] who I see quite often for a cup of tea. He doesn't like publicity.

He was at Tommy Wisbey's funeral and sitting across the church from me. I was with a television lady, Liz Pearson, and she was sitting to my right blocking me from the aisle. Well, she turned out to be Freddie Foreman's 'minder'. I couldn't get past her to have a proper go at that fucking liar Foreman. There was a bit of pushing and shoving. He'd recently said on a television programme that he'd held a gun to my head and that's a fucking lie. And now there he was sitting across the aisle from me. I was ready for him but he ran away and was gone when I got out and never came to the wake.

The newspapers didn't know what to make of the row, had no idea what it was about. We're getting on a bit [Foreman was 86 in 2019] so they were on about a battle of pensioners. Well, I wanted to have a proper tear-up with him. He held a gun at my head? What bollocks. I thought I'd get my chance at the reception drinks afterwards but Foreman never showed up.

That wasn't a surprise.

He knew he'd taken a liberty.

And that was a mistake.

I said at the beginning of this book that people taking liberties was never acceptable. A lifetime later I am a very different man, but my principles and loyalty are still the same.